JavaScript Programmer's Reference

Jonathan Reid
Thomas Valentine

Apress·

JavaScript Programmer's Reference

ISBN-13 (pbk): 978-1-4302-4629-9

ISBN-13 (electronic): 978-1-4302-4630-5

President and Publisher: Paul Manning
Lead Editor: Ben Renow-Clarke
Technical Reviewers: RJ Owen
Editorial Board: Steve Anglin, Mark Beckner, Ewan Buckingham, Gary Cornell, Louise Corrigan, Morgan Ertel, Jonathan Gennick, Jonathan Hassell, Robert Hutchinson, Michelle Lowman, James Markham, Matthew Moodie, Jeff Olson, Jeffrey Pepper, Douglas Pundick, Ben Renow-Clarke, Dominic Shakeshaft, Gwenan Spearing, Matt Wade, Tom Welsh
Coordinating Editor: Christine Ricketts
Copy Editors: William McManus and Mary Bearden
Compositor: SPi Global
Indexer: SPi Global
Artist: SPi Global
Cover Designer: Anna Ishchenko

Distributed to the book trade worldwide by Springer Science+Business Media New York, 233 Spring Street, 6th Floor, New York, NY 10013. Phone 1-800-SPRINGER, fax (201) 348-4505, e-mail orders-ny@springer-sbm.com, or visit www.springeronline.com Apress Media, LLC is a California LLC and the sole member (owner) is Springer Science + Business Media Finance Inc (SSBM Finance Inc). SSBM Finance Inc is a Delaware corporation.

For information on translations, please e-mail rights@apress.com, or visit www.apress.com.

Apress and friends of ED books may be purchased in bulk for academic, corporate, or promotional use. eBook versions and licenses are also available for most titles. For more information, reference our Special Bulk Sales–eBook Licensing web page at www.apress.com/bulk-sales.

Any source code or other supplementary materials referenced by the author in this text is available to readers at www.apress.com. For detailed information about how to locate your book's source code, go to www.apress.com/source-code/.

For Mom and Dad, who have always been there for me.

—Jon Reid

For my Rock, my Mother

—Thomas Valentine

Contents at a Glance

Contents

About the Authors

Jonathan Reid has been building web-based applications since 1996 and is passionate about creating awesome and compelling user experiences on the web. He is a firm believer in user-centered creative processes and is an advocate for standards and accessibility. Jon has a wide range of experience developing web applications, ranging from genetic analysis software to cutting-edge advertising. Jon teaches courses in JavaScript, jQuery, and jQuery Mobile, and has written extensively on all three topics. Jon bet his career on web technologies early on, and he is happy to see his bet paying off.

Jon is an alumnus of the University of Colorado, Boulder, where he graduated with a degree in physics and mathematics. He currently works as a Senior JavaScript Developer at Google, and lives in Sunnyvale, California with his partner of 15 years. He occasionally tweets as @jreid01 and blogs even more occasionally at webdev.dreamwidth.org.

Thomas Valentine lives in the small town of Selkirk, Manitoba, Canada on the shores of the Red River. His love of the written word has shaped his career and life and will continue to do so for many years to come.

About the Technical Reviewer

RJ Owen is a Product Manager and Design Lead at Convercent in Denver, Colorado. RJ started his career as a software developer and spent ten years working in C++, Java, and Flex before moving to the design and product side of things. He truly loves good design and understanding what makes people tick. RJ holds an MBA and a bachelor's in physics and computer science. He is a frequent speaker at many industry events including Web 2.0, SXSW Interactive, and Adobe MAX

Introduction

JavaScript has seen a huge increase in popularity in the last decade. Originally used to create interactive web pages and handle basic form validation, JavaScript is now the backbone of many complex web applications. As a result, people who can program well with JavaScript are in high demand for a wide range of projects. If you want to work with web technologies, you should know JavaScript.

This book aims to provide both a complete reference for JavaScript and to cover the fundamentals of the language. Our overall goal was to cover all the topics you need to work with JavaScript in projects of any size.

Who is this book for?

This book is aimed at two audiences: people who already know JavaScript and need a solid reference, and people who are just learning the language and want to come up to speed quickly. In either case we assume you have at least a basic background in programming. Chapter 1, in particular, assumes you are coming to JavaScript from a more traditional language, such as C++ or Java.

We also assume you have a basic understanding of HTML, including semantic markup and the various document type declarations—though throughout the book the examples that use HTML are written in HTML 5. We also assume you have a basic understanding of CSS and how to use it to manage the appearance of your web pages.

Finally, we assume you have a basic understanding of the web and its underlying protocols.

If you have never written a line of code in your life, or if you are brand new to web technologies, this might not be the best book for you. But as long as you have a basic understanding of programming and web technologies, this book can help you learn JavaScript.

Overview

This book is divided into two sections. The first section is devoted to teaching the basics of JavaScript and its related technologies. The second section is devoted to reference.

- **Chapter 1** is aimed at the programmer who is coming to JavaScript from another language. JavaScript is a much more dynamic language than most of the common languages, and moving to JavaScript from those languages can present special challenges. First we cover what JavaScript is and how it came to be, and then we dive right into the three main challenges that programmers of other languages encounter: JavaScript's object inheritance and lack of classes, its rules for scoping, and its dynamic typing. All of these features work quite differently in JavaScript than they do in other languages, and we want to get into them immediately. We wind up the chapter by providing some common patterns in JavaScript that use what we have learned.

- **Chapter 2** is an overall reference for the JavaScript language. We start at the beginning, with JavaScript's lexical structure, and quickly move into its operators, how it handles variables, JavaScript's take on objects, arrays, and functions. We wind up the chapter by going over JavaScript's flow control statements. Chapter 2 covers some of the things mentioned in Chapter 1 in more detail. Together they form a solid introduction to the language, all the way from the basics to intermediate concepts like closures.

- **Chapter 3** covers the Document Object Model. While the DOM is not technically a part of JavaScript, we include a chapter on it because chances are a significant amount of the work you'll be doing with JavaScript will involve the DOM. The chapter starts with a brief history of the DOM standard and how it has evolved. Then we dive right into the details: how to access page elements, how to manipulate them (including creating new elements and deleting existing ones), and the event model provided by the DOM (including custom events). We wind up the chapter with a discussion of cross-browser strategies for dealing with variations in the implementation of the DOM from browser to browser.

- **Chapter 4** takes everything we have learned in Chapters 1, 2, and 3 and puts them to work. We've divided the chapter up into sections, and each section covers something different. The first section, Working with JavaScript, covers what you need to get to work with JavaScript. We cover basic workflows as well as tools and debugging techniques. The second section covers increasing the efficiency of your JavaScript applications by closely examining how browsers load and parse scripts, and how you can use that to your advantage. The third section covers asynchronous communication using the XMLHTTP object—otherwise known as AJAX. The fourth section covers an important security limitation imposed by browsers—the single origin policy—and some techniques for working with that policy and still getting your work done. In the firth section we provide a practical example of data caching. Section six is all about choosing JavaScript libraries, and section seven covers the most popular JavaScript library, jQuery. Finally, we wrap up the chapter with a practical example of building your own library using everything we have learned so far in the chapter.

- **Chapter 5** begins the reference section of the book, and covers the objects that are a part of JavaScript.

- **Chapter 6** provides a reference for JavaScript's control statements.

- **Chapter 7** is all about JavaScript operators.

- **Chapter 8** is a DOM reference.

Even though they are reference chapters, we have tried to provide useful, nontrivial examples throughout.

Conventions Used In This Book

Throughout this book, code is presented in a `fixed-width` font. Code examples and syntax definitions are separated from other text and use the same font. In addition, inline mentions of code elements (such as objects, primitive values, etc) are also presented in the same font.

Code Downloads

All of the code snippets and examples are available for download from `http://www.apress.com/9781430246299`. This download includes all of the example code in the book, as well as some extra bits that didn't make it into the book itself. We encourage you to download the code and work with it as you go through the text.

CHAPTER 1

JavaScript Basics

In this chapter we are going to take a different approach from what you'll find in the first chapter of most programming language references. Most books would dive right into the syntax and other details of the language, but we are not going to do that here. JavaScript is a surprisingly difficult language to learn, and a relatively easy one to dislike, so we first want to explore why some people struggle with it, and then we'll provide a different, more intuitive approach to mastering the language.

We will begin by examining the challenges of learning and working with JavaScript. We'll cover a bit of background by examining the language's evolutionary history and implementations. Then, armed with that information, we'll examine the three specific areas where JavaScript is a challenge: its inheritance metaphor, its scoping metaphor, and its typing metaphor. We'll finish up by examining two very common patterns in JavaScript—a topic most books wouldn't cover until much later, but which we think you'll be amply prepared to handle by the end of this chapter. The patterns also serve as good applications of everything you will have learned in the chapter.

As we go through this chapter, we'll cover the bare bones basics of JavaScript as we encounter them, but we encourage you to not get too bogged down in considerations of syntax or other details at this stage. We'll cover those topics in later chapters. For now, concentrate on the bigger picture we're about to paint.

Hard to Learn, Harder to Love

JavaScript is the target of a lot of hate. If you enter "hate JavaScript" or "JavaScript sucks" into your favorite search engine, you'll immediately get back page after page of articles about why the language is terrible. You can read the articles for yourself—and we encourage you to do so—but after reading several of them, you'll notice a pattern that emerges in the complaints. There are a few key things that people dislike about JavaScript:

- Its implementation of objects and inheritance—prototypes vs. classes

- Its scoping rules

- Its handling of data types

And it's true, JavaScript does these three things quite differently from many common languages. To make matters worse, JavaScript employs syntax and structures similar to C or Java, which fosters the understandable expectation that JavaScript should behave like C or Java, but it doesn't. (This is a particular problem with JavaScript's scoping rules, which we'll discuss in more detail later in this chapter.)

Also, because JavaScript is very C-like, a programmer who is familiar with C-like languages (C, C++, Java, C#, etc.) can quickly and easily reach a level of proficiency in JavaScript without ever really understanding its inner workings. It's quite common to encounter talented developers who have been working with JavaScript for years (and who may even consider themselves JavaScript experts) but who really have only a basic understanding of the language and have little command of its true power.

So JavaScript is easy to misunderstand, difficult to master, and has significantly different implementations of three important language features. Add to that issues like varying implementations from browser to browser, and it's no wonder people have a low opinion of the language.

1

Lest we scare you away from the language, it's important to realize that many times this low opinion is due to misunderstanding how JavaScript works, or attempting to apply practices from other languages that don't map well to how JavaScript behaves. We have found that the more a developer is willing to learn about JavaScript, the more they appreciate it. That's true to some extent for any language, of course, but it's especially true for JavaScript. Its dynamic nature and true functionality are difficult to understand but once you do understand it the language starts to take on a beauty and simplicity that very few languages possess.

Our approach to teaching JavaScript is designed to help you form that level of understanding of JavaScript before we even begin covering details like functions, arrays, and flow control. We'll cover those things as well, and in great detail, but before we do we want to address head-on the major things that people find confusing or difficult about JavaScript. In so doing we hope to start you down your journey of mastering JavaScript. The first step in that mastery is understanding the origins of JavaScript and its continuing evolution.

What Is JavaScript?

JavaScript is a programming language that was first released in 1995. Despite its name, JavaScript actually has nothing to do with the Java programming language. From a high level, JavaScript has several notable features:

- *It is a scripting language*: JavaScript programs are "scripts" that are read and executed by an interpreter (or *engine*). This is distinguished from compiled languages, in which programs are read by a compiler and translated into an executable file. (Note that often JavaScript engines themselves are written in a compiled language.) Programs written in scripting languages are highly portable in that they can run in any environment where an interpreter for that language has been built.

- *It is C-like*: JavaScript's basic syntax and structure borrow heavily from C.

- *It is an object-oriented language*: JavaScript differs from most object-oriented languages, though, in that its inheritance model is prototype-based rather than class-based.

- *It has first-class functions*: JavaScript functions are full-fledged objects and have their own properties and methods, and may be passed into other functions as parameters or returned from other functions and assigned to variables.

- *It is dynamic*: The term "dynamic programming language" is broad and covers a lot of features. JavaScript's most dynamic features are its implementation of variable typing (see next point) and its eval() method and other functional aspects.

- *It is both dynamically typed and weakly typed*: JavaScript variables are not type-checked at interpretation time (making JavaScript a dynamically typed language), and how operations occur between operands of mixed types depends on specific rules within JavaScript (making JavaScript a weakly typed language).

- *It is an implementation of a standard*: As described in the following section, JavaScript is actually an implementation of the ECMA-262 standard, just as the C programming language is governed by an ISO standard.

These major features combine to make JavaScript somewhat unique. They also help make JavaScript basics fairly easy to learn if you have a passing familiarity with C-like languages, because you'll have very little problem with JavaScript's syntax or structure.

JavaScript is also heavily influenced by Scheme, another functional programming language that is a dialect of Lisp. JavaScript gets many of its design principles from Scheme, including its scoping.

So how did JavaScript come to have this unique combination of features?

The Evolution of JavaScript and the ECMA-262 Standard

As already mentioned, JavaScript is actually an implementation of a standard. It didn't start out that way, though. In September of 1995, Netscape released version 2.0 of its Navigator browser, which had a new feature: an object-oriented scripting language that could access and manipulate page elements. Created by Netscape engineer Brendan Eich and originally code-named "Mocha," the new scripting language was at first released as "LiveScript." Shortly thereafter it was renamed "JavaScript," to ride on the coattails of Sun's Java programming language.

In 1996, Netscape submitted JavaScript to the European Computer Manufacturer's Association (or ECMA for short; see http://www.ecma-international.org/memento/history.htm) for consideration as a standard. The resulting standard, ECMA-262, was adopted in June 1997. ECMA-262 properly defines the ECMAScript scripting language, and JavaScript is considered a "dialect" of ECMAScript. Another notable dialect of ECMAScript is version 3 or later of ActionScript. Technically, Internet Explorer does not implement JavaScript (due to copyright concerns), but instead implements Microsoft's own dialect of ECMAScript called "JScript."

The latest version of ECMAScript is 5.1, which was published in June 2011. The version trail from ECMAScript 3 to ECMAScript 5 has an interesting political history, including a division between the standards committee (as led by Brendan Eich) and industry stakeholders like Yahoo, Microsoft, and Google. We're not going to get into the details; suffice it to say that in the end all parties agreed to ECMAScript 5 as a unified solution.

As a part of ECMAScript 5, ECMA International published a suite of conformance tests that can be run by any browser and will show which ECMAScript 5 features the browser supports and which features it does not support. This suite, called Test262, is available at http://test262.ecmascript.org/. Note that it can take several hours to run the full suite of tests, which contains around 11,500 individual tests. As of this writing, no browser has a perfect score in Test262; the best scores currently belong to Safari and Internet Explorer, both of which fail only seven tests. Firefox has the worst score, currently failing 170 tests (though that's still quite an impressive achievement). These figures are as of this writing, and may very well change between now and publication. We encourage you to run the test suite on your favorite browsers and explore the tests that fail in each one. This will give you some idea of the differences in JavaScript implementations from browser to browser, and how small they really are.

The evolution of ECMAScript is continuing with the 6th edition, code-named ECMAScript Harmony. Harmony hasn't been officially released yet and, as of this writing, no officially sanctioned release date has been set. However, the specification drafts are all open for public viewing at http://wiki.ecmascript.org/doku. php?id=harmony:specification_drafts, and a quick review of them indicates that Harmony will contain several new features, among which are a syntactic implementation of classes, default parameters for functions, new string methods, and the addition of hyperbolic trigonometry functions to the Math library.

Many browser manufacturers have already implemented some Harmony features, but overall implementation is spotty and varies from manufacturer to manufacturer. For the most part, in this book we'll be covering JavaScript as a dialect of ECMAScript 5.1. Where ECMAScript 5 and Harmony overlap, we'll note the differences so that you can be aware of potential support pitfalls. Also, throughout this book we'll use "JavaScript" as the generic term for the language and its implementations unless we need to refer to a specific implementation or the standard itself.

Thanks to the standardizing influence of ECMA-262, all modern implementations of JavaScript are quite similar. Individual implementations will vary, especially for cutting-edge features, but the core standard is well-implemented.

JavaScript Implementations

JavaScript has been implemented in several different ways. Adobe's Acrobat document system, for example, implements a version of JavaScript that enables users to employ simple scripts in Acrobat documents. JavaScript engines have also been implemented as stand-alone resources on Windows, UNIX, and Linux for quite some time. Shortly after it first introduced JavaScript in 1995, Netscape included a server-side implementation of it in its Enterprise Server. Today, the most notable implementation of server-side JavaScript is in the Node.js software system.

By far the most common implementations of JavaScript are in web browsers. A web browser's JavaScript engine typically implements most of the features specified in the ECMA-262 standard. In addition, browsers often extend JavaScript with other features not specified by the ECMA standard. The most notable of these extensions is the Document Object Model, or DOM, which is a separate standard that is maintained by the World Wide Web Consortium (W3C). It's important to remember that the DOM and JavaScript are separate, independent standards, though much of the work JavaScript does in the browser involves manipulating the DOM. We will cover the DOM in more depth in Chapter 3.

Though JavaScript started its life as a browser-based scripting language, server-side implementations of JavaScript are becoming more and more common. On the server side, a JavaScript implementation will include most of the base features of ECMA-262. And, like browser-based implementations, server implementations can extend JavaScript with other features, such as libraries or frameworks. Though server and browser JavaScript implementations may differ on these extended features, the base features are the same: the JavaScript `Array` object has the same methods and properties whether it is implemented in the browser or on the server (assuming the implementation follows the ECMA standard, of course).

This makes your JavaScript skills particularly valuable. JavaScript is one of the few languages that has both client and server implementations, so learning JavaScript is a good investment. With the use of Node.js on the server side, along with client-side scripts, it is possible to build complex, data-driven applications with rich user interactions using JavaScript as the primary language.

Probably two of the best examples of using JavaScript on both the client and the server are Microsoft's Windows Azure Platform and Windows Software Development Kit for Windows 8 (Windows SDK). Both of them support using JavaScript for both back- and front-end implementations, making it possible to build Windows apps in JavaScript and leverage all the power of Microsoft's platforms.

We will not cover server-side JavaScript with Node.js in this book, but instead will focus on JavaScript in the context of a web browser.

Web Browsers and JavaScript

Modern web browsers are complex pieces of software. Most people think of web browsers as content browsers, as a "window on the Web" so to speak. To a programmer with an understanding of JavaScript, however, a web browser becomes something more powerful: a user interface (UI) platform. Whether you are creating a simple web page or a complex, data-driven application, the browser is your UI platform, and JavaScript is the language it uses.

JavaScript is just one of the many moving parts of a browser. At a very high level, a browser consists of a stack of individual subprograms (or *engines*), each of which has an important function:

- *UI engine*: The actual visual interface presented to the user, with address bar, rendering window, back and forward buttons, the bookmarks toolbar, and so forth.

- *Browser engine*: A controller that works between the UI layer and the rendering engine.

- *Rendering engine*: Responsible for reading HTML documents and their associated assets (such as images and Cascading Style Sheets) and deciding how they should look. The rendering engine is where the DOM lives.

- *Network engine*: Responsible for accessing the network.

- *Data persistence engine*: Manages the application's persistence layer, which is where cookies are stored, and where new HTML 5 features like web databases and local storage exist.

- *JavaScript engine*: Includes interfaces to the data persistence, network, and rendering engines and can observe and modify any or all of them.

Figure 1-1 illustrates how the JavaScript engine is quite separate from the rest of the browser's functions, though it works very closely with other parts of the browser.

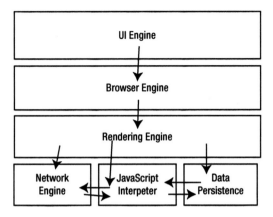

Figure 1-1. *Browser engine stack*

A WORD ABOUT BROWSER VERSIONS

Throughout this book we will be using HTML5 syntax for our HTML markup. Some of the examples will therefore have problems running in older browsers that don't implement HTML5 features. Most of the examples in this book have been tested in the latest stable version of Chrome, but should also work in the latest versions of Safari, Firefox, and Internet Explorer 10.

JavaScript in Web Pages

Web browsers load JavaScript either as blocks of content within the document itself (*inline scripts*) or as linked script files that are loaded separately.

Inline scripts are denoted using the `<script>` tag:

```
<script>
/* Your JavaScript here */
</script>
```

Linked scripts are added using the `<script>` tag as well:

```
<script src="js/init-document.js"></script>
```

This instructs the browser to fetch the referenced file and feed it directly to the JavaScript engine.

■ **Note**   You must use both the beginning and end tags. A self-closing tag is not permitted by the HTML5 standard (though some browsers might permit it).

You can include inline or linked scripts anywhere in the head or body of an HTML document.

Order of Execution

So now we're including JavaScript in our web page, but what is actually happening as the document is loading and being parsed by the browser?

As it turns out, there is an obvious specific parsing order for web browsers: browsers start parsing HTML documents at the top and work their way down, loading specified assets as they come to them. That means that a script (whether inline or linked) can only reference things (styles, other scripts, HTML elements, etc.) that are above it in the document.

Consider the simple HTML page presented in Listing 1-1.

Listing 1-1. Basic HTML Template

```
<!DOCTYPE html>
<html>
    <head>
        <title>JavaScript Developer's Guide</title>
    </head>
    <body>
        <h1>Hello World</h1>
    </body>
</html>
```

This will simply display a "Hello Word" message within the browser. We can demonstrate the order of script execution by adding three scripts, as shown in Listing 1-2.

Listing 1-2. Demonstrating Order of Execution

```
<!DOCTYPE html>
<html>
    <head>
        <title>JavaScript Developer's Guide</title>
        <script>
alert("This is the head.");
        </script>
    </head>
    <body>
        <script>
alert("This is the body, before the message.");
        </script>
        <h1>Hello World</h1>
        <script>
alert("This is the body, after the message.");
        </script>
    </body>
</html>
```

When loaded into the browser, this page will first pop up an alert window that reads This is the head. Note that there is not yet anything in the browser window itself; the browser has not yet parsed the rest of the document.

Next the browser will move down to the body. The next alert message will appear, but the browser window will still be empty. Then the "Hello World" headline will appear in the browser window, and then the last alert message will appear.

This example demonstrates not only the order of execution but also the important fact that JavaScript can block the parsing of the document. In our case, we're using the blocking function alert(), but if we were instead loading a complicated script in the head that took some time to download and parse, it would block the parsing of the rest of the document. Similarly, scripts in the body can cause delays in displaying the whole document. For complex JavaScript applications, the combination of parsing order and blocking can cause some undesirable effects. We'll explore some techniques for overcoming these problems in Chapter 4.

Brief Digression: Understanding and Running Examples

As we mentioned, we're not going to cover the details of syntax in this chapter—that's what the rest of the book is for. But before we jump into the deep end, we do want to cover a few important details about syntax and running these examples:

- *Variable declaration*: Throughout these examples we'll declare variables using the var keyword. The syntax is simple: var variableName declares the variable variableName and gives it the special value of undefined. Optionally, you can provide a value for your variable as part of the declaration: var variableName = myValue will both declare variableName and assign it the value myValue. You'll learn more about the var keyword in the "Scoping in JavaScript" section, later in this chapter, but we wanted to touch on it briefly before diving in.

- *Dot notation*: JavaScript uses dot notation to access properties and methods on objects: myObject.propertyName references propertyName on myObject, and myObject.methodName() invokes methodName on myObject.

- alert: Browsers provide an alert function to JavaScript that gives a quick way to display a string. When you call the alert method and pass it a string as a parameter, the browser performs the following steps:

  a. It pauses the execution of the script.

  b. It pops open a small window that displays the string you provided. The popup window includes a button labeled OK that, when clicked, dismisses the popup window.

  c. When the popup window is dismissed, the browser resumes execution of the script at the next statement after the alert.

- This makes alert an easy way to inspect variables and properties of a script with minimal effort. It also has the virtue of working on just about every browser in existence, even very old ones.

Running the Examples

There are a couple of ways you can run these examples. Probably the easiest is to take the template in Listing 1-1 and add a <script> tag after the <H1> tag. Then copy and paste the examples into the script tag, save the file, and load it into a browser.

Many browsers also provide a JavaScript console that you can use to enter the examples directly. However, the JavaScript console will evaluate your code at the time when you press Enter, and many of our examples are broken up into multiple lines. We don't recommend using the console, but if you want to give it a try, access the console on your favorite browser (typically Control- or Option-Shift-J is the keyboard shortcut, but it varies); for example:

- In Chrome, you can access the console via the "customize and configure Google Chrome" menu. Choose Tools ➤ JavaScript Console. You'll also see the keyboard shortcut for accessing the console (Control-Shift-J for Windows). You can type the code samples directly here.

- In Firefox, choose Tools ➤ Web Developer ➤ Error Console. You can type the code samples in the box labeled Code. If you want to use a console, be sure to type in entire valid statements before pressing Enter. To learn what constitutes a statement in JavaScript, you can skip ahead to Chapter 2.

JavaScript's Three Difficult Features

As we mentioned, there are three main features of JavaScript that people find problematic: the way it implements inheritance, the way it implements variable scope, and the way it implements data types. Rather than shy away from these features, we're going to dive directly into them.

Prototypal Inheritance

JavaScript is an object-oriented language, but, unlike most object-oriented languages, its inheritance is based on prototypes rather than classes. This difference is often misunderstood, and can be difficult to explain.

The biggest difference is that in JavaScript there is no such thing as classes. You can build class emulation with JavaScript, but out-of-the-box JavaScript has no classes. There are only objects, and you instantiate new objects from other objects.

Inheritance in JavaScript is handled through a special property on every object, called the prototype. The prototype property references all the properties and methods it inherited from its parent object—including its prototype. When you attempt to access a property or method on an object, JavaScript first looks to see if it exists in the local copy. If it doesn't, JavaScript checks the prototype. If it doesn't find the requested item in the prototype, it checks the prototype's prototype, and so on, all the way on up the inheritance chain.

You can override properties and methods in the prototype. That will essentially break the prototype chain at that point, so that object and any children instantiated from it will inherit the override, and no further searching up the prototype chain will be done.

In a way, the prototype chain can be thought of as a one-way linked list. The prototype is the reference to the previous element in the list.

One of the major aspects of prototypal inheritance is that if you change an inherited property or method on an object, its children will also reflect that change even after they've been created. This is because the children's prototypes all refer back to the parent properties and methods.

Another major aspect of prototypal inheritance is that you can change the prototype of any of the global objects, thus adding your own properties and methods to them—or even overriding their existing ones. Note however that overriding existing properties and methods of the global objects can be dangerous. Remember that those properties and methods were defined by a standard, so if you make them do something else, then you could lose the benefit of standards compliance. As a result, it's generally considered bad practice to override those properties and methods unless you are very careful about what you are doing.

Listing 1-3 provides a very simple example of prototypal inheritance.

Listing 1-3. Simple Example of Prototypal Inheritance

```
var myParent = {
    a: 10,
    b: 50
}

var myChild = Object.create(myParent);
var myGrandChild = Object.create(myChild);

alert(myGrandChild.a); // will alert 10
myParent.a = 20;
alert(myGrandChild.a); // will alert 20
alert(myChild.a); // will alert 20
```

We'll talk a bit more about the syntax of Object.create in a moment; for now, just concentrate on what the script is doing: first, it creates a parent object with the properties a and b, and then it creates a child object from that parent, and a grandchild object from the child. We now have three objects, each inheriting from its parent. When we check the grandchild object for the value of a, JavaScript traverses the prototype chain until it finds the property in the parent.

Since the prototype is just a reference, adding properties to a parent immediately makes them available in the child, as demonstrated in Listing 1-4.

Listing 1-4. Adding a Property to a Parent Makes It Available to the Children

```
var myParent = {
    a: 10,
    b: 50
}

var myChild = Object.create(myParent);
var myGrandChild = Object.create(myChild);

myParent.c = "hello";
alert(myChild.c); // will alert "hello"
alert(myGrandChild.c); // will alert "hello"
```

This example is similar to Listing 1-3, but we are adding a new property to the parent object after the children have been instantiated.

In some browsers, you can even examine the prototype directly because they provide a __proto__ property on the object, which you can view through the console (see Figure 1-2).

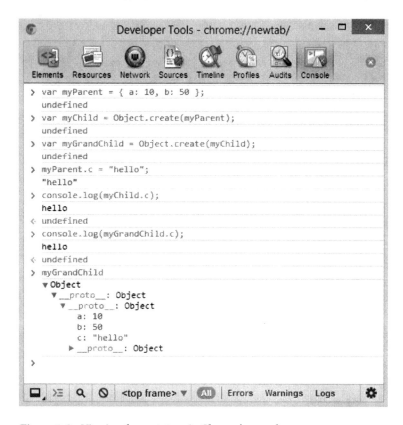

Figure 1-2. *Viewing the prototype in Chrome's console*

In Figure 1-2, we see that myGrandChild is an object, and when we expand it, we see that it has a __proto__ property. When we expand that, we see it has another __proto__ property, and when we expand that, we find the a and b properties. There is also another __proto__ property, which refers to the global Object object...thus, all of our objects inherit all of the properties and methods of the global Object object.

The idea of prototypal inheritance is simple, but it's surprisingly easy to misunderstand. Compounding the problem is that in earlier versions of JavaScript, the methods and syntax for creating new objects from other objects, shown in Listing 1-5, closely resembled the syntax of languages with classic inheritance.

Listing 1-5. Old Syntax for Creating New Objects and Modifying the Prototype

```
function myObject() {}; // constructor function
var myInstance = new myObject; // instantiate a new instance
alert(myInstance.prop1); // will alert "undefined" because it doesn't exist
myObject.prototype.prop1 = "Here I am";
alert(myInstance.prop1); // will alert "Here I am"
```

Not only is this somewhat inelegant, the new keyword led people to think of things in terms of classical inheritance, which only further confused the issue. And it required that any object from which you were planning on creating children be a function.

ECMAScript 5 defines a new property on the global Object: Object.create(). This method takes an object as a parameter, and returns a new object with the parameter object as its prototype. This syntax is tidier, as shown in Listing 1-6, and also helps clarify the inheritance chain and removes the need of directly accessing the prototype property.

Listing 1-6. Improved Syntax for Creating New Objects

```
var myObject = {};
var myInstance = Object.create(myObject);
alert(myInstance.prop1); // will alert "undefined" because it doesn't exist
myObject.prop1 = "Here I am";
alert(myInstance.prop1); // will alert "Here I am"
```

This new method works in modern browsers, but if you find yourself working with an older JavaScript engine that doesn't support this version of the standard (most notably, Internet Explorer 8 and earlier), you can always use the snippet shown in Listing 1-7 to provide the same functionality.

Listing 1-7. A Method for Adding the create Method to Object If It Doesn't Exist

```
if (typeof Object.create !== 'function') {
    Object.create = function (o) {
        function F() {}
        F.prototype = o;
        return new F();
    };
}
```

Listing 1-7 checks to see if Object.create exists, and if it doesn't, it adds it to the global Object object. This is a good example of a safe way to extend global objects.

SHIMS

Listing 1-7 is an example of what is what is known as a *shim* or *polyfill*, terms that refer to small scripts that add missing functionality to a particular environment, or that repair incorrect implementations. Listing 1-7 is a shim for a JavaScript shortcoming; there are also shims for various CSS issues and even HTML issues.

Shims are commonly included in JavaScript libraries—in fact, many libraries got their start as just collections of various shims.

Scoping in JavaScript

Another much-misunderstood and often-maligned feature of JavaScript is its scoping: how JavaScript limits and allows access to its variables. Because JavaScript closely resembles C in many ways, it's natural to think that it uses block-level scoping like C, an example of which is shown in Listing 1-8.

Listing 1-8. Block-level Scoping in C

```
#include <stdio.h>
int main() {
  int x = 1;
  printf("%d, ", x); // 1
  if (1) {
    int x = 2;
    printf("%d, ", x); // 2
  }
  printf("%d\n", x); // 1
}
```

In C, each code block (if statement, for loop, etc.) is its own scope: a variable defined in one scope is not available in another. It's logical to assume that JavaScript employs block-level scoping because it uses syntax very similar to C…but it doesn't.

Instead, JavaScript uses what is called *functional scope*, meaning that scope is declared by functions. A variable defined in a function is available anywhere within that function, even in other blocks such as if statements, for loops or nested functions. As a demonstration, here's a listing that creates a functional scope and tests variables within:

Listing 1-9. Demonstrating Nested Functional Scope

```
function testScope() {
    var myTest = true;
    if (true) {
        var myTest = "I am changed!"
    }
    alert(myTest);
}

testScope(); // will alert "I am changed!"
```

The example shown in Listing 1-9 creates a simple testScope function. Within it we declare a variable, myTest, which gives it scope to be available anywhere within that function. Then we redeclare the variable within an if statement block and give it a different value. Finally, we test to see what the results are: the script will alert I am changed!

In C or another language with block-level scope, a similar example would alert true because the myTest redeclaration in the if statement would be limited in scope to that block.

If we tried to access the myTest variable outside of the testScope function, it would fail, as shown in Listing 1-10.

Listing 1-10. Demonstrating Functional Scope

```
function testScope() {
    var myTest = true;
    if (true) {
        var myTest = "I am changed!"
    }
    alert(myTest);
}

testScope(); // will alert "I am changed!"
alert(myTest); // will throw a reference error, because it doesn't exist outside of the function
```

Outside of the testScope function, myTest doesn't exist. You can make it exist though, as shown in Listing 1-11.

Listing 1-11. Demonstrating Global Scope

```
var myTest = true;
function testScope() {
    if (true) {
        var myTest = "I am changed!"
    }
    alert(myTest);
}

testScope(); // will alert "I am changed!"
alert(myTest); // will alert "I am changed!"
```

By defining the myTest variable outside of the testScope function, it becomes available everywhere. This is what is called the *global scope*. Global functions and variables are available anywhere. This is a very powerful feature of JavaScript, but it is easy to abuse. Generally speaking, it's considered bad practice to clutter the global scope, mostly because it can lead to variables with the same name clobbering each other's values as scripts execute, causing all sorts of difficult-to-debug problems. Instead, it's recommended that variables be limited as much as possible to private scopes.

Limiting Scope

So far, we have been carefully declaring our new variables with the var keyword. But the var keyword is optional in JavaScript; you can simply declare a new variable by providing it a value, as demonstrated in Listing 1-12.

Listing 1-12. Declaring a Variable Without the var Keyword

```
var myNewVar = 1; // Using var to declare a variable.
myOtherNewVar = 2; // var is optional.
alert(myNewVar); // will alert 1
alert(myOtherNewVar); // will alert 2
```

However, when you declare a variable without the var keyword, JavaScript assumes that you mean you defined the variable in a higher scope and you want to access that variable. So JavaScript will look up to the containing scope to see if the variable was declared there using the var keyword. If it wasn't, JavaScript keeps looking up the scope chain until it reaches the global scope. If it reaches the global scope and still hasn't found a declaration using the var keyword, JavaScript will assign the variable to the global scope for you, as shown in Listing 1-13.

Listing 1-13. Cluttering the Global Scope

```
function testScope() {
    myTest = true; // now myTest is global.
    alert(myTest);
}
testScope();  // will alert "true"
alert(myTest); // will alert "true" as well, because now myTest is global.
```

This feature of JavaScript is called *implied global scope*. It basically means that variables that are not specifically limited in scope are assumed to be global.

To limit the scope of a variable, use the var keyword in its declaration, as shown in Listing 1-14. Using the var keyword instructs JavaScript to limit the scope of the variable to the current one. This prevents accidentally cluttering the global scope.

Listing 1-14. Limiting Scope with var

```
function testScope() {
    var myTest = true;
    function testNestedScope() {
        var myTest = false;
        alert(myTest);
    }
    testNestedScope();
    alert(myTest);
}

testScope(); // will alert false, and then true.
```

In Listing 1-14, we're defining two different myTest variables in different scopes. Within the testNestedScope function, myTest has a local definition that overrides the higher scope. This prevents two variables with different names from clobbering each other's values.

You might be wondering what would happen if we swapped the two lines within the testNestedScope function, as shown in Listing 1-15—in other words, what would happen if we try and access a variable before it was defined in a given scope?

Listing 1-15. Accessing a Variable Before It Was Defined in a Given Scope

```
function testScope() {
    var myTest = true;
    function testNestedScope() {
        alert(myTest);
        var myTest = false;
    }
    testNestedScope();
    alert(myTest);
}

testScope(); // will alert "undefined", and then true.
```

Listing 1-15 will alert undefined and then true. Why? That is, why doesn't the first line in testNestedScope alert true? After all, myTest is set to true in a higher scope, so why isn't it available there?

The reason is that we are limiting the scope of myTest within the testNestedScope variable by defining it with the var keyword. But when we access it before we give it a value, it is set to "undefined." So this code is the equivalent of the code shown in Listing 1-16.

Listing 1-16. More Explicit Equivalent of Listing 1-15

```
function testScope() {
    var myTest = true;
    function testNestedScope() {
        var myTest;
        alert(myTest);
        myTest = false;
    }
    testNestedScope();
    alert(myTest);
}

testScope(); // will alert "undefined", and then true.
```

Listing 1-16 illustrates what happened in Listing 1-15 by explicitly declaring the variable without a value at the very beginning of its scope. In JavaScript, any variable declared in a given scope is available anywhere within that scope, even before it is given a value. This feature of JavaScript is often called *hoisting*: a variable is "hoisted" to the beginning of the scope where it is declared. Because of hoisting, it's often considered a good practice in JavaScript to explicitly declare your variables at the beginning of their scope, even if you don't access them until much later.

Closures

In most languages, once a function returns, all of its local variables are *deallocated*—removed from memory and no longer available. In JavaScript, this doesn't have to happen. Because of JavaScript's dynamic nature and scoping rules, you can code situations where local variables within a function will remain available even after that function has finished executing. Consider the example presented in Listing 1-17.

Listing 1-17. Causing a Scope to Be Maintained After Its Function Has Finished Executing

```
function greet(myName) {
    var myAlertString = "Hello " + myName; // Local variable
    function doAlert() {
        alert(myAlertString);
    }
    return doAlert; // return the new function
}

var greetKitty = greet("Kitty"); // greetKitty is now a function
greetKitty(); // will alert "Hello Kitty"
```

Listing 1-17 is a somewhat contrived example, and there are some unusual things going on here, so let's go through them one at a time. The first strange thing is that we're returning a function from our function. This seems a little strange, but it's not that unusual in JavaScript. Remember, in JavaScript, functions are objects, so you can return them and even assign them to variables just as easily as any other object.

Our greet function takes a name as a parameter, concatenates it into a string in a local variable, then defines a local function that alerts that string. Then it returns that local function. When we call the greet function, we assign the returned function to a variable, and then execute the returned function.

What's special about this situation is that the greet function is called and completely executes at the time when we assign its result to the greetKitty variable. In most languages, the myAlertString variable would at that point be deallocated and unavailable. But in JavaScript it's still there, because we have created a specific situation where it needs to remain so that when we execute the returned function, everything will behave as expected. In other words, both the returned function and its immediate nonlocal functional scope are retained, even though the function that created them has finished running. This is a side effect of the variable scoping in JavaScript: the interpreter will maintain a scope until it is no longer needed.

That goes for the private scope we created as well. Listing 1-18 demonstrates this by saying "Hello" to a different cat.

Listing 1-18. The Privacy of a Maintained Scope

```
function greet(myName) {
    var myAlertString = "Hello " + myName; // Local variable
    function doAlert() {
        alert(myAlertString);
    }
    return doAlert; // return the new function
}

var greetKitty = greet("Kitty"); // greetKitty is now a function
greetKitty(); // will alert "Hello Kitty"
var greetMax = greet("Max"); // greetMax is now a function
greetMax(); // will alert "Hello Max"
greetKitty(); // will alert "Hello Kitty"
```

Both the greetMax and greetKitty functions have access to their own maintained scope, and those scopes are private from each other and the global scope.

The result of this particular example happens because of the scoping rules of JavaScript. If we allow the use of a global variable, as shown in Listing 1-19, then we no longer have a private, maintained scope for each function.

Listing 1-19. Using a Global Variable

```javascript
function greet(myName) {
    myAlertString = "Hello " + myName; // Now a global variable
    function doAlert() {
        alert(myAlertString);
    }
    return doAlert; // return the new function
}

var greetKitty = greet("Kitty"); // greetKitty is now a function
greetKitty(); // will alert "Hello Kitty"
var greetMax = greet("Max"); // greetMax is now a function
greetMax(); // will alert "Hello Max"
greetKitty(); // will alert "Hello Max"
var greetLenore = greet("Lenore");
greetLenore(); // will alert "Hello Lenore"
greetKitty(); // will alert "Hello Lenore"
greetMax(); // will alert "Hello Lenore"
```

In Listing 1-19 we have changed the situation by not enforcing a scope limit on the myAlertString variable. This allows JavaScript to imply that it's a global variable, which gets overwritten each time the greet function is called.

Maintaining a function and its parent scope even after its parent function has finished executing is called *closure*. Closures are an enormously important and powerful feature of JavaScript, and we will be using them extensively throughout this book.

Because you can use them to enforce privacy, closures are useful for encapsulating functionality and managing scope. They play a part in some of the most common JavaScript patterns, which we'll cover later in this chapter.

Closures are quite powerful, but they have one important drawback: because a closure requires the browser to keep memory allocated for the function and its scope, once a closure is no longer needed, the browser sometimes might not return all of the memory to the system. The primary symptom of this would be a *memory leak*: as the script continues to execute in the browser, the browser consumes more and more memory, eventually consuming all available memory. A memory leak assumes that the browser shouldn't otherwise be consuming more and more memory or is consuming it faster than it should.

Older browses had serious problems with memory leaks due to closures. Modern browsers are much more efficient but can still have problems. You should monitor the memory use of the browser as it runs your scripts to make sure it's not having problems.

One of Those Weak Types, Eh?

As we mentioned earlier, JavaScript is weakly typed. This means that if there is a type mismatch problem in an expression, JavaScript will resolve it according to its own rules. Consider as an example the code shown in Listing 1-20.

Listing 1-20. Demonstration of Weak Typing

```
var myNumber = 5; // Integer
var myString = "7"; // String
var myResult = myNumber + myString; // Type mismatch: integer + string = what?
alert(myResult); // Will alert "57"
```

A statically typed language would throw an error as this script was parsed. But JavaScript resolves the type mismatch itself, allowing the program to continue without crashing.

Many people consider weak typing to be a disadvantage, and indeed it is easy for novice JavaScript developers to make plenty of mistakes with weak typing. However, once you master JavaScript's typing rules, you can use this feature to its full potential and create scripts that are smaller and more elegant than the scripts you might have created with an equivalent strongly typed language.

Basic Data Types and Primitives

We'll begin our exploration of JavaScript typing by reviewing its basic data types. Yes, though it is weakly typed, JavaScript actually does have data types, they're just broader than typical data types. The four basic data types are:

- *Boolean*: Variables or expressions which are either true or false.

- *Number*: All numbers in JavaScript are 64-bit floating-point numbers.

- *String*: Strings of any characters.

- *Object*: Collections of properties and methods.

JavaScript uses these data types as the basis of all of its type management. To determine the type of anything in JavaScript, use the typeof operator, as demonstrated in Listing 1-21 (see Chapter 7 for full details on the typeof operator).

Listing 1-21. Using the typeof Operator

```
var myArrayOfThings = ["hello", 5, true, {}];
for (var i = 0; i < myArrayOfThings.length; i++) {
    alert(typeof myArrayOfThings[i]);
}
alert(typeof myArrayOfThings);
```

This will alert, in order, "String", "Number", "Boolean", "Object", and "Object". (Yes, in JavaScript, arrays are objects.) Note that typeof will return "Function" for a function, though in JavaScript there is no Function type.

In addition, JavaScript has the concept of *primitives*: non-object simple values. JavaScript primitives are the building blocks from which the more complex data types are built. They are

- *Boolean*: The true and false keywords are the Boolean primitives themselves.

- *Null*: The null keyword.

- *Number*: A number by itself is a number primitive.

- *String*: A string of characters enclosed in quotes is a string primitive.

- *Undefined*: A special value representing a variable that has been created with the var keyword, but to which no value has been assigned.

It's important to note that in JavaScript, anything that is not a primitive is an object. Functions, for example, are objects.

You can also convert between primitives and objects in JavaScript. You'll notice that boolean, number, and string primitives have global objects to match (see Chapter 5 for details on the Boolean, Number, and String global objects and how to use them). Consider the example shown in Listing 1-22.

Listing 1-22. So Wait, Is It a Primitive or Not?

```
var myString = "hello there" // primitive
alert(myString.length); // will alert 11...but length is a property of the String object
alert(typeof myString); // will alert "string"
```

This code snippet alerts 11, the length of the string. But why? If "hello there" is indeed a primitive, how come we can access myString.length?

We can do that because, behind the scenes, JavaScript is converting our primitive value to its associated object, thus giving us access to all of the properties and methods of String. This conversion is transient, which is why typeof myString still results in "String" rather than "Object."

This sort of behind-the-scenes conversion happens frequently in JavaScript, which is another reason why it's important to fully understand how JavaScript does it.

Type Conversion in JavaScript

Now that we have all of the basics defined, we can look at how JavaScript actually handles type mismatches. JavaScript has a set of functions it uses to handle conversion from one type to another: toPrimitive(), toNumber(), and toBoolean(). These functions are *abstract*, meaning they are private to the inner workings of JavaScript and can't be directly called by scripts.

The toPrimitive() method takes an input argument, and can also take an optional preferredType argument. It converts nonprimitives (that is to say, Objects) to their closest associated primitive type. If the input argument can decompose to more than one primitive type, the preferredType argument can be used to specify which one to choose. Table 1-1 summarizes the rules that toPrimitive() follows, depending on its input argument type:

Table 1-1. *Rules for toPrimitive*

input Argument Type	Result
Object	If valueOf() returns a primitive, then return that; else, if toString returns a primitive value, then return that; else, throw an error
Everything else	No change

The toNumber() method takes an input argument and tries to convert it to a Number, as shown in Table 1-2.

Table 1-2. *Rules for toNumber*

input Argument Type	Result
Boolean	1 if true, +0 if false
Null	+0
Number	No conversion
Object	toNumber(toPrimitive(object))
String	Converted similarly to parseInt() (see "Miscellaneous Global Functions and Variables" in Chapter 5 for a full explanation of parseInt()), except if the primitive value contains anything other than numbers, a single decimal, or a leading + or –, it returns NaN
Undefined	NaN

The `toBoolean()` method takes an `input` argument and tries to convert it to either `true` or `false`, as shown in Table 1-3.

Table 1-3. *Rules for toBoolean*

input Argument Type	Result
Boolean	No conversion
Null	`false`
Number	If –0, +0, or NaN, return `false`; otherwise, return `true`
Object	`true`
String	If the string is empty, return `false`; otherwise, return `true`
Undefined	`false`

The most common place where type conversion occurs in a script is during the evaluation of an `if (Expression) Statement` conditional, and when using the `==` comparison. In the case of the conditional, Expression is reduced to a boolean using `toBoolean()`. And the algorithm for type conversion for `==` is a simple algorithm defined by the ECMA-262 standard and outlined in Table 1-4.

Table 1-4. *Type Conversion Algorithm for == Operator*

Type of x	Type of y	Result
Null	Undefined	`true`
Undefined	Null	`true`
Number	String	`x == toNumber(y)`
String	Number	`toNumber(x) == y`
Boolean	Any	`toNumber(x) == y`
Any	Boolean	`x = toNumber(y)`
String or Number	Object	`x == toPrimitive(y)`
Object	String or Number	`toPrimitive(x) == y`

There are a couple of important takeaways from this algorithm: first, that `null` and `undefined` are equal to each other and nothing else, and second, that eventually everything else gets reduced to numbers to facilitate comparison.

Even though this algorithm is actually pretty simple, many people don't understand it and, as a result, find the behavior of `==` to be confusing. People find it so confusing that a common recommended best practice for JavaScript coding is to avoid the use of `==` (and `!=`) and instead use `===` (and `!==`) at all times. Listing 1-23 is a version of an example that is often cited as a reason to avoid using `==` in JavaScript.

Listing 1-23. Confusing Type Conversion in JavaScript

```
if ("Primitive String") {
    alert("Primitive String" == true);
    alert("Primitive String" == false);
}
```

This code will first alert `false` and then alert `false` again, so it's not hard to understand why this might cause people to throw up their hands in frustration. Let's walk through it step by step:

1. In the `if` statement, we see JavaScript applying `toBoolean()` on `"Primitive String"`, which evaluates to `true`, so execution moves into the code block.

2. We apply the algorithm to `"Primitive String" == true`, which tells us to check `"Primitive String" == toNumber(true)`, which is the same as `"Primitive String" == 1`.

3. We check `toNumber("Primitive String") == 1`, which is the same as `NaN == 1`, which is `false`.

4. We go through the same thing with `"Primitive String" == false`, which, after a couple of applications of the algorithm similar to step 2, gets us to `NaN == false`, which is also `false`.

Now that we understand the rules, the results of Listing 1-23 actually makes perfect sense.

Consider the common code pattern shown in Listing 1-24, in which we are trying to provide a default for an argument in a function.

Listing 1-24. A Common Mistake: Checking if Something is undefined or null

```
function myFunction(arg1) {
    // Check if arg1 wasn't provided
    if ((arg1 === undefined) || (arg1 === null)) {
        // provide default value for arg1 here
    }
    // Continue with function...
}
```

The common mistake in Listing 1-24 shows a lack of understanding of one of the most basic type conversion rules: `null` and `undefined` are equal to each other and nothing else. Listing 1-25 shows a better way to write this code.

Listing 1-25. A Better Solution to Check if Something is undefined or null

```
function myFunction(arg1) {
    // Check if arg1 wasn't provided
    if (arg1 == null) {
        // provide default value for arg1 here
    }
    // Continue with function...
}
```

You could have checked `arg1 == undefined`, but because `undefined` is a variable, it has two disadvantages: first, comparing with `undefined` entails a scope chain lookup, which usually isn't that big of a deal, but if you're buried deep in scope and/or implementing the check in a long loop, it can have a performance hit; second, there is a slight chance that its value could be overwritten by accident (it's rare, but it happens). It's safer to compare with `null`.

Putting It Together: Two Common Patterns

Every language has common patterns you see used frequently, and JavaScript is no exception. JavaScript's common patterns make use of one or more of the features we've covered in this chapter, so they're excellent practical examples of those features and how powerful they can be. The first pattern is a syntax pattern that you will see used all the time in JavaScript, and which you will use many times yourself. The second is an implementation pattern that is likewise very common, and will help you begin organizing your JavaScript into manageable modules.

Immediately Executing Function Expressions

In other examples in this chapter, we have created functions within functions and then executed them. Is it possible to define a function and then immediately execute it without having to call it separately?

In JavaScript, the notation to call a function is to place a pair of parentheses after the function's name (or after the name of the variable to which it has been assigned—see Chapter 2 for more details on this distinction). So, if we just place a pair of parentheses after a function declaration, will that execute it? For example, would the code in Listing 1-26 work?

Listing 1-26. Attempting to Immediately Invoke a Function

```
function greet(myName) {
    var myAlertString = "Hello " + myName; // Local variable
    function doAlert() {
        alert(myAlertString);
    }()
}

greet("Kitty");
```

The answer is *no*, this doesn't work. When the JavaScript interpreter sees the keyword `function`, it assumes what follows is a declaration to be added to the scope and not an expression to be evaluated. You have to explicitly tell the interpreter that your function is an expression to be evaluated, and you do this by putting parentheses around it, as shown in Listing 1-27.

Listing 1-27. Immediately Invoked Function

```
function greet(myName) {
    var myAlertString = "Hello " + myName; // Local variable
    (function doAlert() {
        alert(myAlertString);
    })()
}

greet("Kitty");
```

This will actually work as you would expect. You don't even have to name your function, either, as shown in Listing 1-28.

Listing 1-28. Immediately Invoked Anonymous Function

```
(function() {
    // do stuff here
})();
```

You can also pass variables into the invocation, as shown in Listing 1-29.

Listing 1-29. Passing Variables into an Immediately Invoked Anonymous Function

```
(function(var1, var2) {
    // do stuff here
})(myExternalVar1, myExternalVar2);
```

Immediately invoked anonymous functions are useful because they provide a way to exploit closures and manage scope. Everything within the expression is private unless you specifically return something to the global scope, which makes it a lot easier to keep your global scope clear of unneeded clutter. The immediately invoked anonymous function pattern is used throughout JavaScript development, most notably in the module pattern.

The Module Pattern

Imagine you are working on a large JavaScript application with many other developers. You need a way to encapsulate sections of code so that they can have a private namespace, so that you can avoid conflicts with existing code. How would you do this? With the module pattern, of course.

The module pattern uses an immediately invoked function to create a closure for all of your encapsulated code. You can have private members, and you can even publish public APIs. The basic pattern is shown in Listing 1-30.

Listing 1-30. Module Pattern

```
var Module = (function() {
    var _privateVariable = "This is private",
        _otherPrivateVariable = "So is this",
        public = {}; // This object will be returned
    function privateMethod() {
        alert("This method is private as well");
    }

    public.publicProperty = "This is a public property";
    public.publicMethod = function() {
        alert("This is a public method");
    }
    return public;
})()

alert(Module._privateVariable); // will alert "undefined"
// Module.privateMethod(); // would throw an error if we let it run
alert(Module.publicProperty); // will alert "This is a public property"
Module.publicMethod(); // will alert "This is a public method"
```

The module pattern is an excellent example of using closure to manage scope. Within the module there is a private scope that is self-contained and safe from modification.

That's not all. You can even easily extend the module by reprocessing it through an immediately invoked function. All you have to do is pass the original module into the new immediately invoked function as an argument, as shown in Listing 1-31.

Listing 1-31. Extending the Module

```
var Module = (function(oldModule) {
    oldModule.newMethod = function() {
        alert("This is a new method!");
    }
    return oldModule;
})(Module)
```

You can also create submodules on modules, as shown in Listing 1-32.

Listing 1-32. Creating Submodules

```
Module.sub = (function() {
    var _privateSubVariable = "This is a private variable in the submodule",
    public = {};
    public.publicSubVariable = "This is a public variable in the submodule";
    return public;
})();
```

Because it makes such great use of JavaScript's dynamic features, the module pattern is highly flexible. In fact, if you take a look at the source code for modern JavaScript libraries (jQuery, for example), you'll see that many of them are built using this pattern.

Summary

In this chapter we tackled head-on the things that people find most difficult about JavaScript. We didn't shy away from the fact that many people don't like JavaScript because of these things, and we explained JavaScript's history and continuing evolution so that you understand how JavaScript ended up this way. Having read this chapter, you now should understand the following:

- The three things that people have the most trouble with when learning JavaScript are scoping, inheritance, and types.

- JavaScript's inheritance is prototypal rather than class-based.

- JavaScript's scoping is based on functions rather than code blocks.

- JavaScript's scoping and functional nature allow you to create closures.

- JavaScript handles types in very specific and well-defined ways.

You should also be familiar now with immediately executed function expressions and the module pattern, and how the module pattern employs closure to maintain scope and enforce privacy.

With this chapter under your belt, you are ready to dig deeper into the nuts and bolts of JavaScript. In the next chapter we will cover the details that we glossed over in this chapter, from expressions and statements to objects, and all the way to functions and flow control.

CHAPTER 2

▓ ▓ ▓

JavaScript Nuts and Bolts

In Chapter 1 we covered some of the basics of JavaScript. We delved quite deep into a few of the concepts that people struggle with when learning the language. We didn't really address the language as a whole, though, which is what we'll do now. In this chapter we'll dive into the details we glossed over in Chapter 1 and get to the nuts and bolts of the language. We'll also discuss some of the things we touched on in Chapter 1 in more detail.

This chapter will provide you with a solid grounding in the JavaScript language, and will do so in a way that's both accessible to novices to the language and still a valuable reference for the experienced JavaScript developer. Our hope is that, as you progress in your JavaScript development skills, you'll refer to this chapter both to remind yourself of the basics and to dive into specific topics more deeply.

We will begin by reviewing some basic matters of formatting JavaScript code, especially as related to the examples in this book. Then we will cover expressions and statements, the two most basic building blocks of JavaScript from which all JavaScript programs are built. With that groundwork laid, we can then discuss creating more complex statements with operators. We will talk about variables and how to manage them in your JavaScript programs. Then we will discuss objects and arrays, which will give you the building blocks for everything else. Then we will have an in-depth discussion of functions: what they are, and how to make them, and we will gain some important insights into the dynamic nature of JavaScript. Finally, we will cover how to control our programs with conditionals and loops.

By the end of this chapter, you should have a solid understanding of JavaScript's lexical structure and syntax, and should feel comfortable using its basic constructs for flow control and functionality.

▓ **Note**   Throughout this chapter, we will be referring to, and even quoting directly, the ECMA-262 standard, the current version of which is ECMAScript Language Specification, 5.1 Edition. You are encouraged to explore the standard itself at www.ecma-international.org/ecma-262/5.1/ (which also provides a link for a downloadable PDF version), as this is an excellent way of expanding your understanding of JavaScript.

Formatting JavaScript Code

Formatting code is one of the many subjects that will invariably result in a roomful of angry developers shouting at each other. (I once saw someone nearly throw a chair in the middle of an argument about indenting with spaces vs. tabs.) Even though it's a touchy subject, this reference would be remiss without at least laying the groundwork for future arguments, as well as defining the conventions we will use throughout this book.

Broadly, JavaScript uses C-like formatting. Most notably, JavaScript uses curly brackets ({ }) to denote blocks of code, like loops or logical flow control.

JavaScript also uses two styles of comment delimiters. The double-slash (//) is the single-line delimiter, which indicates that everything from that point to the end of the line is a comment. JavaScript also uses /* to denote the beginning of a multiline comment and */ to indicate the end. Anything contained within those delimiters, regardless of new lines, is considered a comment.

Whitespace, including indentation, for the most part is unimportant. To quote Section 7.2 of the ECMA-262 standard: "White space characters are used to improve source text readability and to separate tokens (indivisible lexical units) from each other, but are otherwise insignificant." JavaScript doesn't care if you indent with tabs or spaces, or even if you indent at all. Similarly, JavaScript imposes no requirements for new lines. In fact, it's common to "compress" JavaScript by removing all whitespace and running everything together on one line for the sake of reducing file size (see Chapter 4 for more information on compressing JavaScript).

JavaScript uses semicolons (;) to terminate statements. However, semicolons can be considered optional because JavaScript interpreters practice automatic semicolon insertion (ASI), which means they attempt to correct code that would be nonfunctional without semicolons by automatically inserting them as needed. As a result you can choose to write your JavaScript without using many (or even any) semicolons, and instead rely on ASI. Traditionally, it has been considered a best practice to explicitly use semicolons to terminate statements. However, with the advent of newer meta-scripting languages like CoffeeScript, many people now prefer to write terse code that employs a minimum of semicolons and instead relies on ASI as much as possible.

From a practical standpoint, either method is acceptable in that either method will help produce consistent, functional code. However, as with anything involving programming style, there have been many heated arguments recently about explicit semicolon use versus relying on ASI.

Relying on ASI

ASI follows a well-defined set of rules laid out in the ECMA-262 standard (Section 7.9 of Edition 5.1). If you would like to write JavaScript without semicolons, you are encouraged to review the standard so you know exactly what you are doing. We won't cover the rules in detail here, but if you would like to rely on ASI, there are some important things to bear in mind.

Broadly, if the JavaScript engine encounters a new line (or a curly brace, though ASI is invoked mostly for new lines) that is used to break up tokens that otherwise don't belong together, JavaScript will insert a semicolon—but only if it needs to do so in order to create syntactically valid code: code that the interpreter can successfully parse and execute. But the interpreter does not care if the code results in an error when it is executed. It only cares that the code can be executed.

To illustrate this, consider the two lines of JavaScript shown in Listing 2-1.

Listing 2-1. JavaScript with No Semicolons

```
myResult = argX - argY
myFunction()
```

If the interpreter were to encounter this code, it would determine that indeed a semicolon is needed to make this code functional, and it would insert one (Listing 2-2):

Listing 2-2. Result of ASI on Listing 2-1

```
myResult = argX - argY;
myFunction()
```

On the other hand, consider the two lines of code in Listing 2-3.

Listing 2-3. More JavaScript with No Semicolons

```
myResult = argX - argY
[myResult].myProperty = "foo"
```

In this case, the interpreter would not insert a semicolon because, even though there is a new line, a semicolon isn't needed to make the code functional. Instead, the interpreter would assume we meant what you see in Listing 2-4.

Listing 2-4. What the Interpreter Thinks Listing 2-3 Means

```
myResult = argX - argY[myResult].myProperty = "foo";
```

If you actually run the example, your browser will throw a Reference Error complaining about an invalid assignment. The = operator is JavaScript's assignment operator, and JavaScript expects assignments to be formed such that the left operand takes the value of the right operand. In this example, JavaScript is unable to determine what you even mean in the left operand, let alone be able to use the result to assign a value.

This is a contrived example, but it does expose the main consideration when relying on ASI: you have to understand the rules in order to use it effectively, whereas explicitly using semicolons leaves no doubt. And not only do you have to understand the rules, anyone who will be working with you on your code will have to understand them as well.

Be Consistent

Every programmer has their own personal opinions about programming style, which is fine; what's important is to pick one way of doing things and be consistent. Consistently written code is much easier to read and understand than code written with multiple bracketing styles, inconsistent indentation rules, and variable naming conventions. To that end, in this book we employ the following styles for the sake of consistency:

- *Semicolons*: We use semicolons explicitly (instead of relying on ASI).

- *Brackets*: We use the so-called "one true bracketing style," where opening brackets are placed on the same line as their associated statements, and closing brackets are on their own line at the same indention as their associated statements.

- *Variable naming*: By and large, properties are nouns and methods are verbs. In some examples, we rely on a variation of "Hungarian notation," wherein variable names are prefixed with an indication of their type or functionality (e.g., `intCounter` or `strMessage`), just for the sake of being even more explicit about the variable's use or role within the example.

These particular choices aren't meant to be singled out as better than others. When deciding which styles to use in your projects, you should pick what works best for you, your team, and your situation. Consistency is what is important.

Expressions and Statements

Expressions and statements are the first things to understand really well about JavaScript because they are the basic building blocks for JavaScript programs. The distinction between expressions and statements is simple, but subtle.

Expressions

Conceptually, expressions are like words or phrases in a spoken language. They are the simplest building blocks of a program. In JavaScript, an *expression* is any section of code that resolves to a value. Since literal expressions evaluate to actual values, JavaScript supports the same broad types of expressions as it does of variables: boolean, number, string, and object. Expressions can be as simple as just stating a value, or they can be mathematical or logical operations, as shown in Listing 2-5:

Listing 2-5. JavaScript Literal Expressions

```
10           // Literal expression, resolves to 10
"Hello World" // Literal expression, resolves to the string "Hello World"
3+7          // Mathematical expression, resolves to 10
```

You can also write compound expressions. A *compound expression* is an expression in which one (or more) of the items in the expression is another expression. Compound expressions can be as complex and as nested as needed, as in Listing 2-6:

Listing 2-6. Compound Expressions

```
(3+7)/(5+5)                      // evaluates to 1
Math.sqrt(100)                   // evaluates to 10
```

One of the most common places you'll encounter expressions is in a conditional, as demonstrated in Listing 2-7.

Listing 2-7. Compound Expression in a Conditional

```
if ((myString === "Hello World") && (myNumber > 10)) {
                                 // conditional code here
}
```

In this example, we have a compound expression consisting of two expressions, one testing the value of myString and the other testing the value of myNumber, which will evaluate to either true or false. Those expressions are included in a single logical AND expression, so if both evaluate to true, the conditional code will execute. (We'll talk more about nested multiple expressions in a bit; for now, just concentrate on each individual expression as the boolean that it represents.)

Finally, though an expression can stand on its own, as shown in Listing 2-8, such an expression typically is not very useful.

Listing 2-8. A Not-So-Useful Literal Expression

```
var myNumber = 10,
    myOtherNumber = 20;

"hello world";                   // um, okay?

if (myOtherNumber > myNumber) {
    alert("Condition was true!"); // will alert because conditional is true
}
```

This code will execute without throwing an error, and will alert "Condition was true!" as expected. The literal expression on the third line of Listing 2-8 is perfectly valid, though it is not doing anything useful. To actually do something, literal expressions are usually combined with operators: an assignment (using the = operator), a conditional (using logic operators), and so forth.

The bottom line about expressions (even compound expressions) is that they only represent values. If you want to actually do anything with those values, you need to use a statement.

Statements

In JavaScript, a *statement* is a collection of one or more expressions that performs a specific action. To return to the spoken language analogy, if expressions are words and phrases, then statements are full sentences. Conceptually, the simplest type of statement is an expression that has a side effect, such as variable assignment or a simple mathematical operation. See Listing 2-9 for some examples.

Listing 2-9. Simple Statements

```
var x = 5,      // variable assignment, a statement
    y = 3,
    z = x + y; // mathematical operation, also a statement
```

Sometimes these simple statements are referred to as *expression statements* to underline the fact that they are essentially expressions with side effects. However, that term can confuse the subtle distinction between expressions and statements, so in this book we will not use it.

Just as JavaScript has compound expressions, it also has compound statements. A *compound statement* is a collection of statements in a block of code, often enclosed in curly brackets. Excellent examples of compound statements are if statements and loops, shown in Listing 2-10.

Listing 2-10. if Statements and Loops Are Compound Statements

```
if (expression) {
    // conditional statement--often a compound statement because it contains multiple statements.
}
for (expression) {
    // repeated statement--often a compound statement because it contains multiple statements.
}
```

Note, however, that not every section of code enclosed in curly brackets is necessarily a statement. Object literals, for example, are expressions, not statements, despite being multiple expressions enclosed in brackets, as you can see in Listing 2-11.

Listing 2-11. An Object Literal Is Not a Statement

```
{
    prop1: "value",
    prop2: "value2"
}
```

However, as long as you remember that expressions (even compound expressions) represent values and nothing else, the fact that an object literal is not a statement should be clear because an object literal is simply the specification of an actual object value. For more information on object literals, see the "Objects" section later in this chapter.

Operators

Operators, perhaps unsurprisingly, perform operations on expressions. Operators perform their function ("operate") on operands. Most JavaScript operators are *binary*, meaning they take two operands, typically in this format:

```
operand1 operator operand2
```

Probably the most commonly used binary operator in JavaScript is the assignment operator, =. Other examples include mathematical operators and most logical operators.

A few JavaScript operators are *unary*, meaning they take only one operand; for example:

```
operand operator
```

or

```
operator operand
```

The order of operand and operator depends on both the operator in question and, sometimes, what you're trying to do with the operator. Examples include the logical NOT operator or the mathematical negation operator.

In addition, JavaScript has one *ternary* operator, known as the *conditional operator*. It takes three operands and performs a conditional test:

```
conditionalExpression  ? valueIfTrue : valueIfFalse
```

The conditional operator allows you to write more terse code than if you explicitly used an `if-then-else` statement and can be used anywhere you would use a standard operator.

JavaScript operators fall into the following broad categories:

- *Arithmetic operators*: Perform arithmetical operations on their operands, such as addition, multiplication, etc.

- *Assignment operators*: Modify variables, either by assigning their values or altering their values according to specific rules.

- *Bitwise operators*: Treat their operands as a set of 32 bits, and perform their operations in that context.

- *Comparison operators*: Compare their operands and return a logical value (true or false) based on whether or not the comparison is true.

- *Logical operators*: Perform logical operations on their operands and are often used to link together multiple comparisons.

- *String operators*: Perform operations on two strings, such as concatenation.

- *Miscellaneous operators*: Operators that don't fall into any of the above categories. This category includes the conditional operator and operators such as the void operator and the comma operator.

We're not going to cover every single operator in detail in this chapter; that reference is available in Chapter 7. However, there is one important operator concept we want to cover here: precedence.

Precedence

If you have multiple operators in one statement, how do you determine the order in which to execute them? Do you evaluate them strictly left to right? Are there other rules? Different orders of execution can produce different results depending on the operators and their operands, so it's important to have a standard way of approaching this problem.

Consider the example in Listing 2-12 involving mathematical operators.

Listing 2-12. Multiple Mathematical Operators in a Single Statement

```
var myVar = 5 + 7 * 3 + 4 - 2 * 8;
alert(myVar); // what will this alert?
```

If you evaluate the statement in Listing 2-12 from left to right, performing each operation as you come to it, you end up with 304. However, the example actually alerts 14, because some operators are evaluated before others according to a set of rules known as *precedence*. In this example, multiplication has a higher precedence than addition or subtraction, so that statement is actually evaluated as shown in Listing 2-13, which uses parentheses to indicate precedence explicitly by grouping together the operations as they are actually evaluated.

Listing 2-13. Using Parentheses to Demonstrate Precedence Explicitly

```
var myVar = ((5 + (7 * 3)) + 4) - (2 * 8);
alert(myVar); // will alert 14
```

As it happens, mathematical operator precedence in JavaScript follows the precedence rules of mathematics itself: items in parentheses or brackets are evaluated first, followed by exponents and roots, followed by multiplication and division, followed by addition and subtraction.

Listing 2-14 provides another example, involving just addition and subtraction, two operators that are of the same precedence.

Listing 2-14. Multiple Operators of the Same Precedence

```
var myVar = 5 + 6 - 7 + 10;
alert(myVar); // what will this alert?
```

What's the value of myVar? It depends on the order in which you execute the operations. It would be 14 if you evaluated it from left to right, or it would be –6 if you evaluated it as $(5 + 6) - (7 + 10)$.

When you have multiple operators of the same precedence together, they will evaluate according to their associativity: either left to right, or right to left. In the case of mathematical operators, they are all evaluated left to right, so the value of myVar is 14.

Because JavaScript has more than just mathematical operators, it has slightly more complex precedence rules than those that come with mathematics, as you can see in Table 2-1.

Table 2-1. *Operator Precedence in JavaScript*

Precedence	Operator Type	Associativity	Individual Operator(s)
1	Member	Left to right	., []
	New	Right to left	new
2	Function call	Left to right	()
3	Increment	Not applicable (unary)	++
	Decrement	Not applicable (unary)	--
4	Logical NOT	Right to left	!
	Bitwise NOT	Right to left	~
	Unary +	Right to left	+
	Unary negation	Right to left	-
	Typeof	Right to left	typeof
	Void	Right to left	void
	Delete	Right to left	delete
5	Multiplication	Left to right	*
	Division	Left to right	/
	Modulus	Left to right	%
6	Addition	Left to right	+

(continued)

Table 2-1. (*continued*)

Precedence	Operator Type	Associativity	Individual Operator(s)
	Subtraction	Left to right	-
7	Bitwise shift	Left to right	`<<, >>, >>>`
8	Relational	Left to right	`<, <=, >, >=`
	In	Left to right	`in`
	Instanceof	Left to right	`instanceof`
9	Equality	Left to right	`==, !=, ===, !==`
10	Bitwise AND	Left to right	`&`
11	Bitwise XOR	Left to right	`^`
12	Bitwise OR	Left to right	`|`
13	Logical AND	Left to right	`&&`
14	Logical OR	Left to right	`||`
15	Conditional	Right to left	`? :`
16	Yield	Right to left	`yield`
17	Assignment	Right to left	`=, +=, -=, *=, /=, %=, <<=, >>=, >>>=, &=, ^=, !=`
18	Comma	Left to right	`,`

Understanding operator precedence is important; otherwise, your statements might produce unexpected results. Even so, many JavaScript best practices and style guides recommend that, for complex statements with multiple operators, you explicitly state with parentheses the precedence you are intending. Generally, that makes for more readable code and easier maintenance, though if you have an extremely complex statement, you can end up with lots of parentheses. In that case, it might be worthwhile to break up the single statement into one or more statements, to be fully explicit and reduce the overall number of parentheses.

Variables

Broadly speaking, a *variable* is a named storage location with an associated value. You access the value associated with the storage location by using the name. Each language has its own implementation of variables: how to declare them, what their scope is, and how they are managed.

Declaring Variables in JavaScript

In JavaScript, variables are declared using the var keyword, as shown in Listing 2-15.

Listing 2-15. Declaring a Variable in JavaScript

```
var myVar = 1;
```

You can also simply access variables as needed without formally declaring them using the var keyword (Listing 2-16).

Listing 2-16. Creating a New Variable by Accessing It

```
var myVar = 1;
myOtherVar = 2;
```

Either way of declaring variables is syntactically valid, but they have different meanings for the variable's scope (described in the following section).

It's common practice to declare many variables at once. You can use the var keyword for each variable, or you can use the var keyword once and separate the variable declarations with commas. It's also common practice to place each variable declaration on its own line, as shown in Listing 2-17, for improved readability.

Listing 2-17. Declaring Multiple Variables at Once

```
var myObject = {},
    intCounter = 0,
    strMessage = "",
    isVisible = true;
```

JavaScript style guides typically recommend declaring all variables in a given scope at the beginning of that scope, mostly because it helps prevent problems of variable mis-scoping. It also helps JavaScript code compressors, which will take the list of variables and run search and replace on each item to change variable names to single- or double-letter names, thus further reducing the size of the file.

Understanding Variable Scope in JavaScript

Just as each language has rules for creating variables, each language has rules that govern where variables can be accessed. This is known as *variable scope*. Basically, scoping rules determine the answer to the question, "If I create this variable here, where else will I be able to access it?" Variable scope is an important concept of any language because it influences just about every aspect of working with the language, from debugging to optimization.

As mentioned in Chapter 1, JavaScript has functional scope: when you formally declare a variable using the var keyword, it is limited in scope to the current functional scope and all of the functional scopes contained within the current functional scope. In other words, if you declare a variable within a given scope, you will be able to access it within a subscope but not within any containing scope. Listing 2-18 provides an example to illustrate this concept.

Listing 2-18. Functional Scope in JavaScript

```
function myFunction() {
    var myVariable = "Here"; // myVariable is now limited in scope to myFunction and any scopes we
                                create within myFunction

    // Create a new function within myFunction to demonstrate scope nesting
    function myInternalFunction() {
        alert(myVariable);
    }
    myInternalFunction();    // call myInternalFunction when myFunction is called
}
myFunction();                // will alert "Here"
alert(myVariable);           // will throw an error; myVariable is not defined outside of myFunction().
```

When you declare a variable in a particular scope, that scope is often referred to as the *local scope* for that variable. As you nest functions within one another, you create nested functional scopes that are often referred to as *scope chains*.

Whenever you access a variable in your program, the JavaScript engine will look throughout the current scope to see if it is defined there. If it doesn't find a definition there, it goes up to the containing scope and looks there, and so on, up the chain to the topmost scope of the program. This is often referred to as a *scope chain lookup*, or sometimes just *scope lookup*.

The topmost scope of any JavaScript program is called the *global scope*. Any variable declared in the global scope will be available to all scopes in the program, as demonstrated in Listing 2-19.

Listing 2-19. Global Scope in JavaScript

```
var myVariable = "This is a global variable";
function myFunction() {
    myVariable = "Global variable has been changed inside a function";
    alert(myVariable);
}

alert(myVariable);            // will alert "This is a global variable"
myFunction();                 // will alert "Global variable has been changed inside a function"
alert(myVariable);            // will alert "Global variable has been changed inside a function"
```

You can always override higher scope declarations by re-declaring varibles in a particular functional scope. This essentially creates a new variable limited in scope to that functional scope; this is often referred to as *local scope precedence*. To demonstrate local scope precedence, see Listing 2-20.

Listing 2-20. Local Scope Precedence

```
var myVariable = "This is a global variable";
function myFunction() {
    var myVariable = "Global variable has been overridden inside a function";
    alert(myVariable);
}

alert(myVariable);            // will alert "This is a global variable"
myFunction();                 // will alert "Global variable has been overridden inside a function"
alert(myVariable);            // will alert "This is a global variable"
```

Because of the precedence of local scope, JavaScript variables (and function declarations, described later in the chapter) are available immediately at the beginning of their scope block, whether or not they have been defined yet. If you attempt to access JavaScript variables before their initialization, you will get an undefined value, but they will be there, and the script will not throw an error. This can be quite unexpected behavior, especially in the case of overriding variables that have been declared in a higher scope as illustrated in Listing 2-21.

Listing 2-21. Local Scope Overriding Higher Scope

```
function testScope() {
    var myTest = true;        // myTest is now present in this top level scope.
    function testNestedScope() { // Create a sub-scope within the main scope
        alert(myTest);        // Access myTest...but from which scope?
        var myTest = false;   // Redefine myTest in this sub-scope.
    }
    testNestedScope();
    alert(myTest);
}

testScope();                 // will alert "undefined", and then true.
```

When we execute this example, it first alerts "undefined" and then alerts "true." The first alert occurs because, within the `testNestedScope()` function, we redefined the variable `myTest` so that it is now within that scope. This makes its new value available everywhere within that scope, effectively erasing the value of the variable from the higher scope everywhere within that function. This is called *hoisting*: A variable declaration (not its assignment, just its declaration) is automatically "hoisted" to the beginning of its containing scope. In other words, when a new scope is created, JavaScript immediately declares all of the local variables before doing anything else, including assignments and function calls. As a result, Listing 2-21 is parsed as if it were written as show in Listing 2-22.

Listing 2-22. Explicitly Hoisting Variables

```
function testScope() {
    var myTest = true;
    function testNestedScope() {
        var myTest;
        alert(myTest);
        myTest = false;
    }
    testNestedScope();
    alert(myTest);
}

testScope();            // will alert "undefined", and then true.
```

Because of variable hoisting, many JavaScript best practices and style guides recommend defining all variables at the beginning of their scope before they are accessed, thus explicitly stating what hoisting does invisibly.

If you access a variable without declaring it using the var keyword, JavaScript will still perform a scope chain lookup. If it reaches the global scope and still has not found the variable declaration, it will assume the variable is meant to be global in scope and will add it there. This is known as *implied global scope*, an example of which is shown in Listing 2-23.

Listing 2-23. Implied Global Scope

```
function myFunction() {
    myVariable = "Declared in function, default global scope";
    alert(myVariable);
}

alert(typeof myVariable); // will alert "undefined" because it wasn't created yet
myFunction();             // will alert " Declared in function, default global scope "
alert(myVariable);        // will alert "Declared in function, default global scope "
```

For details on variable scope, including related topics like closures, see the "Scoping in JavaScript" section in Chapter 1.

Managing Variables in JavaScript

JavaScript tries to make variable management as easy as possible for the programmer. Once you declare a variable, you don't need to explicitly undeclare it to free memory—in fact, JavaScript provides no mechanism for doing so. The interpreter will manage the variables itself, deallocating their memory when all references and any closures are completely finished.

As mentioned in Chapter 1, JavaScript is a weakly typed language, which means it will manage variable type mismatches in expressions according to a specific set of rules. Because JavaScript is constantly managing variable types behind the scenes, one of the most important aspects of understanding JavaScript is understanding how it manages types, so be sure to review Chapter 1 closely. To recap, JavaScript has four broad data types:

- *Boolean*: True or False values.

- *Number*: All numbers in JavaScript are 64-bit floating-point numbers.

- *String*: Strings of any characters.

- *Object*: Collections of properties and methods.

In addition, JavaScript employs the concept of *primitives*: non-object, simple variables, which themselves can be booleans, numbers, or strings. Anything that is not a primitive is an object—though JavaScript will transparently change primitives to their associated object types and back again as needed.

When it comes to copying variables, JavaScript handles primitives and objects differently. Primitives are passed from one variable instance to another directly. Objects, on the other hand, are passed by reference: setting a new variable equal to an existing object does not copy that object wholesale into the new variable; rather, it only makes the new variable a pointer to the original object. See Listing 2-24 for an example.

Listing 2-24. Direct Assignment of Primitives and References to Objects

```
var myObject = {};
var myOtherObject = myObject;   // myOtherObject is now a reference to myObject
myObject.bar = "bar";           // This changes myObject directly
myOtherObject.foo = "foo";      // This changes myObject via reference
alert(myObject.foo);            // will alert "foo"
alert(myOtherObject.bar);       // will alert "bar"
var myInt = 5;                  // Primitive
var myOtherInt = myInt;         // myOtherInt is now its own primitive, there is no reference
myOtherInt++;
myInt--;
alert(myOtherInt);              // will alert 6
alert(myInt);                   // will alert 4
var myPrimitiveString = "My Primitive String";
var myOtherPrimitiveString = myPrimitiveString;
myOtherPrimitiveString += " is now longer."
alert(myOtherPrimitiveString); // Will alert "My Primitive String is now longer."
alert(myPrimitiveString);      // Will alert "My Primitive String"
```

Because JavaScript manages type mismatches transparently, sometimes, as you can see in Listing 2-25, it's easy to confuse what's a primitive and what's an object:

Listing 2-25. Type Conversion Between Objects and Primitives of the Same Data Type

```
var myStringObject = new String("This is an object");
var myOtherStringObject = myStringObject;
myOtherStringObject += " which I just changed into a primitive"; // Type change, so no longer a
                                                                 reference!
alert(myStringObject);         // will alert "This is an object"
alert(myOtherStringObject);    // will alert "This is an object which I just changed into a primitive"
```

Two objects will return equal in an equality check if they reference the same object in memory, even if the two objects are otherwise identical, as shown in Listing 2-26.

Listing 2-26. Objects Are Only Equal If They Reference the Same Object in Memory

```
var myObject = {};
var myOtherObject = {};
var myThirdObject = myObject;
alert(myObject == myThirdObject);          // will alert "true"
alert(myOtherObject == myThirdObject);     // will alert "false"
alert(myObject == myOtherObject);          // will alert "false"
```

JavaScript only provides methods for making references to objects; there is no method for copying an object. However, if you should need to, it's not difficult to iterate through an object and copy all of its methods and properties to a new object.

Objects

In just about every object-oriented programming language, an *object* is a collection of properties, and JavaScript is no different. Properties can be either primitives or other objects, including functions. JavaScript objects can be arbitrarily deep, meaning you can have objects that have properties that are objects, which in turn have properties that are objects, and so on, as deeply as you wish.

Inheritance

As covered in detail in Chapter 1, JavaScript uses prototypal inheritance rather than classes. Each object has a special prototype property that serves as a pointer to the object from which it was created. When you attempt to access a property on the object, the interpreter checks to see if the desired property exists within the current object. If the property does not exist, the interpreter checks the prototype. If the property is not there, the interpreter checks the prototype's prototype, and so on, until it either finds the property or reaches the end of the prototype chain and returns an error. (See Chapter 1 for details and examples of prototypal inheritance.)

Accessing Properties and Enumeration

JavaScript provides two ways of accessing properties on objects, as demonstrated in Listing 2-27.

Listing 2-27. Accessing Object Properties in JavaScript

```
var myObject = {};
myObject.property1 = "This is property1"; // access via dot notation
myObject["property2"] = 5;                 // access via square brackets
alert(myObject["property1"]);              // will alert "This is property1"
alert(myObject.property2);                 // will alert 5
```

The ECMA-262 standard specifies that these two methods are exactly the same:

Properties are accessed by name, using either the dot notation:

```
MemberExpression.IdentifierName
CallExpression.IdentifierName
```

or the bracket notation:

```
MemberExpression[ Expression ]
CallExpression[ Expression ]
```

The dot notation is explained by the following syntactic conversion:

```
MemberExpression.IdentifierName
```

is identical in its behaviour to

```
MemberExpression[ <identifier-name-string> ]
```

and similarly

```
CallExpression.IdentifierName
```

is identical in its behaviour to

```
CallExpression[ <identifier-name-string> ]
```

where `<identifier-name-string>` *is a string literal containing the same sequence of characters after processing of Unicode escape sequences as the IdentifierName.*

ECMA-262 Edition 5.1, Section 11.2.1, "Property Accessors"

The benefit of this dual notation is that you can easily programmatically access object properties using the square bracket notation without necessarily knowing the names of all the properties. As an example, consider the need to enumerate all the properties of an object. You don't know what they are, so you can't access them using dot notation. Instead, you just query the object for each of its properties and access their values using brackets, as shown in Listing 2-28.

Listing 2-28. Traditional Method for Enumerating an Object in JavaScript

```
// Assuming the existence of targetObject, which has many unknown properties:
var thing,
    strMessage = "";
for (thing in targetObject) {
    strMessage += "targetObject." + thing + " = " + targetObject[thing] + "\n";
}
alert(strMessage); // will alert all of the properties in targetObject
```

In Listing 2-28, we are iterating over all the properties in `targetObject` using a `for` loop (see the section "for Loops," later in the chapter, for details about for loops). We build a string containing each property and its associated value, one per line, and then alert the string. This will only include the noninherited properties of an object. That's the traditional method for enumerating properties in JavaScript. With newer versions of JavaScript, it's possible to enumerate objects using different methods. In Version 5 of ECMA-262, the global `Object` object has two new methods: `Object.keys()` and `Object.getOwnPropertyNames()`. (See Chapter 5 for details on these two methods and how they differ.) Now we can enumerate an object as shown in Listing 2-29.

Listing 2-29. New Method for Enumerating an Object in JavaScript

```
// Assuming the existence of myObject, which has many unknown properties:
var arrKeys = Object.keys(myObject),
    strMessage = "",
    i = 0,
    arrKeysLength = arrKeys.length;
```

```
for (i = 0; I , arrKeysLength; i++) {
    strMessage += "myObject." + arrKeys[i] + " = " + myObject[arrKeys[i]] + "/n";
}
alert(strMessage);
```

Creating Objects

JavaScript has three main ways of creating objects: using a constructor function, using literal notation, or using `Object.create()`.

Using Constructor Functions

The traditional method for creating new JavaScript objects is to create a constructor function and use it to make new objects as desired. To make a constructor function, you simply create a function as you ordinarily would, and add properties to it as needed, as shown in Listing 2-30.

Listing 2-30. Basic Constructor Function

```
function myConstructor() {
    this.property1 = "foo";
    this.property2 = "bar";
    this.method1 = function() {
        alert("Hello World!");
    }
}
```

You'll notice in this constructor that we are using the `this` keyword to add new properties to the object. Details on the subtleties of the `this` keyword within functions are provided later in the chapter, in the section "Functions." In the context of constructor functions, the keyword `this` refers to the object that is being created by the constructor.

To create a new instance from the constructor, use the `new` operator, as shown in Listing 2-31.

Listing 2-31. Creating a New Instance from a Constructor

```
var myObject = new myConstructor();
myObject.method1(); // will alert "Hello World!"
```

The new operator performs the following steps:

1. It creates a new empty object that inherits from the operand's prototype,

2. It sets that new object as the execution scope of the operand (so within the operand, the `this` keyword refers to the new empty object),

3. It invokes the operand, so the operand can then modify the new object as needed,

4. It returns the value that the operand returns, or if the operand does not return anything, it automatically returns the new object it created in step 1 and that the operand modified in step 3.

If you're coming to JavaScript from a background in class-based languages like Java or C++, you may be thinking, "Hey, that looks kind of like a class!" You're correct, this method does superficially resemble classes. You can continue down this road and fully emulate classes in JavaScript using this method in combination with others. However, you are encouraged to try and leave behind the idea of classes when working with JavaScript so that you can better take advantage of the language's dynamic nature.

Using Literals

Another way of creating objects in JavaScript is to use literal notation. *Literal notation* is a way for you to provide values literally for an object during creation. In JavaScript, literal notation is very common, and we'll be covering it several times in this chapter.

To create an object literally, begin by defining it as you ordinarily would with the var keyword, as shown in Listing 2-32, and then use curly brackets to enclose properties, which should be key/value pairs separated by commas.

Listing 2-32. Creating an Object Using Literal Notation

```
var myObjectLiteral = {
    property1: "one",
    property2: "two",
    method1: function() {
        alert("Hello World!");
    }
}
myObjectLiteral.method1();                      // will alert "Hello World!"
```

Because we have created the object literally, we can use it immediately. Literal notation is thus the best way to create singletons in JavaScript. Objects created this way can still be extended later by adding properties and methods as desired, as shown in Listing 2-33.

Listing 2-33. Extending an Object

```
myObjectLiteral.property3 = "New property"; // adds a new property to the previously created object
```

Using Object.create()

Finally, the latest versions of JavaScript provide a third method for creating new objects: the create() method on the global Object object. As shown in Listing 2-34, the method takes an object as its parameter and returns a new object with the parameter object as its prototype.

Listing 2-34. Using Object.create() to Create New Objects

```
var myObjectLiteral = {
    property1: "one",
    property2: "two",
    method1: function() {
        alert("Hello world!");
    }
}
var myChild = Object.create(myObjectLiteral);
myChild.method1();                              // will alert "Hello world!"
```

This method can create a new object from any object, even a constructor function.

Which Method Should I Use?

Which method to use is largely a matter of taste, though sometimes the choice will be dictated by convention or situation. Some JavaScript libraries, for example, make heavy use of Object.create(). Or, if you are doing extensive work with JSON, you might find it makes more sense to use literals to manage your singletons. And if you really feel you need classlike behavior in your JavaScript programs, then constructor functions are the easiest way to get there.

Arrays

In JavaScript, as in most languages, arrays are essentially indexed data structures, with a value associated with each index. JavaScript array indices all start from 0, so the second item in an array actually has an index of 1, and the length of an array is equal to the last index + 1.

Dynamic Length

In keeping with JavaScript's dynamic nature, its arrays have dynamic lengths. This means that you can add and remove items from arrays, and the length of the arrays will change as needed. Thus, you cannot generate boundary errors when you are adding or removing items from arrays. And if you attempt to access an element that does not exist, the interpreter will return undefined instead of throwing an error. A common mistake in JavaScript is to attempt to retrieve something from an array that does not exist, resulting in undefined, and then attempting to do something with that value without first checking to see if it is undefined. Depending on what you attempt to do with the value, the interpreter might throw an error at that point, but it will not throw an error at the point when the array was accessed out of bounds.

JavaScript arrays have a length property, which contains a number that indicates the length of the array. As elements are added to and removed from the array, this number increases or decreases as needed. The length property can also be set directly, as shown in Listing 2-35; doing so will either remove existing items from or add undefined items to the end of the array, as appropriate.

Listing 2-35. Dynamic Lengths of JavaScript Arrays

```
var arrColors = ["red", "orange", "yellow", "green", "blue", "indigo", "violet"];
alert(arrColors.length); // will alert 7
arrColors.length = 10;   // adds three new elements to the array, each set to "undefined"
alert(arrColors[8]);     // will alert "undefined"
arrColors.length = 6;    // arrColors is now ["red", "orange", "yellow", "green", "blue", "indigo"]
```

Accessing and Assigning Values

In JavaScript, arrays can contain any valid data type: objects, functions, booleans, and so forth. Data types can be mixed within arrays, too, meaning you can have an array made up of an object, a boolean, a number, and a string.

Array values are accessed using the square bracket notation described for objects: the name of the array, followed by a set of square brackets that contain the index of the desired value; for example, in Listing 2-36, myArray[2] will access the third item in the array myArray.

Listing 2-36. Accessing Arrays

```
var myArray = new Array();
myArray[0] = "foo";
myArray[1] = "bar";
myArray[3] = 4;
```

```
alert(myArray.length);        // will alert 4
alert(myArray[2]);            // will alert "undefined"

var testVar = myArray[498]; // testVar is now "undefined" and no error will be thrown
alert(testVar);               // will alert "undefined"
```

Arrays are actually special cases of JavaScript objects. You can add properties to arrays just like you can any other object, as demonstrated in Listing 2-37.

Listing 2-37. Assigning Values

```
var myArray = new Array();
myArray[0] = "foo";           // assign "foo" to the first element of the array
myArray[1] = "bar";           // assign "bar" to the second element of the array
myArray["foo"] = "bar";       // create the property "foo" on myArray and give it the value of "bar"
alert(myArray.length);        // will alert 2
myArray["2"] = 7;             // assign 7 to the third element of the array
alert(myArray.length);        // will alert 3
var strMyIndex = "3";
myArray[strMyIndex] = 8;      // will assign 8 to the fourth element of the array
alert(myArray.length);        // will alert 4
```

Listing 2-37 demonstrates how JavaScript will coerce the type of a non-numeric index to a numeric value if it can, and then use that as an index. Otherwise, it will use the supplied value as the key for a new property on the array object itself.

Because of this behavior, it's often said that JavaScript has "associative arrays." This isn't strictly true, because JavaScript arrays cannot have non-numeric indexes. If you add something to an array with a non-numeric index, as shown in Listing 2-38, you are simply adding it as a property on the array object itself, not adding elements to the array.

Listing 2-38. Array Elements vs. Properties

```
var myArray = new Array();
myArray["foo"] = "bar";       // adds a property, not a new element
myArray["new"] = "old";       // adds a property, not a new element
alert(myArray.length);        // will alert 0, because no elements have actually been added to the array.
myArray[0] = 0;               // Adds a new element to the array
alert(myArray.length);        // will alert 1
```

Creating Arrays

There are two ways to create arrays in JavaScript: using the global Array object as a constructor, as shown in Listing 2-39, or using literal notation, as shown in Listing 2-40.

Listing 2-39. Creating Arrays with the Constructor

```
var myArrayObject = new Array(4);             // creates an array with 4 undefined elements
var myOtherArray = new Array(4, 2, 5, 2, 7); // creates an array with those values
alert(myArrayObject.length);                  // will alert 4
alert(myOtherArray.length);                   // will alert 5
```

Listing 2-40. Creating Arrays with Literal Notation

```
var myLiteralArray = [];                    // Creates an array of length 0 with no elements
var myOtherArray = [1, "foo", {}, true];    // Creates an array of length 4 with a number,
                                               a string, an object, and a boolean
```

When using the Array object as a constructor, you can supply an optional single numeric value, which will cause the constructor to return an array initialized with the specified number of slots. Each slot will be set to "undefined." If you provide more than one comma-delimited argument, the constructor will return an array with each of the arguments as an indexed value, in order, starting from 0.

Creating arrays using literal notation is similar to creating objects with literal notation.

Listing 2-40 demonstrates that you can have multiple data types within a single array. You can even have objects as your array values, just as you can have arrays as properties of objects.

JavaScript also supports multidimensional arrays, as arrays of arrays, as shown in Listing 2-41.

Listing 2-41. Multidimensional Arrays

```
var row1 = [0, 1, 2];
var row2 = [3, 4, 5];
var row3 = [6, 7, 8];
var array3by3 = [row1, row2, row3];
alert(array3by3[2][1]);                 // will alert 7
```

Iterating over Arrays

Because arrays are numerically indexed, one of the most common things to do with them is to run through their members in order, often doing something with each one. The most common way to iterate over an array is in a for loop, as shown in Listing 2-42. (See "for Loops," later in the chapter, for details on for loops and how to optimize them.)

Listing 2-42. Iterating over an Array Using a for Loop

```
var myColors = ["red", "orange", "yellow", "green", "blue", "indigo", "violet"];
for (var i = 0; i < myColors.length; i++) {
    alert(myColors[i]);                 // will alert each color one at a time
}
```

In this example, the for loop will continue until the iterator i reaches myColors.length -1. Each time through the loop, JavaScript will alert the value stored at that index. This is by far the most common pattern for iterating over arrays, and it is very fast, even for very large arrays.

You might be tempted to use a for-in loop, as we did when enumerating objects, but remember that arrays can have properties as well as values, and a for-in loop would iterate over all of those items. Also, there's no guarantee that the loop would go through all of the indexed values in order, or do them all at once.

Commonly, you will want to do something with each element in the array. If you know for certain that none of the elements in your array will be undefined, you can use a slightly different version of a for loop, as shown in Listing 2-43.

Listing 2-43. Another Way to Iterate over an Array

```
var myColors = ["red", "orange", "yellow", "green", "blue", "indigo", "violet"];
for ( var i = 0, color; color = myColors[i]; i++) {
    // Inside of the loop, the variable color will contain the value at the current index
    alert(color); // will alert each color one at a time
}
```

The advantage of this method is that, within the loop, the variable color is already set to a value at the current index, saving you the trouble of getting it yourself. Note that if one of the array elements is undefined, then your variable will likewise be undefined within the loop.

With newer versions of JavaScript, arrays have a forEach() method that you can use to iterate over them, as shown in Listing 2-44. The method takes a function expression as an argument, and it executes that function once per array element. The function expression can take an optional parameter, which will be set to the array value at the current index.

Listing 2-44. Third Way to Iterate over an Array

```
var myColors = ["red", "orange", "yellow", "green", "blue", "indigo", "violet"];
myColors.forEach(function(color) {
    alert(color); // will alert each of the colors, one at a time
});
```

If you have an array that you wish to modify as you are iterating over it, you will need to be careful that you don't skip elements. Consider the example provided in Listing 2-45.

Listing 2-45. Modifying an Array During Iteration

```
var myColors = ["red", "orange", "green", "green", "blue", "indigo", "violet"];
for (var i = 0; i < myColors.length; i++) {
    if (myColors[i] === "green") {
        myColors.splice(i, 1); // the splice() method removes the item at index i (see Chapter 5 for
        details on the splice() method)
    }
}
```

In this example, we start by examining each member of the myColors array one at a time, starting with "red". When the loop reaches i = 2, myColors[i] will be "green" and the conditional will cause that element to be removed from the array. As a result, the array will go from being 7 elements to being 6, and the second "green" element will go from being at index 3 to being at index 2. Then, in accordance with for loop functionality (see "for Loops," later in the chapter), the index will be incremented, going from 2 to 3, and the loop will continue. This will cause the second "green" element to be missed.

Whenever you modify an array while iterating over it, you have to consider this possibility. There are two ways to deal with it. One is to decrement the counter i inside the if statement, so that if a match occurs and an element is popped out of the array, i will decrement by 1, then increment by 1, thus avoiding skipping the element.

Another, more elegant solution is to iterate over the array in reverse, as demonstrated in Listing 2-46.

Listing 2-46. Iterating over an Array in Reverse

```
var myColors = ["red", "orange", "green", "green", "blue", "indigo", "violet"];
for (var i = myColors.length - 1; i >= 0; i--) {
    if (myColors[i] === "green") {
                myColors.slice(i, 1); // the slice method removes the specified element from the array.
    }
}
```

In Listing 2-46 we are starting at the end of the array and working backward. First we test index `i = 6`, then `i = 5`, and so on. At `i = 3`, we encounter a "green" element, which will be removed from the array. This will reduce the array length by 1, and the "blue" element (and all elements that follow) will have their indices reduced by 1. Then, the counter will decrement by 1, going to `i = 2`, and we will hit the other "green" element in the array. By going through the array in reverse, you avoid having to manage the counter manually.

Array Methods and Properties

Arrays have several methods and properties for managing their elements. For example, throughout this chapter we've used the `length` property of arrays. There are several other properties and methods as well; for a detailed description of all array methods and properties, along with examples, see Chapter 5.

Functions

Functions are reusable blocks of code that can be called from other areas of the program. In JavaScript, functions are also first-class objects, meaning they can be manipulated like any other object in the language: they can have properties and methods, can be returned from functions, can be passed as arguments, and so on. The object nature of functions in JavaScript is one of the most important keys to understanding the language's dynamic nature.

JavaScript provides two ways to create new functions: via declarations and via expressions.

Function Declarations

JavaScript provides a `function` keyword that can be used to declare functions. It works similarly to the `var` keyword for declaring variables, and it's useful to consider it in the same context. According to the ECMA-262 standard, a function declaration is of the form:

```
function Identifier (FormalParameterList optional) { FunctionBody}
```

The `FormalParameterList` is optional (JavaScript functions are not required to have parameters).

This will create a function with the name `Identifier()`, which will be visible both in its parent's scope and in its own scope. Listing 2-47 shows a simple function declaration.

Listing 2-47. Simple Function Declaration

```
function saySomething(strMessage, strTarget) {
    alert(strMessage + " " + strTarget);
}
saySomething("Hello", "world"); // will alert "Hello world"
```

Note that because the function name is available in its own scope, a function can call itself, allowing for recursion. Listing 2-48 provides an example that shows we can easily implement the mathematical concept of factorials, where a number $N! = N(N–1)(N–2) \ldots (N–(N–1))$.

Listing 2-48. Recursive Functions

```
function factorial(number) {
    if (number <=1) {
        return 1
```

```
    } else {
        return number * factorial(number - 1);
    }
}
alert(factorial(5)); // will alert 120
```

Like variable declarations, function declarations are hoisted to the beginning of their scope. In fact, they are parsed and evaluated before all other statements, meaning they will be available immediately within their defined scope, even before they are defined in the code. (See "Understanding Variable Scope in JavaScript," earlier in the chapter, for a full explanation of hoisting.) As a demonstration, consider the common JavaScript interview question presented in Listing 2-49.

Listing 2-49. Common Interview Question Demonstrating Function Declaration Hoisting

```
function myFunction() {
    function myInternalFunction() {
        return 10;
    }
    return myInternalFunction();
    function myInternalFunction() {
        return 20;
    }
}
alert(myFunction()); // What will this alert?
```

If you answered "It will alert 20," then congratulations, you're hired! The function myInternalFunction() is defined twice, with the second one replacing the first. It doesn't matter that you accessed the function in the middle of the two definitions, because the definition is hoisted to the top of its scope. It's the equivalent of Listing 2-50.

Listing 2-50. Equivalent to Listing 2-49

```
function myFunction() {
    function myInternalFunction() {
        return 10;
    }
    function myInternalFunction() {
        return 20;
    }
    return myInternalFunction();
}
alert(myFunction()); // What will this alert?
```

Because function declarations are hoisted to the top of their scope, you can access them before you can declare them. Just because you *can*, however, doesn't mean you *should*; many JavaScript style guides recommend against this practice because it can lead to obfuscated or confusing code. Whether or not you make use of it, though, function declaration hoisting exists and you should bear it in mind when determining the scope of your functions.

Function Expressions

The other way you can create functions in JavaScript is with function expressions. As with any expression, a *function expression* represents a value; in the case of a function expression, the value is a function object. Commonly, function expressions are then assigned to variables so that they can be accessed.

According to the ECMA-262 standard, a function expression is of the form:

```
function Identifier optional (FormalParameterList optional) { FunctionBody }
```

which in turn results in code like

```
var myFunction = function foo() {
    // function body here
}
```

You'll notice that the Identifier is optional. JavaScript allows the creation of unnamed function expressions, known as *anonymous functions*. Anonymous functions are quite common in JavaScript. It's commonplace to not provide identifiers when creating function expressions, because the variable serves as a way to invoke the function. Most of the time, unless the function will need to call itself, an anonymous function is assigned to a variable as part of a function expression:

```
var myFunction = function() {
    // function body
}
```

You'll also notice that this definition looks almost exactly the same as the definition for a function declaration (introduced in the previous section). This means it's possible to have exactly the same code serve as either a function declaration or a function expression, depending on context:

```
function myFunction() {
    // function body
}
```

In general, in the context of an assignment (like a variable assignment) or an expression (as in an anonymous function provided as the parameter of another function), or if there is no Identifier, then the interpreter will assume the code is a function expression. Otherwise, the code will be part of a function body (or the global context) and will be interpreted as a function declaration. Listing 2-51 shows examples of each.

Listing 2-51. Function Declarations vs. Function Expressions

```
// This is not an assignment, there is an Identifier, and it's in the
// global scope, so it's a function declarationfunction myFunction() {
    // function body
}

// This is part of an assignment, so it is a function expression
var myOtherFunction = function foo() {
    // function body
}

// Part of a new expression, so it is a function expression
new function myThirdFunction() {
    // function body

    // This is part of a function body, so it is a function declaration
    function myInternalFunction() {
        // internal function body
    }
}
```

Assignment function expressions are hoisted just like variable declarations, but only their declaration expression is hoisted, not their assignment expression. As an example, consider another common JavaScript interview question, shown in Listing 2-52.

Listing 2-52. Hoisting for a Function Expression

```
function myTestFunction() {
    var myInternalFunction = function() {
        return "Hello World.";
    }
    return myInternalFunction();
    var myInternalFunction = function() {
        return "Second Definition.";
    }
}
alert(myTestFunction()); // What will this alert?
```

In this example, the code will alert "Hello Word." The second assignment expression does not get hoisted, so the assignment of myInternalFunction() is to return the string "Hello World."

Invoking Functions

So far in the book we've been invoking functions, but we've never really defined the specific syntax. The syntax is important because there are actually a few ways to invoke functions in JavaScript, and how you invoke a function will determine its execution context.

In JavaScript, when you invoke a function, the function receives a pointer to its execution context, which will be set to the this keyword, which can be accessed within the function.

In JavaScript, there are three ways to invoke a function:

- Using the function invoker, (), which works with both functions and methods (functions attached to objects)

- Using the new keyword, as when constructing a new object

- Using the apply() and call() methods

Invoking Functions Using the Invoker

In JavaScript the function invoker is a pair of parentheses, (). Any expression that evaluates to a function can be invoked using the invoker. To pass parameters to the invoked function, you include them in the parentheses as a comma-delimited list.

When you invoke functions using the invoker, the execution context of the function is set to the window object. When you invoke a method, the execution context is set to the parent object. Listing 2-53 provides some examples.

Listing 2-53. Testing the Execution Context of Functions and Methods

```
var myObject = {
    myMethod : function() {
        alert(this === myObject); // Test to see if this does indeed refer to the parent object of a
        method.
    }
}
```

```
function myGlobalFunction() {
    alert(this === window);     // Test to see if this refers to the window for functions
    function mySubFunction() {
        alert(this === window); // Test to see if this refers to window as well.
    };
    mySubFunction();
}
```

```
                                // Invoke our tests
myObject.myMethod();            // will alert "true"
myGlobalFunction();             // will alert "true" and then alert "true" again.
```

In listing 2-53, we set up an object with a method, and within that method we test to see if the this keyword does in fact refer to the parent object. Then we create a global function that both tests to see if its this keyword is set to window, and defines its own subfunction. The subfunction tests to see if its keyword is set to the window object as well.

In the case of methods, having this refer to the parent object is one of the main features of JavaScript's object-oriented paradigm. It enables you to easily access and modify the parent object with its methods.

Invoking Functions As Constructors

A function can also be invoked by using the new operator, as shown in Listing 2-54. Any expression that evaluates to a function can be invoked in this way.

Listing 2-54. Invoking a Function Using the new Keyword

```
function myFunction() {
    alert('Hello world!');
}
new myFunction;            // will alert "Hello world!"
```

Even though you can invoke any function using the new operator, it's meant to be used for constructing new objects. When you invoke a function in this way, JavaScript creates a new empty object that inherits its prototype from the operand, and sets it as the execution context of the function. As a result, when you are building a constructor function, the this keyword will refer to the new object you're creating. Then your constructor function can either explicitly return the new object, or the new operator will automatically return it for you.

This invocation method gives you the power to create any arbitrary object constructor you need, as demonstrated in Listing 2-55.

Listing 2-55. Constructor Function Used to Construct an Object

```
// A common convention for constructors is to capitalize their first letter.
function Kitty() {
    this.soft = true;
    this.temperature = "warm";
    this.vocalize = function() {
        alert('Purr, purr, purr');
    }
}
```

```
var myKitty = new Kitty;              // create a new kitty.
alert(myKitty.soft);                  // will alert true
alert(myKitty.temperature);           // will alert "warm"
myKitty.vocalize();                   // will alert "Purr, purr, purr"
```

In this example, when we invoke the Kitty() function using the new keyword, JavaScript first creates a new empty object and passes it into the function as its execution context. Then, the function executes, adding the properties soft and temperature and the method vocalize() to the object. Finally, the object is returned so that it can be assigned to the myKitty variable.

This syntax looks remarkably like the syntax you would see for instantiating an object from a class. But don't forget: JavaScript has no classes, only objects. If you come from a background in class-based object-oriented languages, don't let this familiar syntax lull you into thinking you're dealing with classes.

Invoking Functions Using apply() and call()

Finally, all JavaScript functions have two methods that can be used to invoke them: apply() and call(). These methods allow us to specify any context we want for a function.

The apply() and call() methods have similar syntax:

```
myFunction.apply(thisContext, arrArgs);
myFunction.call(thisContext, arg1, arg2, arg3, ..., argN);
```

Both methods take a thisContext parameter, which is an object or reference that specifies the execution context of the function. If you don't specify the parameter, JavaScript will execute the function in the global context, the same as if you had passed a reference to the window object.

The difference between the two methods is how you specify arguments for the function. With the apply() method, you specify the arguments in an array, and with the call() method you supply them as a comma-delimited list. Otherwise the two methods work exactly the same way.

Listing 2-56 provides an example of using these methods to invoke a function.

Listing 2-56. Using call() and apply() to Invoke a Function

```
var contextObject = {
    testContext: 10
}
var otherContextObject = {
    testContext: "Hello World!"
}

var testContext = 15;                 // Global variable

function testFunction() {
    alert(this.testContext);
}

testFunction();                       // This will alert 15
testFunction.call(contextObject);     // Will alert 10
testFunction.apply(otherContextObject); // Will alert "Hello World!"
```

In Listing 2-56, we create two context objects with the same property set to different values: one is set to the number 10, the other to the string "Hello World!". Then we create a global variable with the same name as the property and set it to 15. Finally, we create a function that alerts the value of this.testContext.

When we invoke the function using the invoker, the execution context is the window object, so the function alerts the value of the global variable. When we use the call() method and provide the first context object as the new execution context, the function alerts the value of the property for that object. Similarly, when we use the apply() method and provide the other context object, the function alerts that property.

Conditionals

JavaScript provides a fairly standard set of features for conditional execution of code: testing expressions and, based on the results, executing specified statement blocks.

if Statements

The basic form of an if statement in JavaScript is:

```
if (conditionExpression) { statementBlock }
```

Explicitly, if the conditionExpression evaluates to true, the code in the statementBlock will be executed. If you have just one line of code in your statement block, the brackets are optional.

JavaScript if statements can be expanded using the else keyword, allowing for logic branches:

```
if (conditionExpression) {
    statementBlock1
} else {
    statementBlock2
}
```

Here, if the conditionExpression evaluates to true, statementBlock1 will execute; otherwise, statementBlock2 will execute.

You can chain if statements together in this way:

```
if (conditionExpression1) {
    statementBlock1
} else if (conditionExpression2) {
    statementBlock2
} else if (conditionExpression3) {
    statementBlock3
} else {
    statementBlock4
}
```

In this example, if conditionExpression1 is true, then statementBlock1 will execute and the control of the program will move to the end of the chain. If conditionExpression1 is false, then conditionExpression2 will be evaluated. If it is true, statementBlock2 will execute and then the control of the program will once again move to the end of the chain. As a result, statementBlock4 will only execute if conditionExpression1, conditionExpression2, and conditionExpression3 all evaluate to false; otherwise, it will never execute. See Listing 2-7 for an example of a chain of if...else statements:

Listing 2-57. An if-then-else Block

```
function alertGenres(authorName) {
    if (authorName === "Neil Gaiman") {
        alert("Fantasy");
    } else if (authorName === "Octavia Butler") {
        alert("Science Fiction");
    } else if (authorName === "Roger Zelazny") {
        alert("Science Fiction and Fantasy");
    } else {
        alert("Unknown author.");
    }
}

alertGenres("Roger Zelazny");     // will alert "Science Fiction and Fantasy"
alertGenres("Arthur C. Clarke"); // will alert "Unknown author."
```

In Listing 2-57, we built a simple function that tests an author's name and, if it recognizes it, alerts the name of the genre in which that author wrote. If the author is not recognized, the function alerts "Unknown author."

switch Statements

switch statements provide an alternative to extensive if-else-if-else-if-else chains and are particularly useful when a single conditionExpression is being tested and can have multiple results. The following is the format for a switch statement:

```
switch (expression) {
    case result1:
        statementBlock1
        [break;]
    case result2:
        statementBlock2
        [break;]
    case result3:
        statementBlock3
        [break;]
    default:
        statementBlockDefault
}
```

In a case statement, the expression is expected to resolve to one of the case labels. This in turn will cause execution to move to that label and begin executing the statementBlocks from that point. An optional break statement will stop execution of the blocks. If the expression does not resolve to a matching label, then the interpreter will look for a default label and, if present, will execute its associated statementBlock.

To demonstrate, Listing 2-58 provides a trivial example.

Listing 2-58. Trivial Example of a switch Statement

```
var myColor = "yellow";
switch (myColor) {
    case "red":
        alert("myColor was set to red");
        break;
    case "yellow":
        alert("myColor was set to yellow");
    case "green":
        alert("myColor was set to green");
    default:
        alert("myColor was an unknown color");
}
```

In Listing 2-58, myColor resolves to "red" so the switch statement will alert "myColor was set to red". Because the "red" code block includes a break statement, execution of the switch statement ends, and the program continues after the closing bracket. If myColor were instead set to "yellow", then the switch statement would move to the "yellow" case and alert "myColor was set to yellow". Then, because the "yellow" code block does not have a break statement, the program will execute the "green" case, and then the default case.

Loops

The most common tasks you will need to perform with any programming language typically are repetitive or iterative tasks. Imagine, for example, that you want to check all of the links on a given HTML page to see if any of them contain a particular text value. JavaScript has a set of looping statements to handle those situations.

Generally, a *loop* is a statement block that executes repeatedly until a specified condition is met. JavaScript has four basic kinds of loops: for loops, for-in loops, while loops, and do loops.

for Loops

Probably the most commonly used loop statement is the for loop. Generally, a for loop executes its statement block over and over again until the specified condition is false. At that point the program moves execution to the next statement after the close of the loop. A for loop will execute its condition check before executing its statement block for the first time, so it is possible (if the condition check is false that first time) for the statement block to never execute.

The syntax for a for loop is:

```
for (initialExpression; conditionExpression; incrementExpression)
    statementBlock
```

A for loop executes as follows:

1. The initialExpression is executed. Typically this is used to define and initialize counting variables, but it can be any valid expression. The initialExpression is also optional.

2. The conditionExpression is evaluated. If the expression evaluates to true, then statementBlock will execute. If the expression evaluates to false, the loop will terminate without executing the statementBlock. The conditionExpression is technically optional; if you omit it, the interpreter assumes the condition is always true, and thus will always execute the loop, meaning you would have to manually break out of the loop.

3. After statementBlock executes, incrementExpression is executed. This expression is optional as well. Once it has executed, step 2 is repeated.

Listing 2-59 provides a trivial example to demonstrate for loop execution.

Listing 2-59. Simple for Loop

```
for (var i =0; i < 10; i++) {
    alert(i); // will alert 0 through 9 one at a time
}
```

In this example, the loop executes as follows:

1. A variable i is declared and set to 0.

2. The loop checks to see if i < 10 and, if it is, executes its statement block (in this case, alerting the value of i).

3. i is incremented by 1, and step 2 is repeated.

Note that because the conditionExpression is evaluated each time the loop executes, if it is an expensive statement, it could cause a significant performance problem in your program, especially if the loop is executed hundreds or thousands of times. It's a good idea to keep the conditionExpression as simple as possible. For example, consider the loop in Listing 2-60.

Listing 2-60. Potentially Expensive Loop

```
for (var i = 0; i < someArray.length; i++) {
    // do things
}
```

In Listing 2-60, at the beginning of every time through the loop, we check the length property of the someArray array. This isn't terribly expensive, but if someArray is several thousand items, it could add up. Listing 2-61 provides a simple optimization.

Listing 2-61. Optimized for Loop

```
var someArrayLength = someArray.length,
    i = 0;
for (i = 0; i < someArrayLength; i++) {
    // do things
}
```

In Listing 2-61 we have stored the length of the array in a variable, thus simplifying the conditionExpression. We have also moved the variable declaration of i outside of the loop to explicitly define its scope. These are minor improvements, but if the array is long, the benefits could add up quickly.

for-in Loops

JavaScript also has a for-in loop statement. This construct is specifically intended to enumerate object properties:

```
for (var variable in objectExpression) { statementBlock }
```

Any expression that evaluates to an object can be used in objectExpression; most often it's just an object of some sort. On each iteration, one of the properties of the object will be assigned to the variable and then the statementBlock will be executed. An example is shown in Listing 2-62. See the "Objects" section earlier in the chapter for more information and examples on using for-in loops to enumerate object properties.

Listing 2-62. Enumerating an Object

```javascript
var myObject = {
    prop1: "value1",
    prop2: "value2",
    prop3: true,
    prop4: 100
}
var strAlert = "";
for (var prop in myObject) {
    strAlert += prop + " : " + myObject[prop] + "\n";
}
alert(strAlert);
```

This example will alert

```
prop1 : value1
prop2 : value2
prop3 : true
prop4 : 100
```

while Loops

JavaScript also has while loops, which execute their statement blocks as long as their conditional evaluates to true:

```javascript
while (conditionExpression)
    statementBlock
```

As with for loops, the condition is tested each time before the statementBlock is executed. If on the first time through the loop the condition evaluates to false, then the statementBlock will never execute. Listing 2-63 provides an example.

Listing 2-63. Trivial while Loop

```javascript
var counter = 0;
while (counter < 10) {
    alert(counter);
    counter++;
}
```

In this example, the counter variable is incremented within the loop, so when it finally reaches 10, the loop will terminate. This example will result in alerting the numbers 0 through 9, one at a time.

do Loops

Similar to while loops, do loops execute their statement blocks while their condition evaluates to true:

```javascript
do
    statementBlock
while (conditionExpression);
```

Unlike while loops and for loops, in a do loop the statementBlock is executed the first time before the conditionExpression is evaluated. As a result, a do loop's statementBlock will always execute at least once. Listing 2-64 provides an example.

Listing 2-64. Trivial do Loop

```
var counter = 0;
do {
    alert(counter);
    counter++;
} while (counter < 10)
```

Like the previous examples, this example will alert the numbers 0 through 9, one at a time.

Summary

In this chapter we have discussed the basics of working with JavaScript:

- JavaScript expressions are sections of code that evaluate to a value, and statements are blocks of expressions that achieve a particular goal.

- JavaScript has several different kinds of operators: arithmetic, assignment, bitwise, comparison, logical, and string, as well as a few that don't fit into those categories.

- JavaScript has specific precedence for determining which operators should go first in statements with multiple operators.

- Variables declared with the var keyword are limited in scope to the current scope; variables that are declared simply by accessing them are assumed to be global.

- You can access properties on an object with either dot notation or square brackets.

- Objects can be created with either literal notation, constructor functions, or the Object.create() method.

- JavaScript arrays are dynamic, and do not throw out-of-bounds errors.

- You can create functions either as expressions or by declaration.

- How you invoke a function determines its execution scope.

- You can specify execution scope for a function using either the call() method or the apply() method.

- JavaScript supports both if-then-else and switch conditionals.

- JavaScript supports several loop types: for loops, for-in loops, while loops, and do loops.

In the next chapter we will dive deep into the Document Object Model: the representation of an HTML page in JavaScript. We will apply the knowledge from this chapter to creating dynamic web pages, animations, and other effects.

■ ■ ■

CHAPTER 3

The DOM

In this chapter we'll cover the Document Object Model, or DOM. We'll start by addressing what the DOM is and how it has evolved over time. Then we will explore its internal structure and exposed properties and methods in general, followed by a detailed discussion of working with the DOM using JavaScript.

At the end of this chapter you should have a solid understanding of the DOM and its inner workings. You should also have some familiarity with the standards governing it and where to find them, as well as how they evolved. You should understand not only how to handle user events in your scripts, including how to fire them manually, but also how to make custom events of your own.

How I Learned to Stop Worrying and Love the DOM

The Document Object Model is just that: an object that models the document currently loaded into the browser. Every single element in the document will have a corresponding presence in the DOM: every paragraph, every list item (and every list), every span, and so on. This includes elements that might not be visible in the rendered document, such as <script> tags, style sheets, and so forth. Even the document's title will be in the DOM. If it is in the document's markup, it will have a presence in the DOM. In addition, the DOM presents many useful properties for accessing and manipulating these elements.

The DOM also provides an event model for capturing user interactions with the document: keypresses, mouse movements, and so forth. Using DOM events, you can write scripts that respond to user interactions, from simple things like highlighting a paragraph when the user clicks it, to dragging and dropping elements on the screen.

DOM != JAVASCRIPT

JavaScript often comes under fire for being difficult to work withwhen really the specific problem is actually related to the DOM and not JavaScript itself. It's important to understand that the DOM isn't JavaScript. The DOM is an interface to the document provided by the browser manufacturer. The two are closely intertwined and many people make the mistake of assuming they are the same, but they are not.

It's easy to conflate JavaScript and the DOM because most of what you will be doing with JavaScript in the browser will involve manipulating the document that the browser has loaded. But if you were to access a JavaScript interpreter in a different context—for example, using Node.js on a server or workstation—you wouldn't necessarily have a DOM to access.

The DOM is not actually part of JavaScript, nor is it defined by the ECMA-262 standard. Instead, the DOM is governed by its own standard, maintained by the World Wide Web Consortium (W3C). Even though the DOM is not part of JavaScript itself, no JavaScript reference would be complete without mentioning it. Much of what you will be doing in browser-based JavaScript will involve working with the DOM. In fact, the DOM and JavaScript are so tightly intertwined that it's not unusual to see less experienced JavaScript developers refer to DOM features as JavaScript features.

The DOM standard came about directly because of the so-called "browser wars" at the beginning of the Web's history. Back then, browser manufacturers decided how they wanted to parse HTML documents and what (if anything) they wanted to expose to their JavaScript engines. As a result, web development was a nightmare of browser-dependent code and "best viewed in Netscape" and "best viewed in Internet Explorer" banners.

In response, the industry decided to standardize not only the languages that were being used to build the Web (HTML, CSS, and JavaScript) but also how browsers should implement those languages. This promised to level the playing field across all browsers, making it possible to leave behind browser-dependent coding.

The realization of this promise took some time, however. Standardizing the Web was a huge undertaking and, in many ways, is a process that will never be truly "finished." Technologies are continuing to evolve, resulting in standards that change with them, which is hard on the browser manufacturers because they have to aim at multiple moving targets. Even so, the DOM and other web standards paved the way for the modern Web as we know it.

History of the DOM Standard

As previously mentioned, the DOM is governed by its own separate standard, which is owned by the W3C. The DOM standard was originally developed in three main iterations, Level 1, Level 2, and Level 3.

The Level 1 DOM standard was the first to be proposed and provided the foundation for everything else. It had two main features: a generic set of low-level interfaces for representing any structurally marked-up document, and extensions to that generic specification for HTML documents in particular.

HTML: DESCRIPTIVE, STRUCTURAL, SEMANTIC

In general, markup languages are a family of languages that specify a syntax for annotating documents. Broadly, markup languages fall into three categories:

- *Presentational:* Annotations are typically of a low-level (and often not human-readable) format and are used to specify how applications should display the content. Presentational markup is often used by word processors, for example.

- *Procedural:* Similar to presentational, but annotations are of a higher level format. Annotations are typically human readable, and are intended to specify how content should be displayed. Examples include PostScript, troff, and TeX.

- *Descriptive:* Annotations are used to describe individual parts of the document based on their properties. How that content should be displayed is left up to the interpreting application. Examples include Scribe, SGML, and HTML.

HTML's tags annotate content according to their individual structural properties, so HTML is often referred to as a "structural" markup language. It is also often referred to as a "semantic" markup language, because many of the structural annotations refer to the semantic meaning of their target content, such as <p> for paragraph, or <header> for a heading. However, some HTML tags are semantically null and refer only to structure, such as <div> or <span> tags.

The Level 2 DOM standard followed quickly and provided much more depth than Level 1. It actually consists of six separate specifications:

- *Core*: Extends the Level 1 DOM core specification and includes new interfaces for XML. The specification is at www.w3.org/TR/DOM-Level-2-Core/.

- *Events*: Provides the event model that is implemented in most modern browsers. See DOM Events, below, for specifics. Link: www.w3.org/TR/DOM-Level-2-Events/

- *HTML*: Extends the Level 2 Core specification with features specific to HTML and XHTML. Link: www.w3.org/TR/DOM-Level-2-HTML/

- *Traversal and Range*: Provides interfaces for identifying ranges of content within a document, as well as interfaces for moving through the DOM: for example, starting with a given element, find all of its siblings, or all of its children. Link: www.w3.org/TR/DOM-Level-2-Traversal-Range/

- *Style*: Provides interfaces for a document's Cascading Style Sheets (CSS), as well as the styles that have been applied to elements. Link: www.w3.org/TR/DOM-Level-2-Style/

- *Views*: Specifies the views that are presented by the browser to its scripting engines, including JavaScript. Link: www.w3.org/TR/DOM-Level-2-Views/

The Level 3 DOM specification was written as an extension to Levels 1 and 2. It consists of five separate specifications:

- *Core*: Serves as a further extension of Level 1 and Level 2 Core, providing new interfaces and methods. Link: www.w3.org/TR/DOM-Level-3-Core/

- *Events*: Extends the Level 2 Events specification, providing event specifications for keyboard and mouse wheel events, as well as mutation events (events that fire when a DOM node is modified somehow). Link: www.w3.org/TR/DOM-Level-3-Events/

- *Load and Save*: Specifies how to parse XML and produce a DOM tree from it, and how to serialize a DOM tree into XML. Link: www.w3.org/TR/DOM-Level-3-LS/

- *Validation*: Specifies how to keep documents internally consistent as they are changed by various methods. Link: www.w3.org/TR/DOM-Level-3-Val/

- *XPath*: Provides a specification for using XPath to access DOM trees. Link: www.w3.org/TR/DOM-Level-3-XPath/

Finally, the HTML5 family of specifications, which is a W3C Candidate Recommendation as of December 2012, includes DOM specifications that are meant to subsume much of the material in the previous specifications.

At this point, there are a dozen or so documents specifying the DOM standard, some of them subsuming others wholly or partially. To avoid confusion, and to avoid inadvertently tying the DOM standard to the HTML5 language specification (you should be able to use the DOM standard with any structural markup language, not just HTML), the work was begun to consolidate all the disparate parts into one specification. You can view the results in the following two places:

- The December 2012 Working Draft of the DOM4 (http://dvcs.w3.org/hg/domcore/raw-file/tip/Overview.html) at the W3C. This version provides more context as to how the various versions have been merged together, including future plans for consolidation.

- The Living DOM Specification (http://dom.spec.whatwg.org/) at the Web Hypertext Application Technology Working Group (WHATWG).

The WHATWG is a separate group from the W3C that was formed in response to concerns about the W3C's methodologies. A certain amount of tension exists between the two groups, but ultimately they have the same goals, and though they maintain separate versions of the DOM specification, their versions should never disagree. We encourage you to review both versions; they provide slightly different views of the same information.

Browser Dependencies

Just because governing standards exist for the DOM doesn't mean all browsers implement them equally. The DOM standards arose over time, driven by the need to rein in disparate and diverging document model implementations by the browser manufacturers, and even today that standardization is a work in progress. The JavaScript we have studied in the first two chapters is fairly stable across browsers. With the DOM, we will be encountering variations in implementations from browser to browser, and even from version to version of the same browser. Unfortunately, these variations are often quite pronounced and, if left unaddressed, can result in code that will run in one browser but stubbornly refuse to run in others.

The good news is that modern browsers (Internet Explorer 9 and later, Firefox 4 and later, Chrome, Safari, and Opera) implement these standards very well. Older versions of Internet Explorer are the worst offenders for bad implementations, and unfortunately you will often have to provide support for these older versions in your projects. Most often these implementation problems can be mitigated with JavaScript. Even better, there are already dozens of excellent, well-tested JavaScript libraries that do exactly that.

Probably the most popular of these libraries is jQuery, originally created by John Resig and now maintained as an open source project. According to some browser statistics, jQuery is the most widely deployed library on the Web, so it is definitely well tested. We'll cover using jQuery a bit in Chapter 4.

jQuery isn't the only library available; there are plenty of others. One of the first libraries created is called Prototype, which is still widely used and is also an actively maintained open source project. Other libraries of note are Dojo Toolkit, script-aculo-us, MooTools, and Yahoo's YUI Library. And if you want something that provides more support—something more like a framework—there are choices like Sencha Ext JS, Closure Library and AngularJS (both by Google), Backbone.js, and Montage (a newcomer to the JavaScript frameworks scene, but a favorite of ours).

In this chapter we'll be covering the DOM from a standards viewpoint. When we encounter serious divergences in implementation, we'll mention them, but it's safe to assume that the older a browser version is, the greater the chance that it won't implement some aspect of the standards correctly. We'll also discuss mitigation techniques, so you should be able to work through the worst of the problems. Overall, though, if you find yourself in a situation where you have to support many older browser versions, you may find that a well-chosen JavaScript library will prevent many headaches.

If you will be supporting older browser versions, you'll want to assess how well they support the features you'll be needing for your project. Peter-Paul Koch maintains two excellent pages on his QuirksMode web site, one for DOM features (`www.quirksmode.org/dom/w3c_core.html`) and one for DOM events (`www.quirksmode.org/dom/events/`). These pages are a great starting point for assessing your browser support situation.

DOM Structure

Now that you know what the DOM is and how it came to be, you are ready to dive into how it actually works for you. Conceptually, a DOM structure can be thought of as a tree that represents the documents and subdocuments that are loaded into the browser, as well as the individual elements of each document and subdocuments.

The top of the structure is the `window` object, which represents the actual browser window containing the loaded document. Since HTML documents can contain subdocuments through the use of iframes, the `window` object is actually an array-like object. It has a `length` property, representing the number of iframes the document contains, and these iframes can be accessed via indexes (e.g., `window[0]`) or, if the `<iframe>` tags have name attributes, via `window['iframename']`. The `window` object also has a `frames` property that is an array representing the number of iframes present in the document. It is just a reference to the `window` object itself (in other words, `window === window.frames` and `window[0] === window.frames[0]` if a subdocument was present), but it has the virtue of being more explicit. Either syntax will work.

Each subdocument will have its own `window` object, and since any given subdocument can itself contain subdocuments, a subdocument's `window` object will also be an array-like object.

The `window` object has several other useful methods and properties. The `window` object also serves as the global context for JavaScript, as demonstrated in Listing 3-1.

Listing 3-1. The window Object Is the Global Context for JavaScript

```
myVar = 5;          // defined without var keyword, so it is global
alert(window.myVar); // will alert 5
```

Since window provides the global context for JavaScript, you do not need to access the document object explicitly as a property on the window object; instead, you can access it directly (in other words, referencing window.document. title is the same thing as referencing document.title anywhere in your script).

The window object has a document property that is a reference to the document that has been loaded into the browser window. The document object contains the tree representing the elements of the document itself. Every paragraph tag, every span tag, every div tag, and even script tags, the HTML and body tags, and the document title will all have a presence in the document object. If it's in the HTML markup, it will be represented in the document object. In addition, the document object has several methods for accessing elements, and provides the base for events.

Structurally, the DOM consists of *nodes*, with each node representing content (usually a tag, but can also represent comments and metadata) in the HTML document. Because HTML is structural, nodes are organized structurally: an element's node in the DOM can have child nodes that represent tags that the element itself contains. Similarly, a node in the DOM can have a parent node that represents that element's parent tag.

Consider the simple example document shown in Listing 3-2.

Listing 3-2. Simple HTML Document

```
<!DOCTYPE html>
<html>
    <head>
        <title>JavaScript Programmer's Reference</title>
    </head>
    <body>
        <p id="myParagraph">This is my paragraph! <span class="hideme">Lorem ipsum</span> dolor
sit amet.<span></span></p>
        <p class="hideme">Another paragraph!</p>
        <script>
alert(document.title); // will alert "JavaScript Programmer's Reference"
        </script>
    </body>
</html>
```

HTML5 EXAMPLES

Listing 3-2 is the first example where we have shown an entire HTML document instead of just a JavaScript snippet. Because DOM manipulation involves working with HTML documents, we'll be using this format for our examples in this chapter. In particular, we'll be using HTML5, as specified by the DOCTYPE tag.

Note that if you are using a particularly old browser version (e.g., Internet Explorer 6 or Firefox 2), it might have problems with these examples. (If you are using such an old browser version, we encourage you to upgrade if at all possible.)

If you load this document, the browser will alert "JavaScript Programmer's Reference" because the title is referenced by the document.title property.

The nodes within the body are referenced by the `childNodes` property on the document object:

```
alert(document.childNodes); // Depending on browser, will alert something like "[object NodeList]"
```

Nodes within the DOM are represented by array-like node lists. They have a `length` property representing how many nodes are present, and the individual nodes themselves can be accessed via their index.

Each individual node will have properties that vary depending on the element it represents, but essentially any attribute on the element will have a representation as a property on the node. For example, the class attribute on a paragraph tag will be represented in the `className` property on its node.

Using this tree of nodes, you can access any element in the DOM. For example, `document.childNodes[1].childNodes[2].childNodes[3]` represents the second paragraph in our markup:

```
alert(document.childNodes[1].childNodes[2].childNodes[3].className); // will alert "hideme"
```

Individual nodes have a reference to their parent via the `parentNode` property. Since a tag can have only one parent, the `parentNode` property is not an array-like collection but rather a simple property:

```
alert(document.childNodes[1].childNodes[2] == document.childNodes[1].childNodes[2].childNodes[3].
parentNode); // will alert "true" because the body tag is the parent node of the paragraph
```

That's the basic structure of the DOM, but it's pretty unwieldy when it comes to accessing elements. You can access anything, but even with our super-simple document, we're already producing fairly long reference chains. Imagine how long those chains would be if we had a complex document! Fortunately, the DOM provides better ways to access elements than through these long reference chains.

Accessing Elements in the DOM

Typically you want to access an element within the DOM directly and do something with it: hide it, show it, move it, delete it, make it listen for an event, and so on. The DOM provides several different methods for accessing elements either directly or by starting from a known place and traversing the tree.

Probably the most famous and easiest way to access an element is to use the `document.getElementById()` method, as shown in Listing 3-3.

Listing 3-3. Using getElementById()

```
<!DOCTYPE html>
<html>
    <head>
        <title>JavaScript Programmer's Reference</title>
    </head>
        <body>
        <p id="myParagraph">This is my paragraph! <span class="hideme">Lorem ipsum</span> dolor sit
amet.<span></span></p>
        <p class="hideme">Another paragraph!</p>
        <script>
var myPar = document.getElementById("myParagraph"); // myPar is now a pointer to the paragraph.
myPar.innerText = "I have changed the content!"; // Change the text of the paragraph to "I have
changed the content!"
        </script>
    </body>
</html>
```

In this example, we are getting a pointer to a specific node and then updating its innerText property with new content. When this document loads, you will see two paragraphs: the first will read "I have changed the content!" and the second will read "Another paragraph!"

In Listing 3-3, the document.getElementById() method and innerText property are specified by the DOM standard rather than the JavaScript standard. Since they integrate so seamlessly with JavaScript in the browser, you can see how easy it is to mistake them for JavaScript, as mentioned previously.

There are several other methods that the DOM exposes for accessing nodes directly. The getElementsByTagName() method takes a tag name as a parameter and returns a collection of all the nodes it finds in the document that are that sort of tag, as shown in Listing 3-4. The collection is an array-like object, so you can iterate over the individual elements, which are presented in order of parsing in the document, as demonstrated in Listing 3-4.

Listing 3-4. Using getElementsByTagName()

```
<!DOCTYPE html>
<html>    <head>
        <title>JavaScript Programmer's Reference</title>
    </head>
    <body>
        <p id="myParagraph">This is my paragraph! <span class="hideme">Lorem ipsum</span> dolor sit
amet.<span></span></p>
        <p class="hideme">Another paragraph!</p>       <script>
var myPars = document.getElementsByTagName("p"),
  mySpans = document.getElementsByTagName("span"),
  myParsLength = myPars.length,
  mySpansLength = mySpans.length,
  i;

// Give paragraphs a red background color
for (i = 0; i < myParsLength; i++) {
  myPars[i].style.backgroundColor = "red";
}

// Add some content to our empty span, and alert its index
for(i = 0; i < mySpansLength; i++) {
  if (mySpans[i].innerText === "") {
    mySpans[i].innerText = "No longer empty!";
    alert(i);
  }
}        </script>
    </body>
</html>
```

Listing 3-4 will change both paragraphs to be red, add the text "No longer empty!" to the empty span, and alert the number 1, which is the index of the empty span in the collection of spans returned by the getElementsByTagName() method.

Prior to HTML5, getElementById() and getElementsByTagName() were the two methods the DOM standard specified for accessing elements directly. The HTML5 specification adds three new methods: getElementsByClassName(), querySelector(), and querySelectorAll().

The getElementsByClassName() method works like getElementById(), except it takes a class as a parameter and returns an array-like collection of elements that have that class, as shown in Listing 3-5.

Listing 3-5. Using getElementsByClass()

```
<!DOCTYPE html>
<html>
    <head>
        <title>JavaScript Programmer's Reference</title>
    </head>
    <body>
        <p id="myParagraph">This is my paragraph! <span class="hideme">Lorem ipsum</span> dolor sit
amet.<span></span></p>
        <p class="hideme">Another paragraph!</p>
        <script>
var hideme = document.getElementsByClassName("hideme"),
  hidemeLength = hideme.length,
  i;

// Hide all the elements that have a class of "hideme"
for (i = 0; i < hidemeLength; i++) {
  hideme[i].style.display = "none";
}
        </script>
    </body>
</html>
```

In Listing 3-5, we are getting all elements that have a class of "hideme" and then hiding each one by changing its CSS display attribute to "none."

The querySelector() and querySelectorAll() methods provide a lot more flexibility than the other methods. Both methods take any valid CSS selector as a parameter. The querySelector() parameter will return the first element (in markup order) in the document that matches, while querySelectorAll() will return an array-like collection of all elements that match the selector (if there is only one match, the method will return an array-like object with one member; if there are no matches, the method will return an array-like object with no members—that is, a length of 0). This gives us a powerful tool for accessing elements in the DOM, as demonstrated in Listing 3-6.

Listing 3-6. Using querySelector()

```
<!DOCTYPE html>
<html>
    <head>
        <title>JavaScript Programmer's Reference</title>
    </head>
    <body>
        <p id="myParagraph">This is my paragraph! <span class="hideme">Lorem ipsum</span> dolor sit
amet.<span></span></p>
        <p class="hideme">Another paragraph!</p>
        <script>
var emptySpan = document.querySelector("#myParagraph span:last-child"); // Get the last span
emptySpan.innerText = "Not empty anymore!" // And give it some text.
        </script>
    </body>
</html>
```

In this example, we access the last span of the paragraph using the CSS pseudo-selector last-child. When it is run, this example will place the words "Not empty anymore!" in that last span.

One of the interesting things about using querySelector() and querySelectorAll() is that the elements you want to access with JavaScript often are the same elements you want to access with your style sheets. Thus, often you will find that some of the same selectors you're using in your CSS will show up in your JavaScript as queries.

▓ **Caution**   If you intend to write code that relies on querySelector() or querySelectorAll() and are planning to support older browser versions, those versions may not provide these methods for you because the methods are recent additions to the DOM standard. In that case, you could always use a selector library to add the feature. The most commonly used selector engine is called Sizzle, available at www.sizzlejs.com/. It has no dependencies on other libraries and is quite small, very efficient, and well tested (it is the engine included in the jQuery library).

Finally, each node in the DOM possesses these element selection methods, just like the top-level document object does. When you use one of these methods on a DOM node, the method's scope is limited to the children of that node, as you can see in Listing 3-7.

Listing 3-7. Using the Methods on an Element

```
<!DOCTYPE html>
<html>
    <head>
        <title>JavaScript Programmer's Reference</title>
    </head>
    <body>
        <p id="myParagraph">This is my paragraph! <span class="hideme">Lorem ipsum</span> dolor sit
amet.<span></span></p>
        <p class="hideme">Another paragraph!</p>
        <script>
var myPar = document.getElementById("myParagraph"), // Get a reference to the first paragraph
  mySpan = myPar.querySelector("span:last-child"); // Get a reference to the last span in that
paragraph

mySpan.innerText = "Not empty anymore!"
        </script>
    </body>
</html>
```

This example, like Listing 3-6, will add the text "Not empty anymore!" to the last span of that paragraph. In this case, we first get a reference to the paragraph using getElementById() and then search just that paragraph's child elements using querySelector(). This applies to DOM fragments as well (see the next section for details on DOM fragments).

Traversing the DOM

Another way of accessing elements in the DOM is to start at a known place in the DOM tree and then traverse to a different location using parent/child/sibling relationships. We've already seen a basic example of that in the previous section. Fortunately, the DOM provides some convenient properties for traversal:

- Node.firstChild: Reference to the first child of the node
- Node.lastChild: Reference to the last child of the node
- Node.nextSibling: Reference to the next sibling of the node
- Node.previousSibling: Reference to the previous sibling of the node

Listing 3-8 shows an example of these traversal properties.

Listing 3-8. Using Traversal Properties

```
<!DOCTYPE html>
<html>
    <head>
        <title>JavaScript Programmer's Reference</title>
    </head>
    <body>
      <p id="myParagraph">This is my paragraph! <span class="hideme">Lorem ipsum</span> dolor sit
amet.<span></span></p>
      <p class="hideme">Another paragraph!</p>
      <script>
var mySpan = document.getElementById("myParagraph").lastChild;
mySpan.innerText = "Not empty anymore!"
      </script>
    </body>
</html>
```

This example will fill in the last span in the first paragraph with the text "Not empty anymore!"

Now that you know how to access elements in the DOM, the following section covers what you can do with them.

Modifying the DOM

In addition to enabling you to access elements in the document, the DOM provides a flexible framework for manipulating those elements. You can modify existing elements by changing their properties, changing their content, or even moving them completely from one place in the DOM to another. You can also delete elements and create new ones.

Modifying Existing Elements

Probably the most basic modification you might want to make to an existing element is to access and change its properties. Most simple element properties are presented as simple properties on the element's associated node, and you can get and set the values directly.

For example, Listing 3-9 shows how to change the href property of a simple anchor tag directly.

Listing 3-9. Modifying an Element's Properties

```
<!DOCTYPE html>
<html>
    <head>
        <title>JavaScript Programmer's Reference</title>
    </head>
    <body>
      <p id="myParagraph"><a href="http://www.yahoo.com/">This is my link!</a></p>
      <script>
var myLink = document.querySelector("#myParagraph a");
myLink.href = "http://www.google.com";
      </script>
    </body>
</html>
```

In this example, we are modifying the `href` property, changing it from `www.yahoo.com` to `www.google.com`. If you load this example into your browser and click the link, it will take you to Google rather than to Yahoo. Using this technique, you can modify most of the simple properties on an element: `name`, `href`, even the element's `id`.

Modifying Styles

For some properties, the DOM provides a more robust interface. For example, in Listing 3-10, an element's `style` attribute provides a mapping of all of the inline styles on an element.

Listing 3-10. Modifying an Element's style Attribute

```html
<!DOCTYPE html>
<html>
    <head>
        <title>JavaScript Programmer's Reference</title>
    </head>
    <body>
        <p id="myParagraph"><a href="http://www.yahoo.com/">This is my link!</a></p>
        <script>
var myLink = document.querySelector("#myParagraph a");
myLink.style.backgroundColor = "#ff0000";
myLink.style.color = "#fff";
        </script>
    </body>
</html>
```

In this example, we are modifying the link so that the background color is red and the foreground color is white.

When accessing an element's `style` attribute, as shown in Listing 3-11, all you are doing is working with inline styles. The `style` attribute is not a representation of styles applied to the element through a style sheet, as demonstrated in Listing 3-11.

Listing 3-11. The style Attribute Is Only for Inline Styles

```html
<!DOCTYPE html>
<html>
    <head>
        <title>JavaScript Programmer's Reference</title>
        <style>
#myParagraph a {
  background-color: #ff0000;
  color: #ffffff;
}
        </style>
    </head>
    <body>
        <p id="myParagraph"><a href="http://www.yahoo.com/">This is my link!</a></p>
        <script>
var myLink = document.querySelector("#myParagraph a");
alert(myLink.style.backgroundColor); // will alert "" (empty)
alert(myLink.style.color); // will alert "" (empty)
        </script>
    </body>
</html>
```

Both of these alerts will be empty, even though we have set the background color and text color. That's because they were set using a style sheet rather than an inline style.

Similarly, if you modify an element's style attribute, the DOM will insert your changes as an inline style. Examining the element in Listing 3-11, you would see that it now looks something like this:

```
<a href="http://www.yahoo.com/" style="background-color: rgb(255, 0, 0); color: rgb(255, 255,
255);">This is my link!</a>
```

You can determine which styles are currently at work on an element by using the DOM's getComputedStyle() method of the window object, as shown in Listing 3-12. This method takes an element reference and returns an object representing the styles that are currently active on the element, whether they came from a style sheet or an inline style. The object will be of the same format as the style attribute on the element.

Listing 3-12. Using the window.getComputedStyle() Method

```
<!DOCTYPE html>
<html>
    <head>
        <title>JavaScript Programmer's Reference</title>
        <style>
#myParagraph a {
  background-color: #ff0000;
  color: #ffffff;
}
        </style>
    </head>
    <body>
        <p id="myParagraph"><a href="http://www.yahoo.com/" style="color: #00ff00">This is my
link!</a></p>
        <script>
var myLink = document.querySelector("#myParagraph a"),
  styleObject = window.getComputedStyle(myLink);

alert(styleObject.backgroundColor); // will alert something like "rgb(255, 0, 0)"
alert(styleObject.color); // will alert something like "rgb(0, 255, 0)"
        </script>
    </body>
</html>
```

This example will first alert the color applied to the background of the target element—in this case red, or rgb(255, 0, 0). The second alert will show the color of the text. In this case, we have two conflicting styles, one in the style sheet and an inline style. The inline style has the higher specificity, so it wins, and the script will alert green, or rgb(0, 255, 0).

Another common property to change is an element's class. The HTML5 DOM specification includes a robust interface for managing classes: the classList property. When accessed directly, the classList property will return an array-like object containing the classes applied to the element. (If no classes are applied to the element, the object will be of length 0.) Each individual class can be accessed via indexes. In addition, the classList property exposes a set of useful helper methods (seen in use in Listing 3-13):

- classList.add(classname): Adds class classname to the classList.

- classList.contains(classname): Returns true if classname is present in classList.

- classList.remove(classname): Removes class classname from classList.

- classList.toggle(classname): If classname is present in classList, it is removed; otherwise it is added.

Listing 3-13. Using the classList Interface

```
<!DOCTYPE html>
<html>
    <head>
        <title>JavaScript Programmer's Reference</title>
        <style>
.redclass {
  background-color: #ff0000;
}
.greenclass {
  background-color: #00ff00;
}
        </style>
    </head>
    <body>
        <p id="myParagraph" class="redclass">Here is a paragraph.</p>
        <script>
var myPar = document.getElementById("myParagraph");
myPar.classList.toggle("redclass"); // removes redclass from classList
myPar.classList.add("greenclass"); // adds greenclass to classList
        </script>
    </body>
</html>
```

In this example, the background color of the paragraph will be green.

Older versions of browsers will not have the classList interface, and you will instead have to manually modify the class string through the className property. Also, many JavaScript libraries provide methods for managing classes.

Modifying Content

Another common task is accessing and modifying the content of an element. The DOM provides a property to access the actual markup inside an element as well as a property to access just the text contained within that markup:

- Node.innerHTML: Provides an interface to the HTML inside of a node. When simply accessed, it returns the HTML contained within the node. If used as a setter, it erases the HTML contained within the element (and its associated nodes in the DOM) and replaces it with the specified HTML (and adds the associated nodes to the DOM). This interface was originally created by the Internet Explorer team many years ago, and it was so incredibly useful that all other browser teams implemented it before it became part of the HTML5 standard.

- Node.innerText (nonstandard, available in all browsers except Firefox) or Node.textContent (standard, available in modern browsers except Internet Explorer): Similar to Node.innerHTML except it only returns the text of all the elements contained within the node. It does not return any HTML markup. When used as a setter, it erases all content within the node and inserts the supplied text.

Listing 3-14 shows examples of both of these in use.

Listing 3-14. Using innerHTML and innerText

```
<!DOCTYPE html>
<html>
    <head>
        <title>JavaScript Programmer's Reference</title>
    </head>
    <body>
      <p id="firstParagraph">Here is a paragraph.</p>
      <p id="secondParagraph">Here is another paragraph. It contains <span>some other
tags,</span> <a href="http://www.google.com/">as well.</a></p>
      <script>
var firstPar = document.getElementById("firstParagraph"),
  secondPar = document.getElementById("secondParagraph");

alert(firstPar.innerText); // will alert "Here is a paragraph."
alert(secondPar.innerText); // will alert "Here is another paragraph. It contains some other
tags, as well."
alert(firstPar.innerHTML); // will alert "Here is a paragraph."
alert(secondPar.innerHTML); // will alert "Here is another paragraph. It contains <span>some
other tags,</span> <a href="http://www.google.com/">as well.</a>"

firstPar.innerText = "I have changed the text."; // will change the text of the first paragraph
secondPar.innerHTML = "<ul><li>How do I love thee?</li><li>Let me count the ways!</li></ul>";
// will change the HTML inside the second paragraph
      </script>
    </body>
</html>
```

In this example, we first use the properties to see the content of the paragraphs, then we use them to change the content.

■ **Caution** These methods are remarkably useful, but carry with them an important caveat: be very careful with innerHTML, as anything that you put in there will be parsed into DOM nodes and inserted into the DOM. This can present a serious security problem if you are not carefully sanitizing the HTML you are inserting into the DOM. Specifically, be very careful of using innerHTML with any content that comes from the user, or that you do not have complete control over. These methods will insert any HTML, including script tags, so if you blindly insert user-provided HTML into your document, it would be trivial for a user to include a malicious script that could access your application's data and compromise your security completely.

Creating New Elements

In addition to innerHTML, the DOM provides a generic method for creating new elements: the createElement() method. It takes as an argument an HTML tag name, and returns a plain DOM node of the specified type. You can then work with this node as if it were one you had accessed via one of the access methods: you can modify its properties, change its content, and so forth.

The resulting node is not attached to the document, so the DOM also provides the following set of methods for inserting these fragments into the main DOM, thus causing their associated markup to be rendered in the browser window:

- parentNode.appendChild(fragment): Appends the DOM fragment as a child of parentNode, at the end of its existing child nodes (if any)

- parentNode.insertBefore(fragment, targetNode): Inserts the DOM fragment as a child of parentNode and a sibling of targetNode just before it in the document

- parentNode.replaceChild(fragment, targetNode): Replaces targetNode with fragment

Note that the fragment can refer either to a detached fragment created using createElement() (or other methods) or to an existing node within the document. If the latter, these methods will remove the fragment from its previous location before inserting it into its new location. This makes it easy to move nodes from one place to another within the DOM.

Finally, the DOM provides a way to copy existing nodes using the cloneNode() method, seen in Listing 3-15. The cloneNode() method can take an optional boolean argument that, if set to true, instructs the clone to be "deep" and include all child nodes of the target node.

Listing 3-15. Using DOM Methods to Create New Nodes and Add Them to the Document

```
<!DOCTYPE html>
<html>
    <head>
        <title>JavaScript Programmer's Reference</title>
    </head>
    <body>
      <p id="firstParagraph">Here is a paragraph.</p>
      <p id="secondParagraph">Here is another paragraph. It contains <span>some other
tags,</span> <a href="http://www.google.com/">as well.</a></p>
        <script>
var firstPar = document.getElementById("firstParagraph"),
  secondPar = document.getElementById("secondParagraph"),
  targetLink = document.querySelector("#secondParagraph a"),
  myNewList = document.createElement("ul"),
  myNewListItemTemplate = document.createElement("li"),
  myNewListItem = myNewListItemTemplate.cloneNode();

myNewListItem.classList.add("menuitem");
myNewListItem.innerText = "One";
myNewList.appendChild(myNewListItem);
myNewListItem = myNewListItemTemplate.cloneNode();
myNewListItem.appendChild(targetLink);
myNewList.appendChild(myNewListItem);
firstPar.appendChild(myNewList);
        </script>
    </body>
</html>
```

In this example, we start out by creating an unordered list and a list item template using the createElement() method. Then we clone the template, give the clone a new CSS class and some text using the innerText property, and append it to the unordered list. Then we clone the template again and append to it the link from the second paragraph. This removes that link from that location and inserts it into the list item. Finally, we append the list item to the list and append the list to the first paragraph.

Deleting Elements

The DOM gives us a few ways to delete target nodes:

- parentNode.removeChild(targetNode): Deletes targetNode from parentNode.

- parentNode.innerHTML: By setting the innerHTML of a node to an empty string, we can remove all of its children at once.

There are some caveats when it comes to deleting elements from the DOM, however. If the elements have event handlers attached to them, particularly event handlers that make liberal use of closure to maintain their state, simply removing the elements those handlers are bound to will not necessarily clear them out of memory. This is a prime cause of memory leaks in dynamic applications. Be sure to explicitly remove event handlers from elements (and their children, of course) before removing them from the DOM.

Older versions of Internet Explorer (6 and 7 mostly) are particularly bad about not freeing up memory when elements are removed from the DOM. In fact, these older versions of Internet Explorer hold on to some of the memory for each element even after the elements have been removed from the DOM, resulting in a memory leak. Highly dynamic pages, where lots of elements are added and removed from the DOM, will simply grow larger and larger in memory in IE. There is a simple trick to getting around this: the IE proprietary property outerHTML.

The outerHTML property references the HTML of the parents of the element; when used as a setter and given an empty string, it removes the element from the DOM and efficiently from memory. It doesn't completely clear the element from memory, but it does help.

So, for an average element deletion, you should follow steps similar to these (as demonstrated in Listing 3-16):

1. Delete any event handlers from the target element and its children.

2. Delete the element using removeChild().

3. Check if outerHTML is available and, if so, use it to clear the memory in IE.

Listing 3-16. Efficiently Removing an Element from the DOM and from Memory

```
var myTarget = document.getElementById("deleteme");
deleteme.removeEventListener("click", clickHandler, false);

myTarget.parentNode.removeChild(myTarget);

if (typeof document.outerHTML !== "undefined") {
  myTarget.outerHTML = "";
}
```

In the contrived example shown in Listing 3-16, we first get a reference to our target element, then we remove its event handler, and then we remove it from the DOM. Then we check if we are operating in Internet Explorer and, if so, clear the memory associated with the element.

If you're using a JavaScript library, it will probably manage this process for you, especially if it exposes its own API for deleting elements from the DOM.

DOM Events

In addition to providing access to elements, the DOM specifies a framework for handling user interactions with elements. As the user interacts with the elements on the page—mousing over them, clicking them, selecting them, dragging them, typing within them, and so on—the browser translates those interactions into events within the elements. You can then attach an event handler to an element for a specific event; an *event handler* is essentially a block of code that the browser will execute when the event happens.

The DOM provides a simple but robust framework for handling events. . . and Internet Explorer ignores it almost completely until IE9. In versions prior to IE9, Internet Explorer used different methods to bind event handlers, provided a different execution context for events, and even didn't have an entire phase of the event model.

On the positive side, dealing with Internet Explorer's different event model is a common task, so solutions are plentiful and robust. We will discuss some of these solutions at the end of this section, but for now we will just concentrate on how the event model is designed to work.

Event Phases

When the user interacts with an element, the browser checks whether an event handler is registered for that event type on that element. If so, the browser executes that handler.

Because HTML is structural and tags can be nested, the DOM specifies that an event that starts in one element will "bubble up" through its parent elements—after all, an event in a child element might need to be counted in a parent element as well. After an event has occurred on a target element, the browser will then "bubble up" the event to the target element's parent. It will then perform the same check to determine if a handler is registered for the event type and execute it if there is. Then it will bubble up to the next parent, and so on. Eventually the event will reach the trunk of the DOM tree—the body element, which is the ultimate grandparent of any element in the document. At that point, the event will traverse back down the path it just followed to the original target, again checking for and executing registered event handlers at each element, all the way back to the original target element. Once the round trip is completed, the event terminates.

The phase when the event is moving up the DOM tree is called the *bubbling phase*, and the phase when the event is going back down the DOM tree is called the *capturing phase*. You can specify which phase you want your event handler to execute in, giving you great flexibility in handling events on nested elements. For example, if you want to have a click event execute on a parent element before it executes on the original child target, you can register the parent event handler in the bubble phase and register the child event handler in the capture phase.

There is a third phase for events, called *at target*, which is when the event is currently at the target element. There is no way to target this phase directly when binding event handlers, but you can access it via a property in the Event object (see "The Event Object," below).

Event Execution Context

When the browser executes an event handler, it has to provide an execution context for that function. The DOM standard specifies that this context should be the element that the event handler is bound to. So, within an event handler function, the this keyword will be a pointer to the DOM element that the event is executing on.

Also, when an event handler is executed, the browser will pass into it (as a parameter) an Event object that contains several useful properties that provide details about the event: the original target element where the event originated, the mouse location within the target, the mouse location within the page, and so on. In addition, the Event object has some useful methods for modifying the event's propagation behavior (we will cover these in the section titled "The Event Object," below).

Different Events

The DOM standard provides a huge number of events. They can be grouped into six basic groups:

- *Mouse events*: click, mousedown, mouseup, mousemove, etc. These are covered by the DOM MouseEvents module.

- *Keyboard events*: keypress, keydown, and keyup. Covered by the DOM KeyboardEvents module.

- *Object events*: load, error, resize, scroll, etc. Covered by the DOM HTMLEvents module.

- *Form events*: select, change, submit, reset, focus, etc. Also covered by the DOM HTMLEvents module.

- *User Interface events*: focusin and focusout. Covered by the DOM UIEvents module.

- *Mutation events*: Events that are fired as things change within the DOM, such as DOMNodeInserted, DOMAttrModified, etc. Covered by the DOM MutationEvents module.

In addition, browsers on mobile devices might also expose other events related to touch interactions (tap, doubletap, taphold, swipe, etc.) or other occurrences unique to mobile devices (orientation changes, shaking, movement, location, etc.).

Binding Event Handlers

In order for a browser to react to events on an element, you must first bind a handler for that event to the element. Binding an event handler is essentially the same as saying, "When the user interacts with this element in this way, execute this code when the event passes through this phase." The method the DOM provides for that is the addEventListener() method, which takes three arguments: an event type argument (click, keypress, etc.), a listener argument (the code to execute when the event happens), and an optional boolean phase parameter that instructs the event handler to execute either during the capture phase (if set to true) or during the bubbling phase (if set to false, which is the default). (In some older browser versions, the boolean for capture wasn't always optional, so it's considered good practice to always include it.) The event handler can take an event object as a parameter, and you can then access the event object within the handler. You can see an example of binding a click event handler in Listing 3-17.

Listing 3-17. Binding a Click Event Handler to an Element

```
<!DOCTYPE html>
<html>
    <head>
        <title>JavaScript Programmer's Reference</title>
    </head>
    <body>
      <p id="firstParagraph">Click Me!</p>
      <script>
var firstPar = document.getElementById("firstParagraph");

function myEventHandler(event) {
  alert("You clicked me!");
}

firstPar.addEventListener("click", myEventHandler, false);
    </script>
    </body>
</html>
```

When you click the paragraph, the alert box will open.
You can add more than one event handler to an event on a single object:

```
firstPar.addEventListener("click", myFirstEventHandler, false);
firstPar.addEventListener("click", mySecondEventHandler, false);
etc.
```

The event handlers will execute in the order of binding when the event is triggered.

That's the basic pattern for binding event handlers to elements. You can use an inline anonymous function instead of a named function if you prefer, as shown in Listing 3-18, which is also a fairly common pattern.

Listing 3-18. Using an Anonymous Inline Function as an Event Handler

```
<!DOCTYPE html>
<html>
  <head>
    <title>JavaScript Programmer's Reference</title>
  </head>
  <body>
    <p id="firstParagraph">Click Me!</p>
    <script>
var firstPar = document.getElementById("firstParagraph");

firstPar.addEventListener("click", function(event) {
  alert("You clicked me!");
}, false);

    </script>
  </body>
</html>
```

This example will behave exactly the same as the example in Listing 3-17. The difference is only in the named function. Note that if you are going to have a complex event handler, it's probably worth the effort to create a named function for it and pass it as a parameter. If you have an inline event handler that becomes too long (especially if it gets long enough to go across more than one screen), your code can be confusing to read.

Unbinding Event Handlers

To unbind an event handler, use the removeEventListener() method, as shown in Listing 3-19. Just like addEventListener(), removeEventListener() takes three parameters: an event type, the handler function to remove (in the case of named functions), and the boolean phase parameter.

Listing 3-19. Removing an Event Handler

```
<!DOCTYPE html>
<html>
  <head>
    <title>JavaScript Programmer's Reference</title>
  </head>
  <body>
    <p id="firstParagraph">Click Me!</p>
    <script>
var firstPar = document.getElementById("firstParagraph");

function eventHandler(event) {
  alert("I'm unbinding the event handler!");
  firstPar.removeEventListener("click", eventHandler, false);
}
```

```
firstPar.addEventListener("click", eventHandler, false);

    </script>
  </body>
</html>
```

In this example, when you click the paragraph, it will execute the handler, which will then unbind itself. Note also that this example uses a closure: both the firstPar variable and the eventHandler function remain available even after the event handler has been bound and the script has completed execution. That way, when the event handler is called by an event on the target object, it will be able to successfully execute. Maintaining state for event handlers is one of the more common uses of closures in JavaScript development. (See Chapter 1 for more details about closures.)

If you call removeEventListener() with a combination of parameters that doesn't match any event handlers that have been added to the object, the method simply terminates. It does not throw an error or give any indication that it had no effect.

There is no way to unbind an event handler that uses an anonymous inline function. You need to be able to refer to a function name for removeEventListener().

The Event Object

The Event object is passed into the event handler, so if you want to, you can access it within your scripts. The Event object has several useful properties and methods, most notably:

- event.clientX, event.clientY: The mouse coordinates of the event relative to the browser window (if a mouse event).

- event.offsetX, event.offsetY: The mouse coordinates of the event relative to the target element (if a mouse event).

- event.keyCode: The ASCII code of the key that was pressed (if a keyboard event).

- event.target: A pointer to the DOM element where the event originated.

- event.currentTarget: A pointer to the DOM element where the event is currently bubbled (or captured) to. For example, if you had an unordered list consisting of a UL tag containing LI tags, when you click an LI tag, the click event will bubble up to the parent UL tag, then up to the parent of the UL tag, and so on. As the event bubbles up, the currentTarget property will change value to reflect the location of the event in the bubbling process.

- event.eventPhase: An integer code indicating which phase the event is currently in: 1 for capture, 2 for at target, 3 for bubbling.

- event.type: The type of the event ("click", "keypress", etc.).

- event.relatedTarget: Used in some specific events (such as mouseout) to point to the element where the event originated (or that received the event, in the case of mouseout).

- event.stopPropagation(): When this method is called, it stops the event from propagating any further through the DOM. If more than one event handler is registered to this element for this event, however, any remaining event handlers will still execute.

- event.stopImmediatePropagation(): Like stopPropagation(), but when this method is called, it will also stop any remaining event handlers on the current element from executing as well as preventing any further propagation.

- `event.preventDefault()`: If there is a default action associated with the event, calling this method will prevent it from executing. For example, if you registered a click event handler to an anchor tag, calling `preventDefault()` within it would prevent the browser from following the link. In Internet Explorer, this method is not present. Instead, it is replaced with a boolean property `returnValue`, which, when set to false, will cancel the default action.

These properties tell us a lot about the event and give us a lot of flexibility in writing our event handlers. To illustrate, Listing 3-20 offers a simple game of Kitten Rescue.

Listing 3-20. Rescue the Kittens!

```
<!DOCTYPE html>
<html>
  <head>
    <title>JavaScript Programmer's Reference</title>
    <style>
.basket {
  width: 300px;
  height: 300px;
  position: absolute;
  top: 100px;
  right: 100px;
  border: 3px double #000000;
  border-radius: 10px;
}
    </style>
  </head>
  <body>
    <h3>Rescue the kittens!</h3>
    <p>Click on them to put them in their basket!</p>
    <ul id="kittens">
      <li>Rowly</li>
      <li>Fred</li>
      <li>Mittens</li>
      <li>Lenore</li>
    </ul>
    <ul class="basket"></ul>
    <script>
var basket = document.querySelector(".basket"),
  kittens = document.querySelectorAll("li"),
  kittensLength = kittens.length,
  i;

for(i = 0; i < kittensLength; i++) {
  kittens[i].addEventListener("click", function(event) {
    basket.appendChild(event.target);
  }, false);
}
    </script>
  </body>
</html>
```

In this example, we are registering a click event handler to each kitten, so that when you click on a kitten, it is magically transported to the safety of its basket (or, in our case, we simply append it to the target DOM node, which automatically removes it from its original location in the DOM).

In this game, there's a bit of an inefficiency: we assign an event handler to each item separately. We don't actually have to do this; if we want to, we can take advantage of the fact that events bubble up through the DOM using a method called *event delegation*.

Event Delegation

A common pattern you'll see in event handling is event delegation. Basically, delegating an event means allowing the event to be handled by an element that is higher up in the DOM tree than the original target. This can reduce the number of event handlers you have to employ, and thus can have a significant effect on efficiency.

As an example, let's redo our game using event delegation. Instead of applying a separate event handler to each kitten, let's delegate the event handler to the containing element, as shown in Listing 3-21.

Listing 3-21. Kitten Rescue, Event Delegation Version

```
<!DOCTYPE html>
<html>
  <head>
    <title>JavaScript Programmer's Reference</title>
    <style>
.basket {
  width: 300px;
  height: 300px;
  position: absolute;
  top: 100px;
  right: 100px;
  border: 3px double #000000;
  border-radius: 10px;
}
    </style>
  </head>
  <body>
    <h3>Rescue the kittens!</h3>
    <p>Click on them to put them in their basket!</p>
    <ul id="kittens">
      <li>Rowly</li>
      <li>Fred</li>
      <li>Mittens</li>
      <li>Lenore</li>
    </ul>
    <ul class="basket"></ul>
    <script>
var basket = document.querySelector(".basket"),
  kittens = document.getElementById("kittens");

kittens.addEventListener("click", function(event) {
  basket.appendChild(event.target);
}, false);
```

```
    </script>
  </body>
</html>
```

In this example, we let the containing unordered list element handle the click events. Now we have only one event handler, and our code is that much simpler.

Manually Firing Events

The DOM also enables you to trigger events manually. When you manually trigger an event in your code, it behaves exactly as an event that was dispatched by a user.

Manually triggering an event involves three steps:

1. Create an event object of the appropriate type.

2. Configure the object appropriately. The DOM provides several methods for correctly initializing event objects so that they have all the parameters necessary. The DOM also provides a simpler method for initializing event objects for situations where you only need a minimum of information for your event.

3. Dispatch the event on the element.

Let's look at each of those steps in detail.

NEW MANUAL EVENTS ON THE HORIZON

The latest version of the HTML5 specification proposes a new way of modeling events using a global Event object. In this proposal, this Event object can act as a constructor just like Object or Array, and you can create and configure your event objects that way. Although this is not yet approved, it is already being implemented in some browsers. For details on this upcoming functionality, see the "Interface CustomEvent" section in the W3C DOM4 standard, at https://dvcs.w3.org/hg/domcore/raw-file/tip/Overview.html#interface-customevent.

Creating an Event Object

To create an event object, you use the document.createEvent() method. This method takes a single parameter, which is a string representing the DOM event module you are going to be using. The following are the most commonly used modules:

- MouseEvents: Events dealing with mouse interactions, such as click, mousedown, mousemove, etc.

- UIEvents: Used for focus events, which occur when elements are focused and are receiving keyboard input, as in the case of form fields or content editing.

- HTMLEvents: Used for browser-oriented events such as document loading and unloading, as well as content selection, resizing, and scrolling.

- MutationEvents: Events dealing with changes to the DOM, such as DOMNodeInserted, DOMAttrModified, etc.

- KeyboardEvents: Events dealing with keypresses: keyup, keydown, and keypress.

- Event: This is a generic event module that can be used to send any event.

Once you have an event object of the appropriate type, you can configure it as needed.

Configuring an Event Object

The DOM provides convenience methods to help you appropriately configure your shiny new event object. Which method you should use depends on which module your event is a member of.

Events in the MouseEvents module use `Event.initMouseEvent(type, canBubble, cancelable, view, detail, screenX, screenY, clientX, clientY, ctrlKey, altKey, shiftKey, metaKey, button, relatedTarget)`, where the properties are as follows:

- `type`: The actual event type, such as `click`, `mousedown`, etc.

- `canBubble`: A boolean indicating whether or not the event should bubble up through the DOM.

- `cancelable`: A boolean indicating whether or not the event's default action can be canceled using `event.preventDefault`.

- `view`: The event's meta context, which in JavaScript is always the global context, so always pass a reference to the `window` object here.

- `detail`: Specific detail about the event. For MouseEvents, it is the number of mouse clicks in the same location (thus, if `detail` = 2, it was a double-click event).

- `screenX` and `screenY`: The x and y coordinates relative to the body of the event.

- `clientX` and `clientY`: The x and y coordinates relative to the target element of the event.

- `ctrlKey`, `altKey`, `shiftKey`, `metaKey` (Mac OS X): Booleans indicating whether or not those keys were pressed at the time of the event.

- `button`: A number indicating which button was clicked: 0 indicates a left click, 1 indicates a middle button (usually the mouse wheel on modern mice), and 2 indicates a right-click.

- `relatedTarget`: The related target for the event, if appropriate.

Events of the UIEvents module use `Event.initUIEvent(type, canBubble, cancelable, view, detail)`, where:

- `type`: The actual event type.

- `canBubble`: A boolean indicating whether or not the event should bubble up through the DOM.

- `cancelable`: A boolean indicating whether or not the event's default action can be canceled using `event.preventDefault`.

- `view`: The event's meta context, which in JavaScript is always the global context, so always pass a reference to the `window` object here.

- `detail`: Specific detail about the event. For UIEvents, it's usually the number of times the mouse was clicked as part of the event, so this is often set to 1.

Events of the HTMLEvents module use `Event.initEvent(type, canBubble, cancelable)`, where:

- `type`: The actual event type.

- `canBubble`: A boolean indicating whether or not the event should bubble up through the DOM.

- `cancelable`: A boolean indicating whether or not the event's default action can be canceled using `event.preventDefault`.

Events of the MutationEvents module use `Event.initMutationEvent(type, canBubble, cancelable, relatedTarget, previousValue, newValue, attributeName, attributeChange)`, where:

- `type`: The actual event type.

- `canBubble`: A boolean indicating whether or not the event should bubble up through the DOM.

- cancelable: A boolean indicating whether or not the event's default action can be canceled using event.preventDefault.

- relatedTarget: The related target for the event, if appropriate.

- previousValue: The previous value of the modified node.

- newValue: The new value of the modified node.

- attributeName: The name of the modified attribute.

- attributeChange: An integer indicating how the attribute was changed: 1 = modification, 2 = addition, 3 = removal.

When it comes to initializing a KeyboardEvents event, you use Event.initKeyboardEvent(type, canBubble, cancelable, view, ctrlKey, altKey, shiftKey, metaKey, keyCode, charCode), where:

- type: The actual event type.

- canBubble: A boolean indicating whether or not the event should bubble up through the DOM.

- cancelable: A boolean indicating whether or not the event's default action can be canceled using event.preventDefault.

- view: The event's meta context, which in JavaScript is always the global context, so always pass a reference to the window object here.

- ctrlKey, altKey, shiftKey, metaKey (Mac OS X): Booleans indicating whether or not the virtual keypress happened while these keys were pressed.

- keyCode: The ASCII code of the key.

- charCode: The Unicode character of the key.

Note that the nonstandard browser here is Firefox, which instead calls the method initKeyEvent(). Originally the KeybordEvent module was defined in early versions of the DOM Level 2 specification, but it was removed from that specification.

EXTENDING EVENT OBJECTS

Feel free to extend these event objects if you want. They're objects, just like any other objects in JavaScript, so you can add your own properties and methods to them. One of our favorite techniques is to provide an appDetail property to the events, which contains useful information about the event and why it was triggered. This also makes it easy to determine which events were manually triggered and which events were triggered directly by users. It also works great with custom events (described a bit later in the chapter).

Now that you have a configured event, you just have to dispatch it.

Dispatching an Event

Dispatching your event is quite simple. As shown in Listing 3-22, you call the dispatchEvent() method on the target element.

Listing 3-22. Firing a Custom Event

```html
<!DOCTYPE html>
<html>
  <head>
    <title>JavaScript Programmer's Reference</title>
  </head>
  <body>
    <p id="clickme">Click me to see an alert!</p>
    <script>
var myPar = document.getElementById("clickme");
myPar.addEventListener("click", function(event) {
  alert('This is your alert!');
}, false);

// Create and dispatch a new click event
var myClickEvent = document.createEvent("MouseEvents");
myClickEvent.initMouseEvent("click", true, true, window, 0, 0, 0, 0, false, false, false, false,
1, null);
myPar.dispatchEvent(myClickEvent);
    </script>
  </body>
</html>
```

In this example, we are manually firing a click event, so that when you load this page, you'll immediately see an alert as if you had clicked the paragraph. You can click the paragraph to see the alert again.

In Listing 3-22, though, we don't actually need all of those parameters—we set the coordinates to 0 (even though that's not at all accurate), we don't really care about the Cntrl, Shift, or meta keys, and so forth. If you won't be needing all of those properties, you can use the simpler event object generated by the generic Events module. Consider, for example, Listing 3-23, which automates our Kitten Rescue game—because nothing's more fun than making a game that finishes itself.

Listing 3-23. Automating Kitten Rescue

```html
<!DOCTYPE html>
<html>
  <head>
    <title>JavaScript Programmer's Reference</title>
    <style>
.basket {
  width: 300px;
  height: 300px;
  position: absolute;
  top: 100px;
  right: 100px;
  border: 3px double #000000;
  border-radius: 10px;
}
    </style>
  </head>
  <body>
    <h3>Rescue the kittens!</h3>
```

```
    <p>Click on them to put them in their basket!</p>
    <ul id="kittens">
      <li>Rowly</li>
      <li>Fred</li>
      <li>Mittens</li>
      <li>Lenore</li>
    </ul>
    <ul class="basket"></ul>
    <script>
var basket = document.querySelector(".basket"),
  kittens = document.getElementById("kittens");

kittens.addEventListener("click", function(event) {
  basket.appendChild(event.target);
}, false);

// Make JavaScript rescue the kittens!
var allKittens = document.querySelectorAll("#kittens li"),
  allKittensLength = allKittens.length,
  i,
  clickKittenEvent = document.createEvent("Event");

clickKittenEvent.initEvent("click", true, true);

for (i = 0; i < allKittensLength; i++) {
  allKittens[i].dispatchEvent(clickKittenEvent);
}
    </script>
  </body>
</html>
```

In Listing 3-23, we are looping through each kitten and firing a minimally configured click event on them, which we created using the generic Events module. This provides a quick way of firing events, should you need it.

Note, however, that some events require more complex event objects. Keyboard events in particular seem to be sensitive to this. You might need to experiment to find out what you can use.

Custom Events

You can use the DOM event model to dispatch any kind of event you want! Yes, you read that right: you aren't limited to clicks and keypresses. If you want to define your own events, you can do that. Just specify your event type when you use the addEventListener() method to attach the event handler, and then use the generic Events module to create and fire your own events.

Consider our Kitten Rescue game. Imagine that instead of listening for a click event, we listen for a "rescue" event, as shown in Listing 3-24. We can then manually generate rescue events and rescue all the kittens.

Listing 3-24. Custom Events to the Rescue

```
<!DOCTYPE html>
<html>
  <head>
    <title>JavaScript Programmer's Reference</title>
```

```
    <style>
.basket {
  width: 300px;
  height: 300px;
  position: absolute;
  top: 100px;
  right: 100px;
  border: 3px double #000000;
  border-radius: 10px;
}
    </style>
  </head>
  <body>
    <h3>Rescue the kittens!</h3>
    <p>Click on them to put them in their basket!</p>
    <ul id="kittens">
      <li>Rowly</li>
      <li>Fred</li>
      <li>Mittens</li>
      <li>Lenore</li>
    </ul>
    <ul class="basket"></ul>
    <script>
var basket = document.querySelector(".basket"),
  kittens = document.getElementById("kittens");

kittens.addEventListener("rescue", function(event) {
  basket.appendChild(event.target);
}, false);

// Make JavaScript rescue the kittens!
var allKittens = document.querySelectorAll("#kittens li"),
  allKittensLength = allKittens.length,
  i,
  clickKittenEvent = document.createEvent("Event");

clickKittenEvent.initEvent("rescue", true, true);

for (i = 0; i < allKittensLength; i++) {
  allKittens[i].dispatchEvent(clickKittenEvent);
}
    </script>
  </body>
</html>
```

In this example, we just change the click event handler to a rescue event handler, and then we simply create a rescue event and dispatch it from each kitten, just like we did with click events.

Creating custom events is a powerful technique that allows you to create decoupled components in your code. Each component only needs to publish events as things happen to it, and then other components can listen for those events, or not. That way, all components are completely decoupled: components A, B, and C do not need to know anything about one another, or even if they exist or not, but they can still communicate with one another using events.

Cross-Browser Strategies

As we mentioned at the beginning of this section, Internet Explorer pretty much ignores the standard for DOM events up until version 9. Most notably, instead of addEventListener() and removeEventListener(), Internet Explorer uses the methods attachEvent() and removeEvent(). In addition, Internet Explorer doesn't set the proper context for the executing event handler; instead of setting it to the element where the handler was registered, IE sets it to the window object. IE also doesn't support the capture phase for events. And finally, IE doesn't pass an Event object into its event handlers; instead, it tacks it on to the window object.

Fortunately, most of these problems are easy to mitigate with a bit of JavaScript. The lack of a capture phase is difficult to overcome, but the capture phase is not widely used, so if we focus on the registration methods and context problems, we can come up with a fairly simple solution.

What we'll do is create two new functions that we'll use to register our events: addEventHandler() and removeEventHandler(), as shown in Listing 3-25. If we're working in a browser that supports the DOM standard, we'll just alias our functions to the DOM functions and leave it at that. If we're in IE, though, we'll need to do a bit more to fix our context problems.

Listing 3-25. Creating Cross-Browser Event Binding Methods

```
if (document.addEventListener) {
  // DOM events available, so just use them.
  window.addEventHandler = function(targetEl, eventType, handler) {
    targetEl.addEventListener(eventType, handler, false);
    return handler;
  };
  window.removeEventHandler = function(targetEl, eventType, handler) {
    targetEl.removeEventListener(eventType, handler, false);
  }
} else {
  // Internet Explorer. Fix context problems as well as create alias.
  window.addEventHandler = function(targetEl, eventType, handler) {
    var fixContext = function() {
      return handler.apply(targetEl, arguments);
    };
    targetEl.attachEvent("on" + eventType, fixContext);
    return fixContext;
  }

  window.removeEventHandler = function(targetEl, eventType, handler) {
    targetEl.detachEvent("on" + eventType, handler);
  }
}
```

In this example we add two new methods to the global context: addEventHandler() and removeEventHandler(). In IE, for addEventHandler(), we fix our context problem by creating a dummy function called fixContext() and binding that as the event handler. When fixContext() is called by the event, it manually invokes the handler using the apply() method, which enables us to force the target element to be the execution context.

We also mentioned that Internet Explorer doesn't pass in an Event object as a parameter to its event handlers. There's a simple way around that, too, as shown in Listing 3-26: within the event handlers, just check to see if there was an event passed in and, if not, pull it from the window object (which is where IE puts it).

Listing 3-26. Fixing the Other IE Problem

```
function clickHandler(event) {
  if(!event) {
    event = window.event;
  }
  // continue...
}
```

Addressing the lack of a capture phase is more problematic, but these fixes take care of the worst of the problems. If you find you need a more robust solution, many JavaScript libraries handle this problem very well. jQuery in particular fixes all the problems, as well as providing many useful extensions to the event model.

Summary

In this chapter we have covered an important feature in browsers, the DOM, which provides JavaScript with an interface for accessing and manipulating the document that has been loaded into the browser. Here are the important points to take away from the chapter:

- The DOM is a separate standard; it is not governed by the JavaScript standard.

- The DOM has evolved over time, and browser compliance is an ongoing process.

- The DOM is structured like a tree, and everything that is in the HTML document is represented in that tree.

- The DOM can be traversed using parent/child/sibling relationships and convenience methods.

- Nodes in the DOM can be accessed directly using methods like getElementById() and querySelector().

- The DOM provides several important methods for manipulating its members, including ways to change their properties and their content.

- The DOM allows you to create nodes as needed, and work with them as if they were taken from a document.

- The DOM has a rich and flexible event model. . . which Internet Explorer doesn't follow.

- Event handlers can be added to any element, and removed just as easily.

- Event handling can be delegated to elements higher in the DOM because events bubble up through the DOM structure, eventually reaching the body tag.

- Events can be manually fired.

- You can create custom events.

This chapter marks the end of the discussion chapters. In Chapter 4 we'll have some fun applying everything we've covered in the first three chapters in some practical projects.

CHAPTER 4

■ ■ ■

JavaScript in Action

Now that we've covered the basics of JavaScript and the DOM, let's work with our new tools. In this chapter we have picked seven projects that will help you build your own projects, as well as illustrate many of the techniques and JavaScript features we have covered in other chapters:

- Working with JavaScript

- Loading Scripts Efficiently

- Asynchronous Communication using XMLHttpRequest

- Cross-Domain Techniques

- Data Caching

- Choosing a JavaScript Library

- Using jQuery

- Building Your Own JavaScript Library

Working with JavaScript

Although not technically a "project," we wanted to discuss some important aspects of working with JavaScript. Probably the most common questions we get from JavaScript novices have to do with working with JavaScript: which editors are good? How do you debug? What's the best environment to work with? Are there any tricks to working with the language? We wanted to take this opportunity to answer these questions.

Over the years, we've written JavaScript in just about every environment imaginable. One of the great things about JavaScript is that you don't need a lot of tools to work with it. A simple text editor and a browser will suffice to get you started, and for basic projects that's really all you need. Once you start working on projects with a little complexity, though, you'll quickly find yourself wanting more advanced tools.

In this section we want to cover the basic tools of the JavaScript trade. To start we wanted to go over the trinity of JavaScript development tools: integrated development environments, browsers, and personal web servers.

We'll start by talking a little about some of the more popular integrated development environments (IDEs) with JavaScript support. Having a solid IDE with features like syntax highlighting, code completion, refactoring support, and collaboration capabilities can help tame a complex project. There are many available, and it's hard to know which one to pick.

We also want to cover the developer support provided by web browsers. Modern web browsers provide a wide variety of very useful tools for monitoring and debugging the JavaScript that they're running.

Finally we'll cover the most commonly-used personal web servers. You can use your browser's Open File feature to test your scripts, and that's okay for basic work. Asynchronous communication, however, is one of the cornerstones of building JavaScript applications, and it requires a web server. (We cover asynchronous communication in the Asynchronous Communication with XMLHttpRequest section, below.)

Once we've covered the tools of the trade we will talk about how to use them. We'll provide some insights into our usual workflow when working with JavaScript, and then talk a little about methods for debugging your scripts.

JavaScript IDEs

Since JavaScript is essentially text, all you really need to write it is a text editor. Any text editor can serve the purpose, even something simple like the Notepad application on Windows. There are also several code editors available that work well with JavaScript, and some even provide basic features like syntax highlighting. We've used vi to create projects, and know several colleagues who are die-hard emacs users. We're also very fond of TextMate and Sublime Edit, two great editing programs that support a variety of languages.

When you start working with complex projects with many JavaScript files, you'll quickly find that you'll need more features than simple code editors can provide. That's where integrated development environments (IDEs) come into play. (And if you're already familiar with code editing environments for other languages, you'll want the same features for your JavaScript projects.)

An integrated development environment takes a code editor to the next level. A typical IDE will provide features for managing multiple files and file types, grouping them together in projects or applications (the exact term varies), and will often provide features for collaborating with other developers, such as integration with source control systems.

There are several IDEs that support JavaScript development. Typically they all provide a basic set of editing features (e.g. file creation, deletion, renaming, moving; find/replace in a single file or across multiple files; auto indenting). The better IDEs will provide more advanced features like code assist (a feature that acts as a dynamic assistant, providing suggestions or autocompletion based on what you have typed).

In addition, much of the time you won't be working exclusively with JavaScript. If you're working on a typical web project you'll also be working with HTML and CSS, so you'll want the IDE to support those as well. We find, however, that we can live with fewer features for HTML and CSS in an IDE if the JavaScript support is particularly good.

If you're new to using IDEs entirely, we recommend looking through this list and trying a couple of the options. Many developers are passionate about their IDEs and will claim that their choice is the only logical one, but really the choice is one of personal preference. Trying a few IDEs will help you figure out what your preferences are—which features you really like, which ones you can work without—and you can make a choice at that point.

aptana studio

`http://www.aptana.com`

Aptana Studio is our preferred IDE. It's built on Eclipse (see below) and is available as either a standalone install or as an Eclipse plugin. Aptana has all of the features of the base Eclipse IDE (build integration, cross-platform, scriptability, etc). In addition, Aptana has several very useful features for web development in general, and JavaScript development in particular:

- Code assist with JavaScript, HTML, and CSS.

- Code assist with jQuery (which has its own syntax, see Using jQuery, below).

- Out-of-the-box Git integration (Git is a highly popular source control system; see `http://git-scm.com/` for details).

- Built-in CLI, for working with script interpreters like node (or ruby if you're working with Rails).

- JSLint integration (JSLint is a JavaScript syntax and style checker; see `http://www.jslint.com/lint.html` for details).

- Open Source, with an active community. Bug reports are answered quickly and fixes are pushed regularly via the internal updating system.

- Because it is built on Eclipse, many existing Eclipse plugins will work with Aptana (e.g. the SVN plugin).

- Aptana is free.

Aptana also has the fully configurable UI of Eclipse, and also provides a nice library of predefined themes to try and change to your liking. (We're very fond of the "Espresso Libre" theme.)

Aptana is backed by Appcelerator, a company that focuses on creating tools for building mobile applications. See `http://www.appcelerator.com` for details.

Eclipse

`http://www.eclipse.org`

Eclipse is an open-source IDE. Eclipse was built for Java development (and is itself built using Java), but now includes support for many other languages: JavaScript, C/C++, Ruby, Python, PHP, etc. Eclipse is a full-fledged IDE, so it can handle entire projects, and even has integration with popular build systems like Ant. In addition:

- Eclipse is cross-platform. Because it's built with Java, Eclipse runs on many operating systems. This means you can learn Eclipse once and not have to worry about changing from Windows to Mac and having to learn a whole new IDE.

- Eclipse supports plugins. Anyone can create plugins to extend Eclipse's functionality, and many plugins exist for everything from browser debugging to unit testing to SVN and Git integration.

- Eclipse is Open Source and has an active community.

- Eclipse is free.

Out of the box Eclipse provides very little support for working with JavaScript (or HTML or CSS). You can add varying degrees of support through a plugin. The most prominent Eclipse plugin for JavaScript support is Aptana (see above), but if that's too much there are a couple other choices.

We've had good luck with Amateras `http://amateras.sourceforge.jp/cgi-bin/fswiki_en/wiki.cgi?page=EclipseHTMLEditor` which provides basic functionality including code highlighting, content assist, outlining, and validation. If all you're looking for is basic coding support in a lightweight plugin, Amateras is a good choice.

The Eclipse Web Tools Platform is a project that aims to provide tools for all aspects of web development. You can read more at `http://www.eclipse.org/webtools/`. They have a JavaScript Developer's Tools (JSDT) sub-project at `http://www.eclipse.org/webtools/jsdt/` that works very well, and provides basic code editing features as well as integrated debugging, code assist with browser dependencies, code outlining and perspectives, etc. When we are working with a plain Eclipse install and cannot use Aptana, the Eclipse Web Tools Platform is our preferred plugin for JavaScript support.

Microsoft Visual Web Developer and Visual Studio Express

`http://www.microsoft.com/visualstudio/eng/products/visual-studio-express-products`

Microsoft's Visual Studio is an excellent IDE, but quite expensive for a full license. To make their tools (and thus their platforms) easier to access, Microsoft has created a line of "express" versions of Visual Studio. The Visual Studio Express for Web IDE is a great environment for creating HTML/CSS/JavaScript applications. We've worked with the

2010 version (which was called Visual Web Developer) and it provided all the features we needed for integrating web-based UI work with .NET backend work. Features:

- Integrated workflows with full versions of Visual Studio, allowing you to keep the expensive licenses to a minimum without limiting collaboration.

- Code highlighting and syntax checking for JavaScript and HTML.

- SVN and Git integration.

- Unit testing integration.

- Active community of users who are helpful about answering questions and providing suggestions.

- Free.

If you will be building projects for Windows, or will be collaborating with people who do, the Visual Studio line would be a great choice.

WebStorm

`http://www.jetbrains.com/webstorm`

We know many JavaScript developers that swear by WebStorm and will not even consider using another IDE. Its features include:

- Code highlighting and completion.

- Unit testing integration.

- JSlint integration.

- Internal debugger.

- 30-day free trial, $49 for a personal license.

We've not used WebStorm ourselves, but we have seen enough of it over the shoulders of colleagues to be suitably impressed.

Browsers

Probably as important as your choice of IDE is your choice of browser for doing your development. You'll be testing in all of your target browsers, of course, but you'll have one main browser that will be your go-to choice for ongoing work, that will always be running in the background waiting for you to switch back to it and hit refresh to see your latest changes. Which browser you choose as this faithful companion will depend largely on how well it supports JavaScript development.

Not long ago, browsers had very little support for developers. You could view the source of a web page but that was it. Errors in your JavaScript (or HTML or CSS) would pass unremarked, except for inducing unpredictable behavior in your applications. Debugging a complex script was as much a matter of defensive coding and knowledge of arcane idiosyncrasies of the browser as it was a matter of following any sort of set pattern.

Today all the modern browsers (Safari, Chrome, Firefox, and Internet Explorer) have tools for supporting development. Some browsers provide highly advanced features, but all of them provide at least a JavaScript console and the ability to view generated source.

- JavaScript console: They all provide a console where the browser can output error messages. The browsers also provide access to the console to your scripts (see Using the Console, below).

- View generated source: All modern browsers provide a way for you to view the source of a document that results after all of the JavaScript within the page has run. If that JavaScript has modified the DOM, those changes will be reflected in the markup. This feature is enormously helpful in determining if your DOM manipulations are behaving as you expected. Each browser's implementation of this feature is different; consult with your browser's documentation to learn how to use it.

Most browsers have other features that are quite useful, including the ability to monitor HTTP traffic as it happens (which is helpful when you're making asynchronous requests and are wondering if the server you queried returned the response you expected), the ability to step through code line by line, the ability to directly manipulate HTML, CSS, and even JavaScript as the application is running, etc.

In addition to native development support, some browsers (most notably Firefox) have an extensive library of third party add-ons that provide even more features. In fact, third party add-ons were among the first developer tools available. Their popularity helped convince browser manufacturers that providing native tools is a great way to attract developers to using their browsers.

Developer support features evolve constantly because modern browsers are also evolving and push regular and frequent updates. For example, Firefox recently added a 3-D view to their developer tools, which provides a three-dimensional view of the DOM which you can view from different angles.

Chrome

Google Chrome is our go-to browser for web development. The developer tools are robust and feature the ability to apply break points to JavaScript code, run stack traces, profile efficiency, and more. We work with Chrome on a daily basis and have not yet found its developer tools to be wanting.

Firefox

Firefox is probably the most extensible of the web browsers. The latest versions include an impressive set of development tools which includes the highly useful Scratchpad, which enables you to enter JavaScript code and run it in the context of the current tab.

Firefox didn't always have such robust development tools built in, however, so for many years web developers had to rely on plugins to provide that functionality. Probably the most popular is Firebug (`http://www.getfirebug.com`) which provides all the features you need for web development in Firefox: a DOM inspector, script and network monitors, a JavaScript console, etc.

Another favorite Firefox extension is the Web Developer's Toolbar (`https://addons.mozilla.org/en-US/firefox/addon/web-developer/?redirectlocale=en-US&redirectslug= Web_Developer_Extension_%28external%29`). This extension adds a toolbar to Firefox with many useful features: The ability to selectively enable or disable features such as scripts, image display, or Firefox's native popup blocker; inspectors for the DOM, cookies, forms; validation tools, etc.

Internet Explorer

Internet Explorer's development tools are a relatively new addition, but as of version 10 are quite extensive. To access Internet Explorer's developer's tools, hit F12 while viewing a page. This will bring up a window containing the available tools.

Internet Explorer's tools include all of the basic ones: a console, the ability to add breakpoints to your JavaScript, efficiency profiling, network monitoring, etc. In addition, it provides several useful features such as standards validation, which submits the current page to various validators for checking. IE's developer tools also includes an accessibility validator, which submits the current page to the validator at `www.contentquality.com`.

IE's dev tools also help you manage some of Internet Explorer's more quirky aspects. For example, using conditional comments you can write code that targets specific versions of Internet Explorer, the tools provide a way to see what mode you currently are using. You can also change modes, making it easier to test your work in different viewing modes.

(Explaining document modes in IE is a bit beyond the scope of this section; for a really good explanation see http://www.nczonline.net/blog/2010/01/19/internet-explorer-8-document-and-browser-modes/.)

Safari

Safari also has an extensive set of web developer tools. To use them go to Preferences ➤ Advanced and check the "Show Develop menu in menu bar" option. That will add a Develop item to the main menu bar, which is how you access Safari's developer tools.

Safari's developer tools are quite similar to Chrome's, and that makes sense because they both share a common codebase. However, the developers tools do differ between the two browsers. Safari, for example, has the surprisingly useful Snippets editor: From the Develop menu choose "Show Snippet editor" to pop open the editor. The Snippets editor essentially provides a stripped-down browser for you to work with. Type in your HTML, CSS, and JavaScript in the top pane and it will instantly be rendered in the bottom pane. The Snippets editor is great for testing styles and prototyping interactions, giving you a place to quickly try code without having to go through the extra steps of creating a full HTML file.

Web Servers

Now that you have an editor for creating JavaScript and a browser to run it in, you need a way to get your scripts into the browser. Many of the examples in this book can be saved as simple files on your hard drive and then opened directly in the browser, but for real web development you'll want to run your own local server for testing your work. Each operating system has its own options for web servers, and there is even one cross-platform option available.

MacOS

MacOS comes with an Apache web server built in, and prior to Mountain Lion you could activate it via the Sharing pane in the Control Panel. Apple removed the Control Panel interface, but left the server intact. You can manage the server from the command line, or we were able to find at least one person who had posted a custom Control Panel pane that purportedly restored the feature. (We didn't try that, but if you want to give it a try head to your favorite search engine and search for "replacement system preferences pane web sharing" and you should find it right away.)

Windows

Windows has its own web server called Internet Information Services, or IIS. Most of the various editions of Windows 7 and Windows 8 do not come with IIS installed or enabled by default, but you can easily add it to your installation. We can't cover the details here (that would be an entire chapter in and of itself), but searching for "windows 7 IIS install" or "windows 8 IIS install" should get you started.

Xampp

http://www.apachefriends.org/en/xampp.html

Xampp is an easy to install cross-platform version of the Apache web server (configured with PHP), along with the MySQL database and several other useful tools. It's available for Windows, MacOS, Linux, and Solaris. We've had very good luck with Xampp on both Windows and MacOS, and recommend it.

IDE Debugging Servers

Many IDEs have built-in debugging servers. These will allow you to serve a single page, or possibly an entire project, from within the IDE. In addition to simply serving the files, the IDE will also often provide integrated features for debugging your code, like breakpoints, stack traces, and stepping through code, all in the same environment. We've found that the Visual Studio tools for integrated debugging are particularly good, but Aptana's tools are also quite useful. Consult the documentation for your tool for details on how to configure and use your IDE's integrated server.

JavaScript Development Workflow

Now that you've picked an editor, a browser, and a way to serve your files, you're ready to go. At its most simple, a typical JavaScript development workflow looks like the workflow for any other language (write, test, repeat):

1.   Write some code.

2.   Load it in the browser and observe the results.

3.   Repeat, fixing the problems that occurred or adding more features.

As you write more complex JavaScript, you'll need ways to inspect your scripts as they execute. Some IDEs and browser developer tools provide features that help, like inspectors or breakpoints, but there are some basic techniques you can use that give you a lot of what you need.

Using the Browser Console

Throughout this book we've been using alerts to monitor the progress of our scripts. Alerts are fine, but they have the disadvantage of pausing the execution of a script while it waits for someone to click the OK button.

Fortunately, there is a robust alternative to alerts in the browser's JavaScript console. All modern browsers have a JavaScript console that you can access, typically as part of the browser's built-in Developer Tools, see Figure 4-1 for an example. Most browsers have a keyboard shortcut to bring up the console: for Chrome it's Shift-Control-I, for Firefox it's Shift-Control-J. IE also has a console; hit F12 to bring up the Developer Tools and click on the Console tab.

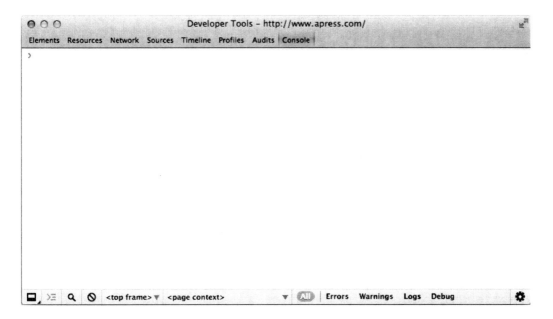

Figure 4-1. *The Screenshot of the Chrome browser console*

Modern browsers expose an interface for the console to JavaScript in the form of the `window.console` object. Each browser's console is different, so each browser's console object is different. But all of them provide methods for outputting your own text to the console:

- `console.log(strText)`: Output the specified text to the console as a simple log.

- `console.warn(strText)`: Output the specified text to the console as a warning.

- `console.error(strText)`: Output the specified text to the console as an error.

Both Firefox and Chrome provide ways to filter the console output so you can view just the types of output you want.

Outputting text to the console has the virtue of not interrupting the execution of your script like an alert would. Now that you know about the console, you can execute any example in this book and replace the alert call with `console.log` and see the same output on the console, rather than as an alert.

Logging to the console provides a great way to keep an eye on the state of your scripts. One of the most common uses is to output the value of variables at different points in your script's execution so that you can see how the variable changes. In Chrome and IE, you can output anything to the console, not just strings. If you output an object, you'll see it enumerated on the console (see Figure 4-2):

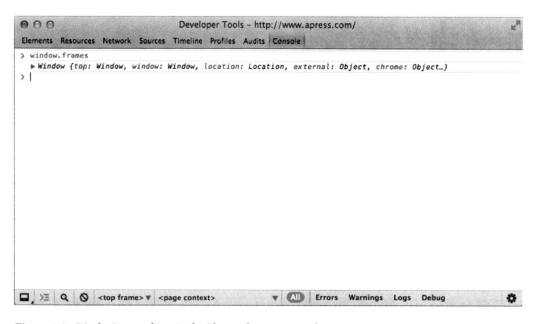

Figure 4-2. *Displaying an object in the Chrome browser console*

In Chrome you can even drill down into an object to an arbitrary depth, including its prototypal inheritances. This is a great way to learn more about JavaScript and the DOM; try outputting the `window` object to the console and poking around in it.

In addition, you can interact directly with the console (see Figure 4-3). At the top of the Firefox console is an input field with a button labeled "Evaluate." In IE's console, it's the input field at the bottom of the window marked with the >> symbol. In Chrome, you just click in the console window.

Figure 4-3. *Entering JavaScript commands into the Chrome browser console*

We are getting a reference to the body of the current document and then hiding it by setting its display property to none.

You can type in any valid JavaScript here and it will execute in the context of the page that's been loaded into the browser window. As an experiment go to any page and type `alert(document.title)` into the console. (Usually you can just press Enter to cause the console to evaluate your code, but sometimes you have to click the Evaluate button in Firefox.) The browser window should alert the title of the page that's loaded. If you enter `window.document` into the console and press enter (or evaluate), the `document` object should appear in the console. In Chrome, when you drill down into this object you'll see HTML markup . . . and as you mouse over the elements Chrome will highlight the corresponding elements in the window. IE will only enumerate the first few properties on an object, and Firefox will only output the results of the `toString()` method of any object.

Breakpoints

One of the most useful tools for debugging scripts is the ability to set breakpoints in the code: specified points at which the browser stops executing the script and allows you to inspect the current state of the scripts and even change things. If you've never used breakpoints as part of your debugging process, we highly recommend giving it a try. It's also useful for examining scripts to learn how they work.

Chrome's developer tools support breakpoints and stepping through JavaScript code line by line. For an excellent tutorial, see `https://developers.google.com/chrome-developer-tools/docs/scripts-breakpoints`.

Firebug also supports breakpoints as part of script debugging.
See `https://getfirebug.com/wiki/index.php/Script_Debugging` for details.

Loading Scripts Efficiently

As you start writing complex JavaScript applications, you'll quickly find that one of the biggest performance issues you'll have is slowness when your application first loads and initializes. Sometimes these problems are due to technical issues, like script blocking or inefficient download order, and sometimes these problems are purely perceptual: you can optimize your application loading process from a technical aspect, but that has side effects (like brief flashes of unmodified content) that result in your application seeming like it is slow, inefficient, or unpolished.

In this section we'll discuss techniques that you can use that will be optimized for both actual speed and perceived speed. The first step is to talk about how browsers download and parse their assets, and then we'll provide four common tips you can use to increase the loading efficiency of your application.

How Browsers Download and Process Content

The details of downloading and processing content aren't specified in any standard, so browser manufacturers are free to implement any methodologies they prefer. As a result, there is some variation from browser to browser (and even from version to version of a given browser) on how that is implemented. Overall, though, there are some general commonalities:

- Browsers parse HTML documents in order. As the browser parses a document, the elements it parses will become available in the DOM and it will begin downloading specified assets (images, external scripts, stylesheets, etc).

- Browsers can download multiple assets in parallel. Older browsers will only download two assets in parallel, but newer browsers can handle up to six.

- Loading an external JavaScript file will block other asset downloads. This is because a script might modify the DOM, or even redirect the browser to a different page, so to avoid unnecessary downloads the browser will not begin any other parallel downloads until the script is loaded, parsed, and executed.

Throughout this book our examples have illustrated document parsing order by always placing the JavaScript at the end of the HTML markup, just before the `</body>` tag. This guarantees that the browser will have parsed the HTML before the script tries to access the elements. If you reverse the order, you'll end up with a script trying to access an element that doesn't exist yet, and usually that results in an error. To demonstrate, consider Listing 3-3 from Chapter 3:

Listing 3-3. Using getElementById()

```
<!DOCTYPE html>
<html>
        <head>
                <title>JavaScript Developer's Guide</title>
        </head>
        <body>
            <p id="myParagraph">This is my paragraph! <span class="hideme">Lorem ipsum</span> dolor
            sit amet.<span></span></p>
            <p class="hideme">Another paragraph!</p>
            <script>
var myPar = document.getElementById("myParagraph"); // myPar is now a pointer to the paragraph.
myPar.innerText = "I have changed the content!";    // Change the text of the paragraph to "I have
changed the content!"
            </script>
        </body>
</html>
```

This simple example illustrates using the getElementByID() method and changing the text of a paragraph. If we place the <script> tag before the <p> tag, the example won't work, as in Listing 4-1:

Listing 4-1. Trying to access a DOM element before it is available

```
<!DOCTYPE html>
<html>
        <head>
                <title>JavaScript Developer's Guide</title>
        </head>
        <body>
            <script>
var myPar = document.getElementById("myParagraph"); // myPar is now a pointer to the paragraph.
myPar.innerText = "I have changed the content!"; // Change the text of the paragraph to "I have
changed the content!"
            </script>
            <p id="myParagraph">This is my paragraph! <span class="hideme">Lorem ipsum</span> dolor
            sit amet.<span></span></p>
            <p class="hideme">Another paragraph!</p>
        </body>
</html>
```

The script will not be able to access the paragraph, so getElementById() will return null. When we attempt to change the innerText property of null, the JavaScript engine will throw an error because null has no properties.

Also, in all of our examples our scripts are inline, meaning they're actually in the document itself. As you write longer and more complex scripts, you'll find it's easier to keep them in separate files rather than placing them inline. Separate files make maintenance and collaboration with other programmers easier, and allow you to leverage deployment options like content distribution networks.

Unfortunately, when you load your scripts as separate files, it means that they will block the parallel download of assets that follow them in the document. That brings us to our first technique for optimizing your applications: load scripts at the end of the document.

Optimization Tip #1: Load Scripts at the End of the Document

One key technique (if an idea this simple can be called a technique) for optimizing your application loading process is to load scripts at the end of the document, after everything else has already been loaded. Then they won't be in a position to block any other downloads, and any elements your scripts may need to access will be present in the DOM.

This technique can sometimes have an undesired side effect: Imagine you have a simple HTML document that you modify heavily with complex JavaScript. You've set up your document structure such that all your scripts are loaded at the end of the document. This results in a simple HTML document loading and appearing in the browser, and then the browser starts to load, parse, and execute your scripts. While the browser is doing that, your unmodified content is being displayed to the user and even worse because script loading is a blocking process, if the user attempts to interact with the page nothing will happen. Then the browser will finish loading, parsing, and executing your scripts and all of a sudden the browser will display the application as you intended. This "flash of unmodified (or unstyled) content," brief though it may be, makes your application appear unpolished and inefficient even though technically your application has been optimized for loading efficiency.

If you find yourself dealing with a flash of unmodified content, remember that it's a perceptual problem. The user is seeing something that they don't expect and doesn't help them, and that gives the perception that your application is at fault. In cases of perceptual inefficiencies, you can often turn it back to your advantage by providing the user with something that is helpful, like a loading screen. A loading screen tells the user that the application is still functioning; it's just not ready yet. If your scripts are otherwise loading and executing efficiently, that's usually enough to buy your application the time it needs to get going.

Creating a loading indicator is easy; just include the markup for it at the very beginning of your document, so that it's the first thing that is parsed and displayed. It can be a simple box in the middle of the screen with the message "Loading…" or it can be a small image. Typically a loading indicator is absolutely positioned in the middle of the screen and blocks access to elements underneath it. To dismiss it all you have to do is place a simple call at the end of your last script to access the loader in the DOM and either remove it or, if you might want to use it again later, to simply hide it.

Here's an example that simulates a loading delay with a timer. In Listing 4-2, we've got a simple loading indicator that covers everything on the screen, and then when the application is "ready" (in this case, when the timer is up) the script hides it:

Listing 4-2. A simple loading indicator

```
<!DOCTYPE html>
<html>
        <head>
                <title>JavaScript Developer's Guide</title>
                <style>
body, h1 {
    margin: 0;
    padding: 0;
}
#container-loading {
    position: absolute;
    /*
     * Radial gradient CSS generated by CSS Background Maker
     * http://ie.microsoft.com/testdrive/graphics/cssgradientbackgroundmaker/default.html
     */
    /* IE10 Consumer Preview */
    background-image: -ms-radial-gradient(center, circle farthest-corner, #9E9E9E 0%, #141414 100%);
    /* Mozilla Firefox */
    background-image: -moz-radial-gradient(center, circle farthest-corner, #9E9E9E 0%, #141414 100%);
    /* Opera */
    background-image: -o-radial-gradient(center, circle farthest-corner, #9E9E9E 0%, #141414 100%);
    /* Webkit (Safari/Chrome 10) */
    background-image: -webkit-gradient(radial, center center, 0, center center, 506,
    color-stop(0, #9E9E9E), color-stop(1, #141414));
    /* Webkit (Chrome 11+) */
    background-image: -webkit-radial-gradient(center, circle farthest-corner, #9E9E9E 0%, #141414 100%);
    /* W3C Markup, IE10 Release Preview */
    background-image: radial-gradient(circle farthest-corner at center, #9E9E9E 0%, #141414 100%);
}

#container-loading div {
    width: 200px;
    height: 100px;
    border: 2px solid #ccc;
    background-color: #fff;
    text-align: center;
    line-height: 100px;
    font-family: arial, helvetica, sans-serif;
    font-weight: bold;
    font-size: 1.5em;
```

```
    border-radius: 20px;
    position: absolute;
}
            </style>
        <script>
function showLoading(boolShow) {
    var loadingIndicator = document.getElementById("container-loading"),
        loadingMessage = loadingIndicator.querySelector("div");
    if (boolShow === true) {
        // Show the loading indicator.
        // Position everything
        loadingIndicator.style.width = window.innerWidth + "px";
        loadingIndicator.style.height = window.innerHeight + "px";
        loadingMessage.style.left = ((window.innerWidth - 200) / 2) + "px";
        loadingMessage.style.top = ((window.innerHeight - 100) / 2) + "px";
        loadingIndicator.style.display = "block";
    } else {
        loadingIndicator.style.display = "none";
    }
}
        </script>
        </head>
        <body>

            <!-- Begin: Loading Indicator -->
            <div id="container-loading">
                <div>
                    Loading...
                </div>
            </div>
        <script>
// Initialize and show the loading indicator.
showLoading(true);
        </script>
            <!-- End: Loading Indicator -->

            <!-- Begin: Rest of document -->
            <h1>Hello World!</h1>
            <!-- Pretend complex markup goes here -->
            <!-- End: Rest of document -->

        <!-- Begin: loading scripts -->
        <!-- Script(s) loaded here -->
        <!-- End: loading scripts -->
        <script>
// Simulate a loading delay with a timer
setTimeout(function() {
    showLoading(false);
}, 2000);
        </script>
        </body>
</html>
```

Note that in this loading indicator we do include two bits of inline JavaScript to handle positioning and layout, as well as hiding and showing the indicator. The first bit of inline JavaScript is in the head of the document, and it sets up a showLoading() function that we can use to show or hide the loading dialog. We could easily have included the function definition in the body, after the loading dialog markup, but the function doesn't need to follow the markup in order to be defined because it doesn't access the elements until it is called. If we define the function in the head, but don't call it until after the elements it accesses are parsed, it will work as expected. We could even pull this simple script out into a separate file and load it using a non-blocking technique if we wanted; see Tip #3.

The other bit of inline JavaScript simply calls the showLoading() function to initialize the loader and show it correctly. Because this script does only one thing, in the name of efficiency it makes sense to keep it inline in the document, rather than pulling it out into a separate file (pulling it out into a separate file would also cause it to block the loading of the complex document that came after).

Loading screens are an easy solution to the problem of blocking scripts, but they come with a couple of caveats. First, they're not really appropriate for every situation. If you're building an informational website, for example, you certainly don't want to make people wait for your site to load. On the other hand, if you are building a complex data-driven web application, a loading indicator can be quite useful.

Second, you should always try to minimize the loading delays so that you'll never need a loading indicator, or so that it will only be on the screen for as brief a time as possible. Our next optimization tip will help you achieve that goal.

Optimization Tip #2: Combine, Minify, and GZip

A common technique for increasing the efficiency of JavaScript applications is to combine scripts into as few files as possible. This reduces the number of HTTP requests the browser has to make, and can have a big impact on the loading speed of your application. Even if you only have a dozen or so JavaScript files, it would be a good idea to look through them and decide which ones could be combined.

If you're hesitant to combine your scripts into one file because it will make them difficult to maintain, that's a legitimate concern. That's why many projects have a publication step that takes a development version of the application and combines the JavaScript files together into one file. That way developers get to keep the more manageable separate files, but the user doesn't have to suffer the extra loading times they would entail. Note that when you do this, it means that the environment you and your fellow programmers are working in is not the same as what your users will be experiencing. The users will be experiencing a more optimized environment, which could result in problems you will not witness. You should test your application regularly in a "compiled" production version to avoid being surprised by bugs at time of deployment.

Another common deployment optimization technique is to minify the combined JavaScript files. Minification is a method where an automated parsing program loads a JavaScript file and then attempts to reduce the overall size of the file by removing comments, removing unnecessary whitespace, and replacing long variable, property, and method names with smaller ones. The result is JavaScript that is very difficult for humans to read, but which browsers have no problem understanding and which is significantly smaller in filesize, thus reducing download times.

Finally, JavaScript files are often compressed using the GZip compression algorithm before they're deployed. Browsers have the ability to accept a GZipped JavaScript file and unzip them internally before processing them. Even though this introduces an extra step for the browser to perform, the time it takes is generally much less than the time it would take for an uncompressed file to be transmitted to the browser, resulting in an overall performance increase. GZip is only applicable for files above 100 bytes or so; files smaller than that will actually get bigger because GZipping does involve some overhead in the file. If your file is big enough, though, the overhead will not be noticeable in comparison to the size savings.

You can just minify or just GZip your JavaScript files, but the best savings in size (and therefore network transmission time) are when you do both. There are several tools available for minifying JavaScript:

- Google's Closure Compiler: Google's Closure Compiler doesn't just minify your JavaScript, it will also optimize it. It removes unused code paths, rewrites inefficient code, and then minifies the results. The output is often much smaller than plain minification, and will run measurably faster. See https://developers.google.com/closure/compiler/ for details on using the Closure Compiler in your project.

- JSMin: One of the oldest minifiers available, but still very good, is Douglas Crockford's JSMin, available at `http://www.crockford.com/javascript/jsmin.html`. It just minifies code, it does not rewrite inefficient code like the Closure Compiler, so provides a slightly less heavy-handed approach. It's written in C, but is easy to build and integrates well into deployment scripts.

- YUI Compressor: Built by Yahoo and part of their YUI library, YUI Compressor is a great choice for minifying your JavaScript. As an added bonus it can also minify CSS files. YUI Compressor can also be included in a Node script, making it super-easy to write your own deployment scripts using JavaScript! See `http://yui.github.com/yuicompressor/` for details on YUI Compressor.

GZipping your files is something you can either do by hand as you deploy, or most modern web servers can be instructed to automatically compress certain file types before transmitting them. The Apache module `mod_deflate` (see `http://httpd.apache.org/docs/2.2/mod/mod_deflate.html`) makes it easy to specify what file types to compress, or even which browsers to compress for. If you're using Xampp, it can be configured to use `mod_deflate` by uncommenting the appropriate directive in the configuration files, see `http://stackoverflow.com/questions/6993320/how-to-enable-gzip-compression-in-xampp-server` for details. For other servers check the documentation to see what's possible.

Optimization Tip #3: Load Scripts In the Document Head Using a Non-Blocking Technique

In Tip #2 we had a small bit of inline script in the head of the document that defined the function for hiding and showing the loading indicator. It was safe to include in the head of the document because it was just a function definition, and did not access the DOM as part of its definition. As you write your scripts, you'll find a significant portion of them will fall into the category of JavaScript that could be loaded in the head of the document because it doesn't access the DOM until called. JavaScript libraries often fall into this category.

If we could load those scripts in the head, we wouldn't have to load them at the end of the document, and that would reduce the amount of time the users would have to look at our loading dialog and maybe even eliminate the need for one entirely. But if we load them as separate files in the head, they'll block anything that comes after.

Fortunately, there is a way to load scripts asynchronously. The reason why scripts block other assets from loading is because they're included as part of the regular document flow. If we inject scripts into the document, they won't be a part of the regular document flow. The browser will still load, parse, and execute them, but they won't be blocking other assets from loading.

Script tags can be injected into a document just like any other DOM element. You just create a new `<script>` tag, set its `src` property, and then append it to the DOM. The moment you append it to the DOM, the browser will begin downloading the script.

As an example, imagine we had several functions we wanted to define—maybe our own personal JavaScript library. And we had several predefined data objects we would like to create, which are defined in a separate file, and maybe there's an analytics package we want to load as well as a third party library being served from a content distribution network. None of these scripts require the DOM in order for them to be executed (though any of them might define methods that when called would access the DOM—but as long as we don't call those methods until the DOM is ready we'll be okay) so we can load them in the head. Listing 4-3 is an example script called manifest-loader.js that would do all of that:

Listing 4-3. manifest-loader.js

```
// Define a manifest array of scripts to load
var defaultManifest = [
  "scripts/js-lib.js",
  "scripts/js-objects.js",
```

```
  "scripts/third-party/omniture.js",
  "http://big.cdn.com/useful-library.js"
]

// Define a function to load a manifest array.
function loadManifest(arrManifest) {
    var i,
        arrManifestLength = arrManifest.length;

    for (i = 0; i < arrManifestLength; i++) {
        var newScript = document.createElement("script");
        newScript.src = arrManifest[i];
        document.getElementsByTagName("head")[0].appendChild(newScript);
    }
}
```

In this example we first create a manifest array of all the URLs we want to load asynchronously. Then we define a function that, when given a manifest array, will loop through the array, create a new script tag, set the src attribute, and then append the script tag to the head of the document, thus causing the script to load asynchronously.

Now we can just load this script into the head of our hypothetical document. We can also include an even smaller inline script that calls loadManifest(defaultManifest) and all of our scripts will begin loading without blocking the rest of the document, as shown in Listing 4-4:

Listing 4-4. Using the manifest loader

```
<!DOCTYPE html>
<html>
    <head>
        <title>JavaScript Developer's Guide</title>
            <script src="scripts/js-loader.js"></script>
        <script>
loadManifest(defaultManifest);
        </script>
        </head>
        <body>

            <h1>Hello World!</h1>

        </body>
</html>
```

It's very important that none of these scripts in the manifest need the DOM to be ready, because it almost certainly not be available when they're loaded. Note that it is possible to determine when the document is ready, but the details vary greatly from browser to browser and even version to version of a given browser. However, it's a common functionality that many JavaScript libraries provide (like jQuery, see below).

If you don't want to build this sort of infrastructure for yourself, you can always look for the features you need in an existing JavaScript library. For example, RequireJS (http://requirejs.org/) takes this technique one step further and allows you to specify dependencies in your JavaScript files, which can be dynamically loaded on an as-needed basis.

Optimization Tip #4: Moderation is Good

Don't fall into the trap of thinking that you absolutely must use any (or all) of these techniques. As you are optimizing your application loading process, you should always look at what makes the most sense for your specific situation. In our loading indicator example above, we kept some scripts inline in the document rather than loading them from external files. We did this because placing them where they are guarantees that they'll be available when we need them (right after the browser parses the necessary part of the document) and because they are small enough that optimizing them wasn't really necessary.

In your projects you should experiment to see what combination of techniques provides the best results. You'll probably find that you'll use a combination of these techniques to balance development needs with deployment requirements across all your target browsers.

As mentioned in Tip #3, if you don't want to build this sort of optimization infrastructure yourself you can always look for the features you need in a JavaScript library or framework.

Asynchronous Communication using XMLHttpRequest

In addition to loading and displaying pages based on user requests (or JavaScript commands), browsers provide another method for accessing servers: the XMLHttpRequest object. This object provides an interface for JavaScript to make requests to web servers and process the responses as needed. The primary difference between this interface and simply loading a page is that these requests can be made asynchronously—they run in the background and will not block user interactions with the main page. In addition, the results of these requests can be processed by JavaScript and incorporated into the current document as needed. Using this technique it is therefore possible to create user interactions that do not require page refreshes, enabling a much more application-like look and feel for a web application.

As you might think from the name XMLHttpRequest, the request can involve XML. And indeed when the technique was first implemented, XML was the preferred way of encoding information. However, the technique can involve any encoded data that is valid for transmission across HTTP: HTML, JSON, or even plain text. The technique also has another name: Asynchronous JavaScript and XML, or AJAX for short.

Originally implemented by Microsoft, the XMLHttpRequest technique was so useful that other browsers quickly implemented it, and it is now a part of the DOM standard at `http://www.w3.org/TR/XMLHttpRequest/`

How It Works

The XMLHttpRequest object performs all of the network access for you, going through all of the necessary steps to contact the server and communicate correctly with it. As it does its work, it will dispatch events at various points—when it has finished communicating with the server, for example, or if an error has occurred. You provide event handlers for those events to correctly process the results.

The basic steps are as follows:

- Create the desired event handler functions.

- Create a new instance of the XMLHttpRequest object and configure it for use (including providing the event handlers).

- Instruct the XMLHttpRequest object to make the request. As it does its work, it will dispatch events at the appropriate times.

Let's go over each of those steps one at a time.

Step 1: Event Handlers

As it goes through its work, the XMLHttpRequest object will dispatch events for which you can provide handlers. As with the DOM interaction events (like click or keypress), the event handler will be called when the event occurs, and will be passed an event object which will contain information about the event. The event types are:

- readystatechange: This event is fired multiple times as the XMLHttpRequest object does its work. When fired, this event will provide a readyState property on the event object that will have one of the following values:

    - 0: Unsent, meaning the XMLHttpRequest object has been created but the request has not been sent.

    - 1: Opened, meaning the open() method has been called and has successfully completed (and thus a request is underway).

    - 2: Headers received, meaning all headers have been received from the server (this includes redirect headers, if any). At this point the status property of the event object is now available, and will have the HTTP response code from the server.

    - 3: Loading, meaning the response is being loaded.

    - 4: Done, meaning the response has been successfully loaded. The response from the server is now located in the responseText property of the event object.

- abort: Fired when the request has been aborted (as when the XMLHttpRequest.abort() method is called).

- error: Fired when an error condition has occurred.

- load: Fired when the request has completed successfully.

- loadend: Fired when the request has completed regardless of success.

- loadstart: Fired when the request is sent.

- progress: Fired during the loading process as it progresses.

- timeout: Fired if a specified timeout period elapses before the request could be completed.

All of these events except the readystatechange event are new to the most recent version of the XMLHttpRequest specification, and so they may not be fully implemented in all of your target browsers. (Webkit, for example, only just implemented the timeout event; see https://bugs.webkit.org/show_bug.cgi?id=74802.) The readystatechange event is the legacy event specified by the original specification and is widely implemented, and it provides all the information we need for handling most success and error situations.

A good readystatechange event handler uses the readyState property to see how far the request has progressed and uses that to act accordingly. It will also use the status property to check for HTTP status messages (like status 404 for file not found). We can see this in Listing 4-5:

Listing 4-5. A simple readystatechange event handler

```
function handleReadyStateChange(objXHR) {
  if (objXHR.readyState === 4) {
    // Request is done.  Was the requested file found?
    If ((objXHR.status !== 200) && (objEvent.status !== 304)) {
      // Something happened..possibly the requested file wasn't found?
      // Tell the user that something went wrong.
      console.error("An error occurred while processing the request.");
```

```
  } else {
    // The requested file was found and sent and the content is now available in
    // the objXHR.responseText property:
    console.log(objXHR.responseText);
  }
 }
}
```

We assume this event handler will be called multiple times as the request progresses, but the only time we want to do anything is if the `readyState` property is 4, meaning the request is Done. Then we check the HTTP status that was returned by the server, located in the `status` property. We're going to assume that any status other than a 200 (success) or 304 (resource not modified) is an error condition; however you could do more detailed error handling based on different status codes if you wanted. (See `http://www.w3.org/Protocols/rfc2616/rfc2616-sec10.html` for a full list of status codes, their meanings, and when they are provided.) Assuming the request was a success, we simply output the result to the console. (Obviously you can do much more with the result than just send it to the console; this is a simple example to illustrate the pattern.)

Step 2: Creating and Configuring the XMLHttpRequest Object

The browser's `XMLHttpRequest` object is an abstract object, meaning it isn't accessed directly but rather is used as a pattern to create new instances. It's these new instances that you use in your scripts to perform the asynchronous requests. You can even have more than one.

To create a new `XMLHttpRequest` object, you simply use the new keyword as with any JavaScript constructor:

```
var myXHR = new XMLHttpRequest();
```

This syntax is valid in all browsers that support this feature with the single exception of Internet Explorer 6. For IE6, the feature is still available but involves evoking a new ActiveX object.

Once you have a new object, you will need to configure it. At the very least, an `XMLHttpRequest` object needs to know a URL to request, what HTTP method to use to make the request (typically GET or POST, but you can also do HEAD requests if you just want to examine the headers of a URL without actually fetching it), any supporting data needed (e.g. form data in the case of a POST), and at least one event handler to execute in case of success.

You start by opening the object using the open() method:

```
myXHR.open(strMethod, strURL, boolAsynchronous);
```

- **strMethod**: The HTTP method to use for the request

- **strURL**: The desired URL to use

- **boolAsynchronous**: A boolean indicating whether or not to perform the request asynchronously. This parameter is optional; if omitted it defaults to true. (If set to `false` this will cause the request to be performed synchronously, and it will pause the browser for the duration of the request just like a regular page load.)

Then, once you have opened the object, you can register your event handler. The most common choice is to register an event handler on the `readystatechange` event:

```
myXHR.onreadystatechange = function() {
    handleReadyStateChange(myXHR);
};
```

This registers our previously-defined handleReadyStateChange() function as the event handler for the readystatechange event. (If you are working only with browsers that implement the latest version of the standard, you can also use the addEventListener() method, just as if this were any other DOM event.)

Step 3: Sending the Request

Sending the request is easy. All you have to do is call the send() method on the configured object:

myXHR.send(postData);

- postData: Data from a form that is being posted as part of the request. In the case of GET requests, this will always be null.

At that point the object will perform the request and trigger event handlers as outlined.

■ **Note**   You can send an XHR request to any server, even one that is on a different domain from the source of your page. However, access to the request result is limited by the Same Origin Policy. Unless the origin of the response and the origin of your script match, your script will be unable to access the response. The "Cross Domain Methods" section of this chapter discusses some techniques for safely getting around these limitations.

Putting It All Together

It's pretty simple to configure and send an XMLHttpRequest, but we can make it even easier in our scripts if we create a single function that can do it all for us.

There are a lot of things we need for a robust XMLHttpRequest object: a URL, the method, any post data, and callbacks for success, error, and timeouts. We could provide each of those things as a separate parameter in a single function, but it would be tidier to gather them all up into a single object and then provide that object as a single parameter to the function, as in Listing 4-6:

Listing 4-6. A configuration object for an XMLHttpRequest function

```
var myXhrDefs = {
    strMethod : "GET",
    strUrl : "http://myhost.com/ajax-test.txt",
    intTimeout: 3000,
    postData: null,
    boolAsync: true,
    successCallback: function(objXHR) {
        // Do things when the request is successful
        console.log(objXHR.responseText);
    },
    errorCallback: function(objXHR) {
        // Do things when there is an error in the request.
        console.error("The XHR failed with error ", objXHR.status);
    },
    timeoutCallback: function() {
        // Do things when a timeout occurs.
        console.error("The XHR timed out.");
    }
}
```

Here we have gathered everything up into one object, even the callbacks which are methods on the object. In Listing 4-7, we can then build a function that uses this object as a parameter to handle our XMLHttpRequests:

Listing 4-7. An XMLHttpRequest function

```
function doXHR(myXhrDefs) {

    // Create and configure a new XMLHttpRequest object
    var myXhr = new XMLHttpRequest(),
        myTimer = null;
    myXhr.open(myXhrDefs.strMethod, myXhrDefs.strUrl, myXhrDefs.boolAsync);

    // Register the error and success handlers
    myXhr.onreadystatechange = function() {

        // If readyState is 4, request is complete.
        if (myXhr.readyState === 4) {

            // Cancel the timeout timer if we set one.
            if (myTimer !== null) {
                clearTimeout(myTimer);
            }

            // If there's an error, call the error callback,
            // Otherwise call the success callback.
            if ((myXhr.status !== 200) && (myXhr.status !== 304)) {
                if (myXhrDefs.errorCallback != null) {
                    myXhrDefs.errorCallback(myXhr);
                }
            } else {
                myXhrDefs.successCallback(myXhr);
            }
        }
    }

    // Handle timeouts (set myXhrDefs.intTimeout to null to skip)
    // If we're working with a newer implementation, we can just set the
    // timeout property and register the timeout callback.
    // If not, we have to set a start running that will execute the
    // timeout callback. We can cancel the timer if/when the server responds.
    if (myXhrDefs.intTimeout !== null) {
        if (typeof myXhr.ontimeout !== "undefined") {
            myXhr.timeout = myXhrDefs.intTimeout;
            myXhr.ontimeout = myXhrDefs.timeoutCallback;
        } else {
            myTimer = setTimeout(myXhrDefs.timeoutCallback, myXhrDefs.intTimeout);
        }
    }

    // Send the request
    myXhr.send(myXhrDefs.postData);
}
```

In this example, we're creating a function that can handle all of our XMLHttpRequest needs. It creates and configures a new XMLHttpRequest object and then registers the provided event handlers as needed. To browsers that do not yet implement the timeout feature for XMLHttpRequest, it implements a timer using setTimeout(). Then it sends the request for us. All we have to do to use the function is set up an object and then call the function:

```
doXHR(myXhrDefs);
```

Pulling all of our XMLHttpRequest code into one function makes maintenance and upgrading easier; instead of manually managing XMLHttpRequest objects in possibly multiple places in our code, we call it in only one spot.

Cross Domain Techniques

All browsers implement a security measure called the Same Origin Policy. This policy allows scripts on a page to access each other's properties and methods as long as they are all served from the same origin: the same protocol (http or https), the same host name, and the same port number (if specified). Scripts from different origins are not allowed to interact with one another. Without this policy malicious scripts could access our pages and data.

Unfortunately, this policy also stands in the way of easily making applications that work with data from multiple origins. There are a few methods for getting around this limitation, however, and because this is a common barrier in JavaScript development we wanted to cover them here briefly.

Note that all of these techniques involve potential security risks, and what risks are involved will vary depending on how you employ them. You should evaluate these techniques carefully for security problems before employing them, to avoid malicious scripts from gaining access to your pages or your data.

Server-side proxy

One of the easiest solutions to implement is to create a simple proxy service that runs on your domain, and use that to do all of your cross-domain queries. From the browser's standpoint all requests are coming from the same origin, so everything is okay.

You can implement the server-side proxy in any language you want, including JavaScript (thanks to node.js). In fact, there are already several proxy servers built using node. We've built simple proxies using both PHP and Java. For a great example, see Ben Alman's Simple PHP Proxy, available at http://benalman.com/projects/php-simple-proxy/

JSONP

JSONP stands for "JSON with padding," a rather confusing name for a technique that gets around the Same Origin Policy by making use of script injection.

One of the exceptions to the Same Origin Policy is that scripts loaded through a <script> tag with a src attribute are exempt, and can access and be accessed by scripts from another origin. For an example of this, see the examples in the Using jQuery section, below, where we load jQuery from a content distribution network, which is definitely a different origin than the example pages. If it weren't for this exception, we wouldn't be able to do this.

Ordinarily when you query a service you'd get back a JSON string as a response. You'd then use JSON.parse() to deserialize the string into an object, and then access the properties on the object to do what you need. The Same Origin Policy prevents this if the service is in a different origin than the querying page.

But what if the service didn't return a simple JSON string, and instead returned a script that could be injected into the querying page? If we did that, the injected script would be exempt from the Same Origin Policy, and we'd be able to access its properties and methods as desired. That's the key to JSONP: the service doesn't return straight JSON for parsing, it returns JSON padded inside a script that is injected into the host document.

There are two different kinds of padding that are typically used in JSONP. One is that the returned script simply does a variable assignment, like so:

```
myResponse = { "foo" : bar, "serial" : 238 };
```

If that's injected into the host document via a script tag, the variable myResponse would become available in the global scope, enabling you to access the properties as needed.

The other way is for the returned script to execute a function call, like so:

```
responseHandler({ "foo" : bar, "serial" : 238 });
```

This executes the responseHandler() function with the desired data as an object literal. (This assumes you have defined a function responseHandler() already, so that the injected script can call it, of course.)

Which kind of padding you will need will typically be specified by the target service. You, in turn, will specify the name of the variable or function in your query to the target service when you inject the script tag, like this:

```
<script src="http://www.service.com/getserial?jsonp=myResponse"></script>
<script src="http://www.service.com/getserial?jsonp=responseHandler"></script>
```

The exact syntax will be provided by the service; it may not be "jsonp=varname" or "jsonp=functionname". (Twitter, for example, specifies that the format should be "callback=functionname"—see https://dev.twitter.com/docs/things-every-developer-should-know#jsonp.)

Step by step, here's how it goes:

- If the service specifies that it will pad the JSON with a function call, create a function that you can use to handle the data. If the service specifies that it will pad the JSON with a variable assignment you can namespace the variable if you wish.

- Create a new <script> tag. Update its src attribute to have the target URL formatted as the service specifies.

- Append the <script> tag to the document. This will cause the browser to go fetch its URL, resulting in a cross-domain call.

Note that this will mean you'll be creating a new <script> tag with every JSONP call. If you're only making a few calls (maybe a dozen or less) that will probably be okay. But if you're relying heavily on JSONP, you'll want to re-use your <script> tags so you don't end up with a bloated DOM and the resulting memory problems. The easiest way to do this is to write a simple function that can handle all of your JSONP calls, as in Listing 4-8:

Listing 4-8. A function that executes JSONP calls and recycles the script tag

```
function executeJSONPQuery(strUrl) {
    // Check to see if a jsonp script tag has already been injected.
    // Also, create a new script tag with our new URL.
    var oldScript = document.getElementById("jsonp"),
        newScript = document.createElement("script");
    newScript.src = strUrl;
    newScript.id = "jsonp";

    // If there is already a jsonp script tag in the DOM we'll
    // replace it with the new one.
    // Otherwise, we'll just append the new script tag to the DOM.
    if (oldScript !== null) {
        document.body.replaceChild(newScript, oldScript);
```

```
    } else {
        document.body.appendChild(newScript);
    }
}
```

This example function takes a URL as a parameter. It creates a new script tag with the URL as its `src` attribute and "jsonp" as its ID. It then looks to see if there is another script tag with that ID. If it finds one, it replaces it with the new one, otherwise it simply injects the new script tag into the DOM. Either way, adding the new script tag to the DOM causes the browser to go load the specified URL as a script.

A great example for using this is Twitter. They provide a robust but simple API for searching tweets that will provide responses in JSONP format. For a simple example, let's just show the last 20 tweets from the author Jon Reid. We'll build a function called `handlejsonpresults()` which will receive an object literal as its parameter. According to the Twitter API documentation, the object will have an array called "results" as one of its properties. Each result is an object representing a single tweet, and has a property called "text" that contains the text of the tweet. In Listing 4-9 we'll loop through the array and create a list item for each tweet, and then append the results to the document:

Listing 4-9. Fetching tweets from the Twitter API and displaying them in the document

```
<!DOCTYPE html>
<html>
    <head>
        <title>JavaScript Developer's Guide</title>
        <script src="http://code.jquery.com/jquery-1.9.1.min.js"></script>
    </head>
    <body>
        <h1>Hello World</h1>
        <p id="clickme">Click here for tweeting goodness!</p>
        <script>
// Attach a click event handler to the paragraph so that it will load
// the tweets.
var clickme = document.getElementById("clickme");
clickme.addEventListener("click", function(event) {

executeJSONPQuery("http://searcexact syntax will be provided by the servim:jreid01&callback=
handlejsonpresults");
});

// Execute a JSONP query, reusing the script tag.
function executeJSONPQuery(strUrl) {
    // Check to see if a jsonp script tag has already been injected.
    // Also, create a new script tag with our new URL.
    var oldScript = document.getElementById("jsonp"),
        newScript = document.createElement("script");
    newScript.src = strUrl;
    newScript.id = "jsonp";

    // If there is already a jsonp script tag in the DOM we'll
    // replace it with the new one.
    // Otherwise, we'll just append the new script tag to the DOM.
```

```
    if (oldScript !== null) {
        document.body.replaceChild(newScript, oldScript);
    } else {
        document.body.appendChild(newScript);
    }
}

// This function is called by the injected scripts.
function handlejsonpresults(objData) {
    var arrTweets = objData.results,
        arrTweetsLength = objData.results.length,
        i,
        myNewList = document.createElement("ul");

    // Loop through the results array and create a list item for
    // each tweet containing its text.
    for (i = 0; i < arrTweetsLength; i++ ) {
        var myLi = document.createElement("li"),
            myTextNode = document.createTextNode(arrTweets[i].text);
        myLi.appendChild(myTextNode);
        myNewList.appendChild(myLi);
    }

    // Now that all of the tweets have been compiled, append the list to the DOM.
    document.body.appendChild(myNewList);
}

            </script>
        </body>
</html>
```

In this example, every time you click on the paragraph the script will execute a JSONP call using our function (and thus recycling the script tag) and append the results to the page.

JSONP is useful, but it's not without its drawbacks. The biggest problem is that it necessarily involves a security risk. You're trusting the target URL to not send a malicious script in response to your request. If the target URL responds with a malicious script, you would inject it into your own page and not even know it. Currently there is no effective way to close that particular security hole, so be very sure you want to open it.

CORS

Created in response to the security concerns with JSONP, CORS is a proposed standard that is gaining some traction. An acronym for Cross Origin Resource Sharing, CORS specifies new HTTP headers that browsers and servers must provide as part of their communication with one another. Though many of the latest versions of browsers support CORS headers, older ones do not, making this a poor choice for projects that will be targeting even slightly out of date browsers.

Post Message

HTML 5 provides a new feature that can be used for cross-domain communication: the Post Message standard. This standard specifies a new DOM method, window.postMessage(), and a new DOM event, message, that are used to communicate between iframes.

An iframe can load a document from a different origin than the host document, but the Same Origin Policy prevents scripts from either document interacting with each other. Post Message, however, provides a secure means for transmitting strings between them.

In the sending document, your script can call the postMessage() method on a pointer to the target document, which can be either a child document or a parent document. The postMessage() method takes as a parameter the string to be transmitted to the target document, along with the desired origin of the target document.

When the target document receives the message, it triggers a DOM message event. You can create a handler for this event and register it to the window object. The event object passed into the handler will contain the string that was sent along with the origin that was specified. You can then make sure that you are received the message from the expected origin.

The Post Message method is widely supported among modern browsers. Older browsers support it as well; Internet Explorer 8 and greater support it, as does Firefox 16+, Chrome 23+, and Safari 5.1+. Post Message enjoys even more support on mobile browsers: Safari Mobile on iOS has supported it since 3.2, and the Android browser has supported it since 2.1.

We cover the postMessage() method in detail in the Chapter 8 under window.postMessage(). See that section for details on syntax and an example.

Data Caching

As you do more asynchronous programming with XMLHttpRequest, it's not uncommon to find yourself wanting to cache data locally for speed and efficiency. This is particularly true with mobile applications, where having a local cache of data can not only speed up your application (because accessing cached data is faster than going over the potentially quite slow network) but also make your application use less battery power (because accessing the network requires power). Even for desktop applications it's common to want to cache commonly used information that doesn't change very often.

Data caches are very simple, and typically consist of an identifier representing the service or data source, a timestamp of the last time the service was accessed, and the data that was returned the last time the service was accessed. Every time you look at the cache, you can see if the data you want is cached; if it isn't, you can simply call the service and cache it with a new timestamp. If there is data in the cache, you check its timestamp. If it was accessed too long ago, you'll know you need to access the service and cache the new results. But if it wasn't accessed too long ago, you can just use the cached data.

We've already built a doXHR() function in the Asynchronous Communication using XMLHttpRequest section above. When we call that method, we provide an object that specifies the URL to call, as well as other information (such as a success method to call, or an error method to call). What would be nice is if we specified a length of time as a property, the doXHR() function would know that we want to cache the data from that URL and it could perform as follows:

- Check to see if there is already data in our hypothetical cache.

- If the data does not exist in the cache, go and fetch the data from the URL, and save it in the cache with the current timestamp.

- If the data does exist in the cache, check the timestamp.

  - If the timestamp is too old, go and fetch the data from the URL and save it in the cache with the current timestamp.

  - If the timestamp isn't too old, just use the data from the cache.

We can easily extend our doXHR() function to handle caching. In our example, we'll use the localStorage feature defined by HTML 5, because it is widely supported (especially among mobile browsers). As covered in detail in Chapter 8, window.localStorage takes key/value pairs and stores them in a cache that persists even if the user closes their browser or reboots their computer, which makes it an ideal choice for our data cache.

We'll begin by extending our XHR definition object in Listing 4-10 to include two new properties: A name for the service we're caching, and a duration for when the cache is valid:

Listing 4-10. An updated version of the XHR definition object

```
var myXhrDefs = {
    intCacheDuration: 14400,
    cacheName: "ajax-test",
    strMethod : "GET",
    strUrl : "http://127.0.0.1:8020/developers-guide/chapter-4/ajax-test.txt",
    intTimeout: 3000,
    postData: null,
    boolAsync: true,
    successCallback: function(objEvent) {
        // Do things when the request is successful
        console.log(objEvent.responseText);
    },
    errorCallback: function(objEvent) {
        // Do things when there is an error in the request.
        console.error("The XHR failed with error ", objEvent.status);
    },
    timeoutCallback: function() {
        // Do things when a timeout occurs.
        console.error("The XHR timed out.");
    }
}
```

The two new properties are `intCacheDuration` (which we will specify in seconds; 14400 seconds is four hours), and `cacheName`, which provides a base name for the cached data. When we cache the information, we'll append "-timestamp" to `cacheName` for the key, and when we cache the data, we'll append "-data" to `cacheName` for the key. (So in this example, our sample URL of ajax-test.txt will use "ajax-test-timestamp" for its timestamp key and "ajax-test-data" for its data key.)

To make use of this new object, in Listing 4-11 we'll wrap our existing doXHR() method within another method, which we'll call doCachedXHR(). This will take the same XHR definition object and either read from the cache or use doXHR() to fetch new information and cache it:

Listing 4-11. The doCachedXHR() method

```
// Either perform an asynchronous call to a service and cache it with a timestamp,
// or if the service has already been called and cached, just use that if the data isn't
// too old.  If the data is too old, perform the asynchronous call again and cache the
// results with a new timestamp.
function cachedXHR(myXhrDefs) {
    var fetchNewData = false,
        now = new Date(),
        lastTimeStamp = localStorage.getItem(myXhrDefs.cacheName + "-timestamp");

    // Does the cache even have the specified item?
    if (lastTimeStamp == null) {
        fetchNewData = true;
    } else {
        // We've cached the service at least once. Check the last timestamp.
```

```
          var timeStamp = new Date(lastTimeStamp);
          if ((timeStamp.getTime() + (myXhrDefs.intCacheDuration * 1000)) < now.getTime()) {
            fetchNewData = true;
          }
      }


      // If we need to fetch new data, we need to extend the existing successCallback method
      // to cache the new results with a new timestamp.
      if (fetchNewData) {
          myXhrDefs.successCallback = (function(oldCallback) {
              function extendedCallback(objEvent) {
                  localStorage.setItem(this.cacheName + "-data", objEvent.responseText);
                  localStorage.setItem(this.cacheName + "-timestamp", now.toISOString());
                  oldCallback(objEvent);
              }
              return extendedCallback;
          })(myXhrDefs.successCallback);

          // Perform the XHR request.
          doXHR(myXhrDefs);
      } else {
          // Just use the cached data.
          var cachedData = localStorage.getItem(myXhrDefs.cacheName + "-data"),
              fakeEvent = {
                  responseText : cachedData
              };
          myXhrDefs.successCallback(fakeEvent);
      }
  }
```

There's a lot going on in this method, including a trick for extending methods, so let's walk through it one step at a time.

At the heart of the method is a simple check: is the data cached or not? If it isn't cached, the method needs to go get the data and cache it. If it is cached but too old, it needs to refresh the cache. If the data isn't too old, we can use it. That simple logic makes up the skeleton of the method.

The first thing we need to do is create a new Date object representing the current time. Then we check to see if the data has even been cached by looking for a timestamp. If the timestamp doesn't exist, we know we need to fetch and cache the data.

If the timestamp does exist in the cache, we need to check to see if it's too old. First, we create a new Date object using the timestamp. Then we can use the getTime() method of the date objects to perform our age comparison—the getTime() method returns the number of milliseconds from midnight, January 1, 1970, so we'll have to convert our intCacheDuration time from seconds to milliseconds before adding them to the timestamp. (This is a great practical example of comparing the values of Date objects.)

If the data isn't too old, we can just use it. But if it is too old, we have to fetch new data. We've defined our successCallback() method on the XHR definition object, but we want to extend that method so that it caches the result of the XHR request. Basically what we do is we overwrite the old successCallback() method with the results that are returned from an immediately executed function expression (IEFE). We pass the old successCallback() method into the IEFE as the oldCallback parameter. So within the IEFE we create a new function that caches the data, then calls the oldCallback function. The IEFE then returns that new function, which takes over the successCallback() method.

We could have just re-written the successCallback() methods in our XHR definition objects, but with this technique you can add the new cachedXHR() method to existing code and not have to modify a bunch of your methods to account for caching. The new method will handle that for you.

We encourage you to test this function to verify that it works the way you expect. You'll need to set up your own personal web server—in this example, we're just using the debugging server that comes with Aptana, which runs on port 8020. We're also using a simple ajax-test.txt file that contains the text "hello world." But you could easily transmit JSON-formatted data, or XML-formatted data.

This function is pretty basic, and could use some more features. For example, what if the browser doesn't support localStorage? You could easily extend this function to use document.cookie in that case; see Chapter 8 for details on using cookies.

JavaScript Libraries and Frameworks

Like any language, JavaScript has a plethora of libraries and frameworks you can use in your projects. These can range from highly specific libraries designed to do one thing, to more generic libraries that enforce their own syntax, to complete frameworks for creating web-based applications in modern browsers.

Generally speaking a library is a collection of re-usable code, often small and optimized, and focused on a specific task such as providing convenience routines for complex tasks or extending the base language with new features. Common examples include mathematical libraries, libraries for accessing databases, and libraries for accessing filesystems.

In the specific case of JavaScript, libraries often extend JavaScript with new features (like animation) as well as convenience routines for more complex tasks (like asynchronous communication). In addition, JavaScript libraries can also focus on overcoming inconsistencies in the implementation of the various standards, allowing you to write code that works in multiple browsers across multiple platforms.

The term framework is a bit harder to nail down because there's no traditional definition as there is for library. As a result, "framework" can mean many different things depending on the language and context in question. In terms of JavaScript, we like to think of frameworks as complex collections of libraries and routines that provide a pre-defined structure for you to fill in as you need. One way we've heard the difference explained is, "Libraries are things your code calls and frameworks are things that call your code."

Choosing a Library

When it comes to choosing a library, the first step is easy: find libraries that do what you need. But many libraries have overlapping features, so how do you choose which one is best for your project? The answer isn't very cut-and-dry, but there are some simple questions to ask yourself to help you choose:

- License: Does the library have a license that is compatible with your needs? Most libraries are open source and allow redistribution, but others do not. You should check the license carefully to make sure it allows you the freedom you need for your project.

- Support: What sort of support is there for the library? Is it under active development? Can you get help if you need it? Some libraries are backed by companies that sell support contracts but most are open source projects with varying degrees of documentation.

- Style: Does the library work well with your programming style? How easy is it to set up and maintain in your project? Some libraries (and many frameworks) enforce their own syntax and style, and you'll want to make sure you're comfortable with that.

- Size: How big is the library? Can the library be minified and GZipped? How expensive is the library when it loads, does it cause noticeable delays?

- Security: Does the library meet your security needs? If it is an open source library, do you see anything questionable in the code for the library? Security is often ignored, but it's as important as any of the other considerations.

- Testing: Does the library have its own unit tests? How will you write tests for code that uses the library? Does that work with your existing testing practices?

Not all of these considerations will be relevant to your situation. Probably the most important are license and support, but thinking about all of them will help you make a good choice.

Here is a brief list of common JavaScript libraries and frameworks. This list isn't meant to be conclusive or even representative, the ecosystem of JavaScript libraries is just too vast to make those claims. However, this list does represent the libraries that we have commonly encountered and worked with, and is meant as a starting point for your own exploration of JavaScript libraries.

Prototype and Scriptaculous

http://www.prototypejs.org/ and http:// script.aculo.us/

Prototype is one of the first JavaScript libraries. It provides support for classes, event delegation, AJAX convenience routines, and extensions to the DOM. Scriptaculous is built on Prototype and provides a rich framework for user interfaces and interactions. It includes support for animation effects, dragging and dropping of DOM elements, and various DOM utilities. Both libraries are well-supported by active communities and are undergoing active development. Both frameworks have their own unit tests, and Scriptaculous includes support for testing your own code.

Dojo Toolkit

http://www.dojotoolkit.org/

The Dojo Toolkit is a lightweight library that provides support for event normalization, simplified AJAX interactions, and DOM manipulation. In addition, Dojo has built-in support for modules, allowing you to encapsulate your code for reuse easily. Dojo also supports dynamic loading of modules, so that applications can load modules as they need them rather than all at once.

jQuery

http://www.jquery.org

jQuery is probably the most widely-used JavaScript library in the world. jQuery enforces a selector-based syntax, and includes features for normalizing events across platforms, simplifying AJAX interactions, basic animation, and a wide variety of convenience routines. See the next section for details on using jQuery.

Sencha ext JS

http://www.sencha.com/products/extjs/

Sencha's ext JS is a framework focused on creating application-like user interfaces for JavaScript applications. It has a rich set of UI widgets and includes support for charting and drawing. The framework also includes an advanced layout engine that allows you to create complex interactive layouts with docking and other features.

YUI

http://www.yuilibrary.com/

YUI is a set of open source JavaScript libraries built and maintained by Yahoo. Yahoo uses YUI in their products, and as a result it is highly performant and well-tested. It includes event normalization, animation, a lightweight application framework, and several UI interactions (like drag and drop and sortables) and widgets (like a rich text editor and a datagrid). YUI has several libraries and all together is quite extensive, but you can pick and choose which libraries you need and create a customized smaller library. YUI also includes CSS libraries; we've had very good luck with their Fonts and CSS normalization libraries.

Closure

https://developers.google.com/closure/

Closure is Google's JavaScript application framework. It includes the Closure JavaScript Library, the Closure Compiler, and Closure Templates. The Closure JavaScript Library includes all the standard features of a JavaScript library, as well as having a wide variety of UI interactions and widgets. Closure uses a strictly namespaced object-oriented syntax, and is probably the most accessible to developers migrating to JavaScript from languages like C#, Java, or C++. Closure also includes the Closure Compiler, which we've mentioned earlier in the chapter. It can compile, optimize, and minify any JavaScript, but works particularly well with JavaScript that uses the Closure Library. Finally, Closure Templates provide a templating solution for both HTML and JavaScript. The entire framework is completely unit-tested and supports (and encourages) unit testing of your own code.

Node.js

http://www.nodejs.org

Node is a server-side JavaScript platform. It's built on Chrome's V8 JavaScript engine and so is not only very compliant with the ECMA-262 standard but is also highly performant. Since Node operates outside of a browser context, it doesn't have any of the usual features you would expect in a JavaScript library: it has no event normalization or DOM manipulation features. Instead, it has a set of APIs for building server features such as web servers, accessing the file system, network operations (including raw socket management), and a module system.

Montage

http://www.montagejs.org

A relative newcomer to the field, Montage is an impressive framework that is built around the latest features of JavaScript, HTML, and CSS. It is focused on building complex applications and includes its own templating system built around HTML and CSS, and has an impressive array of prebuilt UI components that work in both mobile and desktop contexts. Montage itself is built using an MVC pattern, and you will naturally fall into that pattern as you use Montage, so it's a great introduction to MVC applications built with JavaScript. Finally, because it does a lot of the heavy lifting for you behind the scenes, Montage allows you to program pretty much in pure JavaScript without any enforced syntax like selectors, arbitrary namespaces, or other syntactic sugar.

MicroJS

`http://www.microjs.com/`

MicroJS is actually a clearinghouse of small JavaScript libraries that you can combine as needed. The site lets you search for libraries based on the functionality that you need. All of the libraries are quite small, but their licensing, support, style, security and testing vary, so you'll have to explore individual libraries yourself. We mention it here because it's a great starting point for finding libraries that are focused on a single task.

Using jQuery

Created in 2006 by John Resig, jQuery is one of the most widely used JavaScript libraries in the world. There are many libraries available, but jQuery is our preferred choice. It provides a robust and cross-browser API for everything from animation to AJAX.

The biggest benefits of jQuery are:

- jQuery is small. At only 32kb (minified and GZipped) it's remarkably small for such a full-featured library.

- jQuery fixes a lot of browser dependent problems. One of the main reasons jQuery was created was to help overcome the variations in browser implementations of JavaScript and the DOM standard. If you're looking to solve cross-browser issues in your scripts, jQuery is a great candidate.

- jQuery is well-tested. Not only is jQuery well-tested by its own suite of unit tests, jQuery is used on so many sites by so many people that bugs are reported quickly.

- jQuery is fast. The internal coding for jQuery is highly optimized and efficient.

- Writing jQuery code is fast. Because jQuery provides convenient shorthand methods for so many common tasks, writing code in jQuery can take less time than writing equivalent code in straight JavaScript.

- jQuery is easy to use. All you have to do is include the jQuery script in the header of your document and all of its functionality will be available to any scripts that come after.

One of the main caveats to remember with jQuery is that because it abstracts away so much of JavaScript and the DOM that it tends to enforce its own way of doing things. That's fine, but it's not necessarily congruent with how you might approach the same problems in pure JavaScript. We usually recommend that novice JavaScript developers bear that in mind while they're working with jQuery so as to avoid potentially harmful habits. (Many JavaScript libraries enforce their own syntax, so this advice applies to more than just working with jQuery.)

We're not going to cover everything about jQuery in this section—entire books have been written about that. Fortunately, jQuery's online documentation is some of the best available, and you can find it at `http://docs.jquery.com/` You'll find the entire jQuery API documented in detail there, along with examples for just about everything.

How It Works

jQuery works by creating a `jQuery()` function object in the global scope (aliased to `$()` for brevity; you can use either) that you can then use in your own scripts. The `jQuery()` function takes as a parameter a CSS selector for an element in the DOM (just like the DOM standard methods `querySelector()` and `querySelectorAll()`and returns a reference to that element wrapped in a `jQuery` object (similar to how JavaScript will wrap a string primitive with a `String` object to give it needed functionality). The resulting object is often referred to as a "jQuery selector" and it has an impressive set of methods and properties you can access that will affect the element(s) it refers to.

As an example, say you want to hide an element on the page, as in Listing 4-12. In regular JavaScript, you might write something like this:

Listing 4-12. Hiding an element using JavaScript

```
<!DOCTYPE html>
<html>
        <head>
                <title>JavaScript Developer's Guide</title>
        </head>
        <body>
                <h1>Hello World</h1>
                <script>
var myHeadline = document.querySelector("h1");
myHeadline.style.display = "none";
                </script>
        </body>
</html>
```

In this example, we use the `querySelector()` method to get a reference to the headline, and then we set an inline style property of `display: none` on it. As soon as the example loads in your browser, the headline will disappear (you may not even see the headline before it disappears).

In jQuery, you would provide the selector to the `jQuery()` function (we'll use `$()` throughout these examples) and then call the `hide()` method on the result, as in Listing 4-13:

Listing 4-13. Hiding an element using jQuery

```
<!DOCTYPE html>
<html>
        <head>
                <title>JavaScript Developer's Guide</title>
                <script src="http://code.jquery.com/jquery-1.9.1.min.js"></script>
        </head>
        <body>
                <h1>Hello World</h1>
                <script>
$("h1").hide();
                </script>
        </body>
</html>
```

Same result as the previous example in only one line of code. Note that we have included the jQuery library in the head of our example; you must include the library before attempting to use it. jQuery is available via a content distribution network (CDN) thanks to the generosity of MediaTemple. You could just as easily download jQuery and serve your own private copy. See `http://www.jquery.com/download` for details and examples.

In addition to the `hide()` method, jQuery also provides a `fadeOut()` method which causes the target element to fade out of sight, as in Listing 14:

Listing 4-14. The jQuery fadeOut() method

```
<!DOCTYPE html>
<html>
        <head>
```

```
                <title>JavaScript Developer's Guide</title>
                <script src="http://code.jquery.com/jquery-1.9.1.min.js"></script>
        </head>
        <body>
                <h1>Hello World</h1>
                <script>
$("h1").fadeOut();
                </script>
        </body>
</html>
```

When you load this example, you'll see the headline fade out quickly. jQuery also provides a fadeIn() method, shown in Listing 4-15:

Listing 4-15. The jQuery fadeIn() method

```
<!DOCTYPE html>
<html>
        <head>
                <title>JavaScript Developer's Guide</title>
                <script src="http://code.jquery.com/jquery-1.9.1.min.js"></script>
        </head>
        <body>
                <h1>Hello World</h1>
                <script>
$("h1").fadeOut();
$("h1").fadeIn();
                </script>
        </body>
</html>
```

In this example, we first fade out the headline, then we fade it back in. You'll notice that we called the jQuery() function twice to select the element, which is a little inefficient. The jQuery() function is kind of expensive; it has to go and fetch the element and then wrap it in a jQuery object. If you're going to be using the same selector more than once, you can alias it to a variable. Also, almost all jQuery methods return the original selector, so you can chain commands as in Listing 4-16:

Listing 4-16. Chaining jQuery methods for efficiency

```
<!DOCTYPE html>
<html>
        <head>
                <title>JavaScript Developer's Guide</title>
                <script src="http://code.jquery.com/jquery-1.9.1.min.js"></script>
        </head>
        <body>
                <h1>Hello World</h1>
                <script>
$("h1").fadeOut().fadeIn();
                </script>
        </body>
</html>
```

This example has exactly the same result as the previous example, but it is both more efficient (because we only call the jQuery() function once to select the element and then use chaining) and also smaller—it's shorter by 8 characters. That's not a big savings, but on average you'll find jQuery code can be quite terse, resulting in smaller scripts.

Events in jQuery

jQuery started its life as a way to provide cross-browser functionality for JavaScript developers, and one of the most important ways it does this is by providing an event system that works the same in all of its supported browsers. If you'll recall from Chapter 3, the DOM event model is not correctly implemented in Internet Explorer versions lower than 9. jQuery handles those problems for you, so that your event handlers will execute as you expect in all supported browsers.

As of version 1.7, jQuery uses the on() method to attach event handlers, and uses the off() method to remove event handlers. jQuery's on() method has a simple syntax:

```
$(targetSelector).on(events, filterSelector, data, handler);
```

- targetSelector: A selector for the element(s) you wish to attach the event handler to.

- events: One or more event types; multiple event types can be separated by spaces. For example, "click keydown" would specify that the event handler should be fired whenever the user clicks on the target element, or whenever the user presses a key while the target element has keyboard focus. You can also apply namespaces to your events by appending .namespace to an event type (e.g. click.kittenRescue). This allows you to add and remove multiple event handlers of the same type to a given targetSelector.

- filterSelector: a jQuery selector specifying that this event handler should only execute if the specified event types originated on elements that match filterSelector (and are children of targetSelector). This feature allows you to have a lot of flexibility in your event delegation. Note, however, that the selector is checked every time the specified events are dispatched to targetSelector. For most events that happen infrequently that isn't a problem, but for events that fire rapidly many times (like mouseover events) it can cause a performance hit.

- data: Either an object reference or an object literal. This object will be available on the resulting event object in the handler as the event.data property. This feature allows you to pass in arbitrary data into your event handlers.

- handler: a function expression (which can be an anonymous inline function) that accepts an event object as a parameter, and is executed when the specified events fire on the targetSelector.

For an example using jQuery's event system, consider our Kitten Rescue game from Chapter 3. In straight JavaScript it looks like this:

```
<!DOCTYPE html>
<html>
    <head>
        <title>JavaScript Developer's Guide</title>
        <style>
.basket {
    width: 300px;
    height: 300px;
    position: absolute;
    top: 100px;
```

```
    right: 100px;
    border: 3px double #000000;
    border-radius: 10px;
}
        </style>
    </head>
    <body>
        <h3>Rescue the kittens!</h3>
        <p>Click on them to put them in their basket!</p>
        <ul id="kittens">
            <li>Rowly</li>
            <li>Fred</li>
            <li>Mittens</li>
            <li>Lenore</li>
        </ul>
        <ul class="basket"></ul>
        <script>
var basket = document.querySelector(".basket"),
    kittens = document.getElementById("kittens");

kittens.addEventListener("click", function(event) {
    basket.appendChild(event.target);
}, false);

        </script>
    </body>
</html>
```

Here we are delegating the click event handler to the unordered list so that we don't have to attach an event handler to each individual list item.

Written in jQuery, the game would look like Listing 4-17:

Listing 4-17. Kitten Rescue written in jQuery

```
<!DOCTYPE html>
<html>
    <head>
        <title>JavaScript Developer's Guide</title>
        <script src="http://code.jquery.com/jquery-1.9.1.min.js"></script>
    <style>
.basket {
    width: 300px;
    height: 300px;
    position: absolute;
    top: 100px;
    right: 100px;
    border: 3px double #000000;
    border-radius: 10px;
}
        </style>
    </head>
```

```
<body>
    <h3>Rescue the kittens!</h3>
    <p>Click on them to put them in their basket!</p>
    <ul id="kittens">
        <li>Rowly</li>
        <li>Fred</li>
        <li>Mittens</li>
        <li>Lenore</li>
    </ul>
    <ul class="basket"></ul>
    <script>
var $basket = $(".basket");
$("#kittens").on("click", function(event) {
    $basket.append(event.target);
});
    </script>
    </body>
</html>
```

In the jQuery version we first save a reference to the jQuery(".basket") selector so that we can reuse it every time the event handler fires—that way we don't have to get a reference to the basket every time the event fires. Then we attach an even t handler to the unordered list using the on() method. We could have specified a filterSelector of "li" but in this case it was unnecessary, because events can only originate on list items.

Event handlers are removed using the off() method:

```
$(targetSelector).off(events, filterSelector, handler);
```

- targetSelector: the selector specifying the element(s) to remove the event handlers from.

- events: The list of event types, or namespaces, of the event handlers(s) to remove.

- filterSelector: The selector specified when the event was delegated using the on() method.

- handler: The function specified when the event was bound.

Note that you can specify just a namespace to remove all the event handlers that share that namespace on targetSelector. For example, if you added the following hypothetical event handlers with the same namespace:

```
$(targetSelector).on("click.myEventHandler", "li", handleClickEvent);
$(targetSelector).on("focus.myEventHandler", handleFocusEvent);
```

You could remove both by specifying just their namespace:

```
$(targetSelector).off(".myEventHandler");
```

That would remove both the click event handler and the focus event handler at the same time.

A convenient event that jQuery provides is a document ready event that is triggered when the DOM of a given document has been loaded and parsed and is available for manipulation. This event gives you an extra level of flexibility in your scripts; with it you do not need to load your scripts at the end of a document (see the section on Optimization Techniques earlier in this chapter for details). You listen for the ready event on the document just like any other event on any other target element, as in Listing 4-18:

Listing 4-18. Using the document ready event in jQuery

```
<!DOCTYPE html>
<html>
        <head>
                <title>JavaScript Developer's Guide</title>
                <script src="http://code.jquery.com/jquery-1.9.1.min.js"></script>
                <script>
$(document).on("ready", function() {
  $("h1").fadeOut().fadeIn();
});
                </script>

        </head>
        <body>
                <h1>Hello World</h1>
        </body>
</html>
```

In this example, we have a script in the head that accesses a DOM element. Ordinarily, the element wouldn't be ready at the time the script was executed, so we create an event handler for the document's ready event. When that event fires, we know the DOM is parsed and available for manipulation, so we can execute our code.

jQuery UI

jQuery UI is a library of user interface interactions and themable widgets maintained by the jQuery group. It provides a set of easy to use interactions:

- Draggable: Allows you to specify elements as draggable, meaning the user can click and drag them around on the page.

- Droppable: Allows you to specify elements as droppables, meaning they can have draggable elements dropped on them.

- Resizable: Allows you to specify elements as resizable, meaning the user can "grab" an edge (you specify which) and resize the element.

- Selectable: Allows you to select elements, multiselect using modifier keys, and marquee select by dragging and drawing a box around target elements.

- Sortable: Allows you to specify a set of elements can be sorted using drag-and-drop interactions. Elements can be a simple list or a grid.

jQuery UI also has a full set of useful user interface widgets, including a datepicker and a dialog system capable of producing popups and modals. All the widgets are completely customizable in appearance. You can use the themeroller available on the jQuery UI site to roll a custom theme, or you can write custom CSS to make the widgets appear exactly as you want.

For more information about jQuery UI see `http://jqueryui.com`.

jQuery Mobile

jQuery Mobile provides a basic framework for producing mobile web applications. It provides a set of events focused on touch interactions like tapping and swiping, as well as interactions unique to mobile devices like orientation changes. jQuery Mobile also provides a set of mobile-optimized user interface widgets that provide UI features that are common on mobile applications, such as toolbars, expandable and collapsible content areas, sliders, and list views.

jQuery Mobile works a bit differently than other jQuery products. Instead of operating directly on jQuery selectors, jQuery Mobile defines a set of data attributes that you can apply to your markup. These data attributes provide a way for you to specify what the elements are supposed to be: headers, footers, list views, panels, buttons, sliders, etc. You create semantic markup, apply jQuery Mobile data attributes to the elements, and then load in jQuery Mobile and it initializes the elements for you.

For example, consider the very basic two-page mobile application in Listing 4-19:

Listing 4-19. A two page mobile application built using jQuery Mobile

```
<!DOCTYPE html>
<html>
        <head>
                <title>jJavaScript Developer's Guide</title>
        <link rel="stylesheet" href="http://code.jquery.com/mobile/1.3.0/jquery.mobile-1.3.0.min.css" />
        <script src="http://code.jquery.com/jquery-1.8.2.min.js"></script>
        <script src="http://code.jquery.com/mobile/1.3.0/jquery.mobile-1.3.0.min.js"></script>
        </head>
        <body>
                <section id="page1" data-role="page">
                        <header data-role="header"><h1>JavaScript Developer's Guide</h1></header>
                        <div class="content" data-role="content">
                                <p>Here is a sample jQuery Mobile application.</p>
                                <p><a href="#page2" data-transition="slide">Go to next page</a></p>
                        </div>
                        <footer data-role="footer" data-position="fixed"><h1>Apress</h1></footer>
                </section>

                <section id="page2" data-role="page">
                        <header data-role="header"><h1>JavaScript Developer's Guide</h1></header>
                        <div class="content" data-role="content">
                                <p>This is the second page.</p>
                                <p><a href="#page1" data-transition="slide"
                                data-direction="reverse">Go to previous page</a></p>
                        </div>
                        <footer data-role="footer" data-position="fixed"><h1>Apress</h1></footer>
                </section>
        </body>
</html>
```

In this example, we started with basic semantic HTML 5 markup, with sections, headers, footers, etc. Then, using jQuery Mobile's predefined data attributes, we specified pages, headers, content areas, etc. We even specified the transitions between the pages should be a slide transition from page 1 to page 2, and a reverse slide transition when going back from page 2 to page 1.

When you load this application into a browser and jQuery Mobile initializes, it scans for data attributes, applies the necessary modifications to them, and handles all of the page management for you. jQuery Mobile exposes all of its functionality through data attributes, so it's possible to create fairly complex mobile applications with just semantic HTML and never writing a single line of JavaScript.

This is just scratching the surface of jQuery Mobile. For more details, see jQuery Mobile's documentation at `http://jquerymobile.com`.

Building a Library

As with any language, the more you work with JavaScript, the more you'll find you are recreating the same bits of code in your projects. Maybe you have a specific way you like to enumerate objects. Maybe you have a particular way of handling DOM events. Whatever they are, it might make sense to roll these commonly-used bits into your own JavaScript library. So far in this chapter, we've provided a useful set of methods for performing asynchronous requests, caching data, and performing cross-domain requests.

In this chapter we've also introduced you to jQuery, one of the most common JavaScript libraries, so you've had some exposure to what a good library can do for you. What if we wanted to create our own jQuery-like library that included all of the methods we've built in this chapter? We would want our new library to have a selector-based syntax and to support chaining of commands, just like jQuery.

That's actually very easy to to do. In this section we'll create a new library called "jkl" (pronounced "Jekyll," after the eponymous good doctor) because "jkl" is really easy to type. The basic pattern to create our library looks like Listing 4-20:

Listing 4-20. Basic library pattern

```
(function() {
    var window = this,
        undefined;

    jkl = window.jkl = function(selector) {
        return new jkl.jklm.init(selector);
    }

    jkl.jklm = jkl.prototype = {
        init: function(selector) {
            this.selector = selector;
            return this;
        }
    }
    jkl.jklm.init.prototype = jkl.jklm;
})();
```

Here we are once again using an immediately invoked function expression to create a closure that we can use as our own private playground. We want our library to exist entirely in its own namespace, and to expose only one method in the global namespace: the jkl() function. To do that, we have to do a little bit of fancy footwork:

1. We define the jkl() function in the global context (which is the window object). This function calls a constructor function called init() which lives on a subproperty of jkl. This subproperty of jkl, which we're calling jklm (also for ease of typing) is the namespace where we'll be adding our methods.

2. So far everything we've done has been fairly straightforward, but here is the first bit of mind-bending code: we set jkl.jklm to be a reference to jkl's prototype. So any property or method we add to jkl.jklm will be added to jkl's prototype, and will thus be available to jkl(). Another way of looking at it is that we're creating a private namespace within jkl that will have its properties and methods exposed on jkl as if they were defined there originally.

3. Within the jkl.jklm namespace, we create our init() function, which will act as a constructor for our library. Every time someone calls jkl(selector) it will be the equivalent of calling new jkl.jklm.init(selector). Our init() function adds the selector to the newly-constructed copy of jkl, and then returns the results to the global scope.

4. Finally, we set the prototype of jkl.jklm.init to be a reference to jkl.jklm (and thus to jkl.prototype), which closes the prototype circle.

This library doesn't do anything at the moment, because aside from init() it has no methods. We add methods by extending jkl.jklm as in Listing 4-21:

Listing 4-21. Adding a few basic methods to the library

```
(function() {
    var window = this,
        undefined;

    jkl = window.jkl = function(selector) {
        return new jkl.jklm.init(selector);
    }

    jkl.jklm = jkl.prototype = {
        init: function(selector) {
            this.selector = selector;
            return this;
        },

        // Hide the target element.
        hide : function() {
            document.querySelector(selector).style.display = "none";
            return this;
        },

        // Show the target element.
        show : function() {
            document.querySelector(selector).style.display = "inherit";
            return this;
        },

        // Make the target element red
        enredden : function() {
            document.querySelector(this.selector).style.backgroundColor = "#F00";
            return this;
        }
    }
    jkl.jklm.init.prototype = jkl.jklm;
})();
```

Now our library will have three methods: hide(), show() and enredden(). Note that at the end of every method we return this, which allows for method chaining, just like jQuery. We can use our library in Listing 4-22 like this:

Listing 4-22. Using the jkl library

```
<!DOCTYPE html>
<html>
    <head>
        <title>jJavaScript Developer's Guide</title>
        <script src="jkl-0.0.1.js"></script>
    </head>
```

```
    <body>
        <h1>Testing the jkl Library</h1>
        <script>
jkl("h1").enredden();
        </script>
    </body>
</html>
```

In this simple example, we use the enredden() method to change the headline's background to red. Now, in Listing 4-23, we can add the other methods to the library (performing an XHR request, performing a JSONP query, and data caching):

Listing 4-23. Adding other methods to the jkl library

```
(function() {
    var window = this,
        undefined;

    jkl = window.jkl = function(selector) {
        return new jkl.jklm.init(selector);
    }

    jkl.jklm = jkl.prototype = {
        init: function(selector) {
            this.selector = selector;
            return this;
        },
        // Hide the target element.
        hide : function() {
            document.querySelector(selector).style.display = "none";
            return this;
        },

        // Show the target element.
        show : function() {
            document.querySelector(selector).style.display = "inherit";
            return this;
        },

        // Make the target element red
        enredden : function() {
            document.querySelector(this.selector).style.backgroundColor = "#F00";
            return this;
        },

        // Perform an asynchronous request defined by myXhrDefs object.
        doXHR : function(myXhrDefs) {
            // Create and configure a new XMLHttpRequest object
            var myXhr = new XMLHttpRequest(),
                myTimer = null;
```

```
        myXhr.open(myXhrDefs.strMethod, myXhrDefs.strUrl, myXhrDefs.boolAsync);
        // Register the error and success handlers
        myXhr.onreadystatechange = function(objEvent) {
            // If readyState is 4, request is complete.
            if (myXhr.readyState === 4) {
                // Cancel the timeout timer if we set one.
                if (myTimer !== null) {
                    clearTimeout(myTimer);
                }
                // If there's an error, call the error callback,
                // Otherwise call the success callback.
                if ((myXhr.status !== 200) && (myXhr.status !== 304)) {
                    if (myXhrDefs.errorCallback != null) {
                        myXhrDefs.errorCallback(myXhr);
                    }
                } else {
                    myXhrDefs.successCallback(myXhr);
                }
            }
        }

        // Handle timeouts (set myXhrDefs.intTimeout to null to skip)
        // If we're working with a newer implementation, we can just set the
        // timeout property and register the timeout callback.
        // If not, we have to set a timer running that will execute the
        // timeout callback.
        if (myXhrDefs.intTimeout !== null) {
            if (typeof myXhr.ontimeout !== "undefined") {
                myXhr.timeout = myXhrDefs.intTimeout;
                myXhr.ontimeout = myXhrDefs.timeoutCallback;
            } else {
                myTimer = setTimeout(myXhrDefs.timeoutCallback, myXhrDefs.intTimeout);
            }
        }

        // Send the request
        myXhr.send(myXhrDefs.postData);
        return this;
    },

// Execute a cross-domain JSONP query.
executeJSONPQuery : function(strUrl) {
    // Check to see if a jsonp script tag has already been injected.
    // Also, create a new script tag with our new URL.
    var oldScript = document.getElementById("jsonp"),
        newScript = document.createElement("script");
    newScript.src = strUrl;
    newScript.id = "jsonp";

    // If there is already a jsonp script tag in the DOM we'll
    // replace it with the new one.
```

```
            // Otherwise, we'll just append the new script tag to the DOM.
            if (oldScript !== null) {
                document.body.replaceChild(newScript, oldScript);
            } else {
                document.body.appendChild(newScript);
            }
            return this;
        },

        // Perform a cached XHR request.
        cachedXHR : function(myXhrDefs) {
            var fetchNewData = false,
                now = new Date(),
                lastTimeStamp = localStorage.getItem(myXhrDefs.cacheName + "-timestamp");

            // Does the cache even have the specified item?
            if (lastTimeStamp == null) {
                fetchNewData = true;
            } else {
                // We've cached the service at least once. Check the last timestamp.
                var timeStamp = new Date(lastTimeStamp);
                if ((timeStamp.getTime() + (myXhrDefs.intCacheDuration * 1000)) < now.getTime()) {
                  fetchNewData = true;
                }
            }

            // If we need to fetch new data, we need to extend the existing successCallback method
            // to cache the new results with a new timestamp.
            if (fetchNewData) {
                myXhrDefs.successCallback = (function(oldCallback) {
                    function extendedCallback(objEvent) {
                        localStorage.setItem(this.cacheName + "-data", objEvent.responseText);
                        localStorage.setItem(this.cacheName + "-timestamp", now.toISOString());
                        oldCallback(objEvent);
                    }
                    return extendedCallback;
                })(myXhrDefs.successCallback);

                // Perform the XHR request.
                doXHR(myXhrDefs);
            } else {
                // Just use the cached data.
                var cachedData = localStorage.getItem(myXhrDefs.cacheName + "-data"),
                    fakeEvent = {
                        responseText : cachedData
                    };
                myXhrDefs.successCallback(fakeEvent);
            }
            return this;
        },

        // Perform an asynchronous call to the specified URL and load the results into
        // the target element.
```

```
        load : function(strUrl){
            var ptrTarget = document.querySelector(this.selector),
                myXhrDefs = {
                    strMethod : "GET",
                    strUrl : strUrl,
                    intTimeout: 3000,
                    postData: null,
                    boolAsync: true,
                    successCallback: function(objEvent) {
                        // Do things when the request is successful
                        ptrTarget.innerHTML = objEvent.responseText;
                    },
                    errorCallback: function(objEvent) {
                        // Do things when there is an error in the request.
                        console.error("The XHR failed with error ", objEvent.status);
                    },
                    timeoutCallback: function() {
                        // Do things when a timeout occurs.
                        console.error("The XHR timed out.");
                    }
                };

            this.doXHR(myXhrDefs);
            return this;
        }
    }
    jkl.jklm.init.prototype = jkl.jklm;
})();
```

Here we have added our doXHR(), cachedXHR(), and executeJSONPQuery() methods that we have previously defined, basically by copying and pasting their code into our library with very few modifications. The only difference is that at the end of each we return this so that we can chain methods.

In addition, we've added one new method: a shorthand method called load() which will perform an asynchronous call to the specified URL and place the results as the HTML in the target selector. Assuming that on our local development server we have a simple text file called ajax-test.txt that contains the text "hello world", we can use our new load() method in Listing 4-24:

Listing 4-24. Using the new load() method

```
<!DOCTYPE html>
<html>
    <head>
        <title>jJavaScript Developer's Guide</title>
        <script src="jkl-0.0.1.js"></script>
    </head>
    <body>
        <h1>Testing The jkl Library</h1>
        <script>
jkl("h1").load("http://127.0.0.1:8020/developers-guide/chapter-4/ajax-test.txt").enredden();
        </script>
    </body>
</html>
```

When you load this example, the headline will immediately be replaced with "hello world" and then its background color will be set to red. The `load()` method is a great example of how a library can save you a lot of trouble; it's very common to want to fetch information from the server and insert it directly into a target element in the DOM and now our library will do that for us with a single function call. We can even make a `cachedLoad()` method which will use our `cachedXHR()` method to cache the results.

Summary

In this chapter we have tried to address the practical aspects of working with JavaScript.

- We started by giving an overview of popular tools available for working with JavaScript, including IDEs and personal servers. And we discussed some basic techniques for debugging your scripts.

- We discussed how to load your scripts efficiently. We also discussed the difference between perceptual delay and actual delays, and discussed techniques for dealing with both.

- We talked about asynchronous communication using the XMLHttpRequest object, a technique that forms the basis of many JavaScript applications. We even built a reusable method easily employing AJAX in your own projects.

- Because asynchronous communication is limited by the Same Origin Policy, we discussed some common cross-domain techniques that would allow you to bypass the policy with relative safety. As part of that process we built a simple method for efficiently performing JSONP requests.

- We explored a way to cache data in the browser, for efficiency and speed, and built a function that will cache your asynchronous requests as you specify.

- We discussed how to choose a JavaScript library, and reviewed some of the more common JavaScript libraries.

- We did a very quick overview of jQuery and how it works. We couldn't go into jQuery in depth, because it is a very featureful library, but we hope that we piqued your interest. We also touched briefly on jQuery UI and jQuery Mobile.

- Finally, we discussed how to build your own library. By following a simple pattern, it's easy to build your own library of methods that you use frequently.

Each of these projects provided concrete examples of many of the topics covered in this book: closures, events, prototypal inheritance, the Date object, etc.

This concludes the discussion chapters of this book. The next several chapters in the book are reference chapters, starting with a complete reference for JavaScript objects.

CHAPTER 5

JavaScript Global Objects Reference

Since one of the basic features of JavaScript is prototypal inheritance, it has no base classes for things like arrays or strings. Instead, JavaScript has a set of base objects from which other objects of the same type can inherit their properties and methods. These base objects reside in the global scope (which in the browser is the window object) and can thus be accessed at any time.

This chapter provides a reference for the major JavaScript global objects Array, Boolean, Date, Number, RegExp, and String. It also includes documentation for the Math object, which, unlike the other objects, does not serve as a base object for inheritance purposes (you'll never make a new Math object) but rather as a library for mathematical methods and functions. The reference is arranged in alphabetical order by object name, and each object is organized by property and method. In addition, there are several other variables and functions that are kept in the global scope that are quite useful, and we'll cover those in the last section of the chapter, "Miscellaneous Global Variables and Functions."

Array

The JavaScript Array object is a global constructor for arrays. An array is a simple data structure of numerically indexed values. In JavaScript, arrays are accessed using a familiar square bracket notation; for example, arrayName[12] will access the value of the array stored at index 12. JavaScript arrays have the following basic properties:

- JavaScript arrays are zero-indexed, so the first element in an array is at index 0 rather than index 1.

- JavaScript arrays have dynamic lengths, so you do not have to define how many elements an array will have.

- JavaScript arrays do not throw out-of-bounds errors when you access a nonexistent element. Instead, JavaScript returns the value undefined.

- JavaScript arrays can index any type of valid JavaScript element: strings, numbers, other arrays (which is how JavaScript implements multidimensional arrays), even objects. JavaScript arrays can also contain more than one type of element, so you can place objects, strings, and booleans as different elements in a single array.

- JavaScript arrays are themselves objects—they inherit from the global Object object and have access to all of the features of objects.

The Array object has several useful methods for managing arrays. For a detailed discussion of JavaScript arrays, see the "Arrays" section in Chapter 2.

There are two main ways to construct a new array: directly using the Array object as a constructor, or using literal notation.

If you use the Array object as a constructor, the method takes an optional parameter that is an integer representing the array's length. This integer is expected to be between 0 and 2^321; any other value will throw a RangeError exception. If the parameter is supplied, the new array will be initialized with the specified number of elements (each of which will be set to undefined). From a practical standpoint, because JavaScript arrays are of a dynamic length and JavaScript doesn't throw out-of-bounds errors when attempting to access a nonexistent element, there's not much point in creating arrays with predefined lengths.

To construct an array with data, simply include the data as a comma-delimited list within either the constructor or the literal notation.

Syntax

```
var exampleArray = new Array(length);        // Create an array using the Array constructor.
var exampleArray = [];                       // Create a new array literal.
```

Examples

```
// Initialize an empty array
var myArray = new Array();                   // myArray will be empty--have a length of 0.
var myOtherArray = [];                       // Literal notation
var myLongArray = new Array(100);            // length is 100.
alert(myLongArray[47]);                      // will alert "undefined"

// Initializing new arrays with values
var myFilledArray = new Array("this", "and", "the", "other");
var myIntegerArray = new Array(202, 53, 12, 0);
var myOtherFilledArray = ["more", "like", "this"];
var mySmallArrayOfDecimals = [0.1, 0.4];

// Constructing multidimensional arrays
var row1 = [1, 2, 3];
var row2 = [4, 5, 6];
var row3 = [7, 8, 9];
var array3by3 = [row1, row2, row3];          // array3by3 is now a multidimensional array
alert(array3by3[1][1]);                      // alerts 5

// Constructing arrays of objects
var object1 = {
    "myName" : "object1"
};
var object2 = {
    "myName" : "object2"
};
var object3 = {
    "myName" : "object3"
};

var arrayOfObjects = [object1, object2, object3]; // arrayOfObjects now contains the objects
alert(arrayOfObjects[1].myName);             // alerts "object2".
```

Array Properties

The JavaScript Array global object has only a few default properties, and most of those are inherited from Object. Array's only default property that it defines itself is the length property.

length

Each array has a length property that corresponds with the total number of elements in the array. Empty arrays have a length of 0. If an array has elements, then the index of the last element will be length – 1, because JavaScript arrays are zero-indexed.

Syntax

```
exampleArray.length;
```

Examples

```
var myArray = ["this", "is", "an", "array"];
alert(myArray.length);              // alerts 4
alert(myArray[myArray.length]);     // alerts "undefined"; there is no such element with index of 4.
alert(myArray[myArray.length -1]);  // alerts "array".
```

Array Methods

The Array object provides several very useful methods for manipulating arrays.

concat()

The Array.concat() method joins two (or more) arrays together into one new array. It will not affect the target arrays.

Syntax

```
var newArray = exampleArray.concat(array1, array2, ..., arrayN);
```

Examples

```
var array1 = ["bunnies", "kittens", "puppies"];
var array2 = ["velociraptors"];
var array3 = array1.concat(array2); // array3 will now contain ["bunnies", "kittens", "puppies",
"velociraptors"].
```

indexOf()

Array.indexOf() provides an easy way to search arrays for particular values. If the provided element is present in the array, this method will return the index of its first occurrence. If the provided element is not in the array, this method will return –1.

This method also takes an optional integer argument, which is interpreted as a starting index for the search. A positive integer is interpreted as a starting index from the beginning of the array, and a negative integer is interpreted as a starting index from the end of the array. In both cases, the search proceeds to the end of the array.

Syntax

```
exampleArray.indexOf(element, startingIndex);
```

Examples

```
var myArray = ["bunnies", "kittens", "puppies", "ponies", "polar bear cubs"];
var indexOfKittens = myArray.indexOf("kittens");          // 1
var indexOfVelociraptors = myArray.indexOf("velociraptors"); // -1
var indexOfPuppies = myArray.indexOf("puppies", -1);         // this will return -1 because puppies
is not contained within the subset specified by the starting index.
var indexOfPuppiesForReal = myArray.indexOf("puppies", -3);  // 2
```

join()

`Array.join()` concatenates all the elements of an array into a string. The method takes an optional parameter that serves as the separator character(s); if the parameter is not specified, then a comma is used by default.

Syntax

```
exampleArray.join(separator);
```

Examples

```
var myArray = ["bunnies", "kittens", "puppies", "ponies", "polar bear cubs"];
var strCuteThings = myArray.join();                      // strCuteThings now contains
"bunnies,kittens,puppies,ponies,polar bear cubs"
var sentence = myArray.join(" are cute and ") + "are cute!"; // sentence now contains "bunnies are
cute and kittens are cute and puppies are cute and ponies are cute and polar bear cubs are cute!"
```

lastIndexOf()

`Array.lastIndexOf()` provides a useful way to find the last occurrence of an element within an array. If the element is found, this method will return the index of the last occurrence; if the element is not found, it will return –1.

Like `Array.indexOf()`, this method takes an optional integer argument that serves as a starting index. A positive integer is interpreted as a starting index from the beginning, and the search will proceed to the end. A negative integer will be interpreted as an index from the end, and the search will proceed to the beginning of the array.

Syntax

```
exampleArray.lastIndexOf(element, startingIndex);
```

Examples

```
var myArray = ["bunnies", "kittens", "puppies", "ponies", "polar bear cubs", "bunnies", "kittens"];
alert(myArray.lastIndexOf("bunnies"));                  // alerts 5
alert(myArray.lastIndexOf("ponies", 4));                // alerts -1
alert(myArray.lastIndexOf("kittens", -2));              // alerts 1
```

pop()

Array.pop() removes the last element from an array, and returns that element. Compare with Array.shift().

Syntax

```
exampleArray.pop();
```

Examples

```
var myArray = ["bunnies", "kittens", "puppies", "ponies", "polar bear cubs"];
var cubs = myArray.pop(); // myArray is now ["bunnies", "kittens", "puppies", "ponies"] and cubs
is now "polar bear cubs"
```

push()

The Array.push() method provides a way to add new elements to an array. The new elements need to be specified using literal notation. The method returns the new length of the array.

Note that one array can be pushed into another array. This is one way of creating multidimensional arrays. (To concatenate arrays together, use Array.concat().)

Syntax

```
exampleArray.push(element1, element2, ..., elementN);
```

Examples

```
var myArray = ["bunnies", "kittens", "puppies", "ponies", "polar bear cubs"];
var newLength = myArray.push("chinchillas", "sugar gliders"); // newLength is 7
var predators = ["velociraptors", "wolves"];
newLength = myArray.push(predators);                    // newLength is 8 (not 9!)
alert(myArray[7]);                                      // alerts "velociraptors,wolves"
alert(myArray[7][1]);                                   // alerts "wolves"
```

reverse()

Array.reverse() reverses the order of the elements in the array. It does this "in place," meaning the array itself is reversed when this method is called upon it.

Syntax

```
exampleArray.reverse();
```

Examples

```
var myArray = ["bunnies", "kittens", "puppies", "ponies", "polar bear cubs"];
myArray.reverse(); // myArray is now  ["polar bear cubs", "ponies", "puppies", "kittens",
"bunnies"];
```

shift()

Array.shift() removes the first element from an array and returns that item. Compare with Array.unshift() and Array.pop().

Syntax

```
exampleArray.shift();
```

Examples

```
var myArray = ["bunnies", "kittens", "puppies", "ponies", "polar bear cubs"];
var bunnies = myArray.shift(); // myArray is now ["kittens", "puppies", "ponies", "polar bear cubs"]
and bunnies is now "bunnies"
```

slice()

The Array.slice() method removes elements from an array based on the specified range of indices. The method takes two integers as arguments: a start index and an end index. The method will select the elements starting at the starting index and ending at the end index (but it will *not* include the element specified by the end index). Positive integers are interpreted as indices from the beginning of the array, and negative integers are interpreted as indices from the end of the array. The method returns the specified elements as a new array, and does not affect the target array.

Syntax

```
exampleArray.slice(startingIndex, endingIndex);
```

Examples

```
var myArray = ["bunnies", "kittens", "puppies", "ponies", "polar bear cubs"];
var commonPets = myArray.slice(1, 2); // commonPets is now ["kittens", "puppies"];
var carnivores = myArray.slice(4, 5); // carnivores is now ["polar bear cubs"];
```

sort()

Array.sort() will sort the elements of an array. If no argument is specified, the array is sorted in place in ascending alphabetical order.

If ascending alphabetical order is not useful, the method can take as a parameter a sorting function, either as an inline function or as a named function. The sorting function must expect two parameters, a and b (which will be array elements), and compare them. If a is a lower index than b, the function should return −1. If the two are equal, the function should return 0. And if b is a lower index than a, the function should return 1. This makes it possible to do complex sorting of arrays.

Note, however, that complex sort functions can be expensive to run on large arrays because Array.sort() will run the function on every element. Exactly what constitutes "complex" and "large" depends on your specific situation, so if you find that your application is running slow and it is doing a complex sort, this is a logical place to look for opportunities to optimize performance.

Syntax

```
exampleArray.sort(sortMethod);
```

Examples

```
var myArray = ["bunnies", "kittens", "puppies", "ponies", "polar bear cubs"];
myArray.sort(); // myArray is now ["bunnies", "kittens", "polar bear cubs", "ponies", "puppies"]
var arrayOfIntegers = [0, 1, 2, 3, 4, 5, 6, 7, 8, 9, 10, 11, 12, 13];
arrayOfIntegers.sort(); // arrayOfIntegers is now [0, 1, 10, 11, 12, 13, 2, 3, 4, 5, 6, 7, 8, 9],
which is possibly not useful
function mySortingFunction(a, b) {
    return a-b;
}
arrayOfIntegers.sort(mySortingFunction); // arrayOfIntegers is now [0, 1, 2, 3, 4, 5, 6, 7, 8, 9,
10, 11, 12, 13]
```

splice()

`Array.splice()` provides a generic method for manipulating arrays. The method can either add or remove elements from an array, and the target array is manipulated in place. The method will return, as an array object, any elements that were removed from the array.

The method takes three arguments. The first argument is an integer and is the start index for the manipulation, and is required. Like other `Array` methods that take indices as arguments, a positive integer is interpreted as an index from the beginning of the array, and a negative integer is interpreted as an index counted from the end of the array.

The second argument is required, and is either 0 or a positive integer. It specifies how many elements to remove from the array. If set to 0, no elements will be removed.

The third argument is optional and is the new item(s) to be added to the array via a concatenation. This can be a literal list or another array object.

Syntax

```
exampleArray.splice(startingIndex, numberOfElements, item1, item2, item3, ..., itemN);
```

Or

```
exampleArray.splice(startingIndex, numberOfElements, arrayOfNewItems);
```

Examples

```
var myArray = ["bunnies", "kittens", "puppies", "ponies", "polar bear cubs"];
var arrayOfPuppies = myArray.splice(2, 1);          // This just removes "puppies" from myArray.
arrayOfPuppies  is now ["puppies"]
var arrayOfKittens = myArray.splice(1, 1, "maru"); // arrayOfKittens is now ["kittens"] and myArray
is now ["bunnies", "maru", "ponies", "polar bear cubs"];
var arrayOfPredators = ["velociraptors", "wolves"];
myArray.splice(2, 0, arrayOfPredators);            // myArray is now ["bunnies", "maru", "ponies",
["velociraptors", "wolves"], "polar bear cubs"]
```

toString()

Array.toString() concatenates all of the elements of the array together into a comma-delimited string. This method is exactly the same as calling Array.join() with no arguments.

Syntax

```
exampleArray.toString();
```

Examples

```
var myArray = ["bunnies", "kittens", "puppies", "ponies", "polar bear cubs"];
var strCuteThings = myArray.toString(); // strCuteThings now contains
"bunnies,kittens,puppies,ponies,polar bear cubs"
```

unshift()

Array.unshift() will add specified elements to the beginning of an array. Compare to Array.shift() and Array.push().

Syntax

```
exampleArray.unshift(element1, element2, ..., elementN);
```

Examples

```
var myArray = ["bunnies", "kittens", "puppies", "ponies", "polar bear cubs"];
myArray.unshift("chinchillas"); // myArray is now ["chinchillas", "bunnies", "kittens", "puppies",
"ponies", "polar bear cubs"]
```

Boolean

The JavaScript Boolean is an object wrapper for the boolean (true or false) data type. JavaScript also has the boolean primitives true and false; if you attempt to access a Boolean property or method on a boolean primitive, JavaScript will silently wrap it with a Boolean object to provide the requested functionality.

You can construct a new boolean object using the Boolean object as a constructor, which takes an optional parameter. If the parameter is 0, null, "", false, undefined, or NaN (or not specified at all), then the value property of the new Boolean object will be false. Otherwise it will be set to true (even in the case of specifying a string value of "false"). Just remember that when creating Boolean objects with the constructor, the result is an object, not the primitive value. Note that, from a practical standpoint, you'll rarely need to create Boolean objects because JavaScript will wrap boolean primitives for you.

Syntax

```
var exampleBoolean = new Boolean(parameter);
```

Examples

```
var newBooleanObject = new Boolean(false);  // create new Boolean object with a value of false
var newBooleanPrimitive = false;            // create new primitive boolean
alert(typeof newBooleanObject);             // will alert "object"
alert(typeof newBooleanPrimitive);          // will alert "boolean"
```

```
// This alert will happen because objects cast to true, even though the value is false
if (newBooleanObject) {
  alert("newBooleanObject is true!");
}

// This alert will not happen because it is a primitive set to false.
if (newBooleanPrimitive) {
  alert("newBooleanPrimitive is true!");
}
```

Boolean Methods

Boolean objects provide a couple of useful methods for determining their values. These are most often used in casting situations.

toString()

The Boolean.toString() method will return a string representing the value of the boolean (either "true" or "false").

Syntax

```
exampleBoolean.toString();
```

Examples

```
var myBoolean = false;           // Create a new boolean with the false primitive
alert(myBoolean.toString());        // alerts "false"
var myOtherBoolean = new Boolean("false");
alert(myOtherBoolean.toString());    // alerts "true"
var myLiteralBoolean = true;
alert(myLiteralBoolean.toString()); // alerts "true"
```

valueOf()

The Boolean.valueOf() method will return the value of the boolean as a primitive value (as opposed to Boolean.toString(), which returns the value of the boolean as a string).

Syntax

```
exampleBoolean.valueOf();
```

Examples

```
var newBool = false              // Create a new boolean with the false primitive
var otherBool = newBool.valueOf();
alert(typeof otherBool);         // will alert "boolean"
alert(otherBool.toString());     // will alert "false"
```

Date

The Date object is used to return the date, the form of which is generated by its many constructor functions. Each instance of the Date object is a value derived in milliseconds, and is relative to the zero hour point of January 1, 1970. All positive values represent a date after January 1, 1970. All negative values represent a date before January 1, 1970.

When using arguments with the Date object, follow the sequence of year, month, day, hours, minutes, seconds, and milliseconds. The browser stores the time as a millisecond value in the UTC() method. UTC, also known simply as Universal Time, stands for Coordinated Universal Time, which is essentially Greenwich Mean Time taken from the January 1, 1970 point. The time returned to the browser is taken from your operating system, so keep in mind that an incorrect system time may be causing any problems you may be encountering when working with the Date object.

Date objects are complex but provide many convenience methods for managing, comparing, and formatting dates. With a little practice they become easier to use.

Dates are constructed using the Date object as a constructor. The constructor takes an optional argument that can be a single integer (representing the number of milliseconds since the zero hour point of January 1, 1970 and which can be either positive, negative, or 0), a string of information formatted according to the requirements in Date.parse(), or a set of integers representing the desired year, month, day, etc. If no argument is specified, the current date is returned.

Syntax

```
var exampleDate = new Date();
var exampleDate = new Date(milliseconds);
var exampleDate = new Date(string);
var exampleDate = new Date(year, month, day, hours, minutes, seconds, milliseconds);
```

Example

```
var currentDate = new Date();  // No arguments so the current date is returned
alert(currentDate.getDate() ); // alerts the current day of the month (see getDate() method, below).
```

Date Methods

The Date object provides several very useful methods for manipulating and comparing dates.

getDate()

The Date.getDate() method is used to return the day of the month of the Date object.

Syntax

```
exampleDate.getDate();
```

Example

```
var dateObject = new Date();   // Create new date object with today's date.
alert(dateObject.getDate());   // alerts today's day of the month.
```

getDay()

The Date.getDay() method is used to return the day of the week of the Date object. Days are zero-indexed, with Sunday being 0.

Syntax

```
exampleDate.getDay();
```

Example

```
var dateObject = new Date();      // Create new date object for today
alert(dateObject.getDay());       // Alerts today's day of the week
```

getFullYear()

The Date.getFullYear() method is used to return the four digits representing the year, which is taken from the date specified by your operating system, and used by the Date object.

Syntax

```
exampleDate.getFullYear();
```

Example

```
var dateObject = new Date();        // Create new date object with today's date
alert(dateObject.getFullYear()); // Alerts the year
```

getHours()

The Date.getHours() method is used to return the hour of the day, which is taken from the date specified by your operating system, and used by the Date object. The hour returned is based on the 24-hour clock system.

Syntax

```
exampleDate.getHours();
```

Example

```
var dateObject = new Date();      // Create new date object with today's date
alert(dateObject.getHours());     // Alerts the current hour.
```

getMilliseconds()

The Date.getMilliseconds() method is used to return a number between 0 and 999, inclusive, that represents the milliseconds of the Date object.

143

Syntax

```
exampleDate.getMilliseconds();
```

Example

```
var dateObject = new Date();         // Create new date object as of that moment
alert(dateObject.getMilliseconds()); // Alerts the milliseconds at the time when
dateObject was formed.
```

getMinutes()

The Date.getMinutes() method is used to return the minutes of the hour of the day.

Syntax

```
exampleDate.getMinutes();
```

Example

```
var dateObject = new Date();         // Create new date object with today's date
alert(dateObject.getMinutes());      // Alerts the minutes of the hour
```

getMonth()

The Date.getMonth() method is used to return the month of the year, which is taken from the date specified by your operating system, and used by the Date object. The value returned is the numeric representation of the month, not the month name. Months are zero-indexed, so January is 0 and December is 11.

Syntax

```
exampleDate.getMonth();
```

Example

```
var dateObject = new Date();         // Create new date object with today's date
alert(dateObject.getMonth());        // Alerts the month
```

getSeconds()

The Date.getSeconds() method is used to return the seconds of the minute, which is taken from the date specified by your operating system, and used by the Date object.

Syntax

```
exampleDate.getSeconds();
```

Example

```
var dateObject = new Date();         // Create new date object with today's date
alert(dateObject.getSeconds());      // Alerts the seconds
```

getTime()

The Date.getTime() method is used to return the number of milliseconds that have passed since January 1, 1970, the time for which is taken from the date specified by your operating system, and used by the Date object. The value returned is in milliseconds.

This may seem like a strange and arbitrary way of representing dates, but it makes date mathematics (comparisons, addition and subtraction, etc.) quite easy.

Syntax

```
exampleDate.getTime();
```

Example

```
var dateObject = new Date();          // Create new date object with today's date
alert(dateObject.getTime());          // Alerts the milliseconds since January 1, 1970
```

getTimezoneOffset()

The Date.getTimezoneOffset() method is used to return the number of minutes corresponding to the difference between GMT and the time on the client computer, which is the time specified by your operating system, and used by the Date object.

Syntax

```
exampleDate.getTimezoneOffset();
```

Example

```
var dateObject = new Date();            // Create new date object with today's date
alert(dateObject.getTimezoneOffset()); // Alerts the timezone offset
```

getUTCDate()

The Date.getUTCDate() method is used to return the day of the month as specified by your operating system, expressed in UTC time or time without your local offset. The value returned is a value from 1 to 31. UTC stands for Universal Time Coordinated and is the same as Greenwich Mean Time (GMT).

Syntax

```
exampleDate.getUTCDate();
```

Example

```
var dateObject = new Date();          // Create new date object with today's date
alert(dateObject.getUTCDate());       // alerts the day of the month
```

getUTCDay()

The Date.getUTCDay() method is used to return the day of the week (0 to 6, for the seven days of the week), as specified by your operating system, expressed in UTC time or time without your local offset. The value returned is a value from 0 to 6. UTC stands for Universal Time Coordinated and is the same as Greenwich Mean Time (GMT).

Syntax

```
exampleDate.getUTCDay();
```

Example

```
var dateObject = new Date();          // Create new date object with today's date
alert(dateObject.getUTCDay());        // Alerts the day of the week
```

getUTCFullYear()

The Date.getUTCFullYear() method is used to return the four-digit representation of the current year as specified by your operating system, expressed in UTC time or time without your local offset. UTC stands for Universal Time Coordinated and is the same as Greenwich Mean Time (GMT).

Syntax

```
exampleDate.getUTCFullYear();
```

Example

```
var dateObject = new Date();          // Create new date object with today's date
alert(dateObject.getUTCFullYear());   // Alerts the current year
```

getUTCHours()

The Date.getUTCHours() method is used to return the hour of the day, expressed in UTC time or time without your local offset. The value returned is a value from 00 to 23, using the 24-hour time clock. UTC stands for Universal Time Coordinated and is the same as Greenwich Mean Time (GMT).

Syntax

```
exampleDate.getUTCHours();
```

Example

```
var dateObject = new Date();          // Create new date object with today's date
alert(dateObject.getUTCHours());      // Alerts the current hour of the day
```

getUTCMilliseconds()

The Date.getUTCMilliseconds() method is used to return the millisecond portion of the current date, expressed by an integer between 0 and 999 (inclusive), as specified by your operating system, expressed in UTC time or time without your local offset. UTC stands for Universal Time Coordinated and is the same as Greenwich Mean Time (GMT).

Syntax

```
exampleDate.getUTCMilliseconds();
```

Example

```
var dateObject = new Date();            // Create new date object with today's date
alert(dateObject.getUTCMilliseconds()); // Alerts the milliseconds of dateObject
```

getUTCMinutes()

The Date.getUTCMinutes() method is used to return the number of minutes past the last hour, as specified by your operating system, expressed in UTC time or time without your local offset. The value returned is a value from 0 to 59. UTC stands for Universal Time Coordinated and is the same as Greenwich Mean Time (GMT).

Syntax

```
exampleDate.getUTCMinutes();
```

Example

```
var dateObject = new Date();        // Create new date object with today's date
alert(dateObject.getUTCMinutes()); // Alerts the UTC minutes of the hour.
```

getUTCMonth()

The Date.getUTCMonth() method is used to return the month of the year, as specified by your operating system, expressed in UTC time or time without your local offset. The value returned is a value from 0 to 11. UTC stands for Universal Time Coordinated and is the same as Greenwich Mean Time (GMT).

Syntax

```
exampleDate.getUTCMonth();
```

Example

```
var dateObject = new Date();        // Create new date object with today's date
alert(dateObject.getUTCMonth());   // Alerts the month.
```

getUTCSeconds()

The Date.getUTCSeconds() method is used to return the number of seconds past the last minute, the time for which being taken from the time specified by your operating system, expressed in UTC time or time without your local offset. The value returned is a value from 0 to 59. UTC stands for Universal Time Coordinate and is the same as Greenwich Mean Time (GMT).

Syntax

```
exampleDate.getUTCSeconds();
```

Example

```
var dateObject = new Date();        // Create new date object with today's date
alert(dateObject.getUTCSeconds()); // Alerts the seconds past the minute
```

parse()

The Date.parse() method is used to return the time, measured in milliseconds from the date given as date (see syntax) to the present date. The present date is taken from the client operating system. The full date specified must be in the following form:

```
DayOfWeek, dayOfMonth MM YYYY HH:MM:SS TimeZoneOffset
```

The above is the format followed by the toGMTString() method.

Syntax

```
exampleDate.parse(date);
```

Example

```
alert("The number of milliseconds from January 1st, 1970 to Sun, Jan 3 1999 10:15:30 is : " +
Date.parse('Sun, Jan 3 1999 10:15:30') ); // Will alert "The number of milliseconds from
January 1st, 1970 to Sun, Jan 3 1999 10:15:30 is : 915387330000"
```

setDate()

The Date.setDate() method is used to set the day of the month property of the Date object. The Date object will then use this value for its operations. The date and time of your system clock is not consulted with this method.

The day parameter is expected to be between 1 and 31 (inclusive). If you provide 0, the day of the month property will set to the last hour of the previous month. If you provide –1, the day of the month property will set to the hour before the last hour of the previous month. If the month has 30 days, providing 32 will set the day of the month property to the second day of the next month. If the month has 31 days, then providing 32 will set the day of the month property to the first day of the next month.

This method returns an integer representing the number of milliseconds between the new value of the Date object and midnight, January 1, 1970.

Syntax

```
exampleDate.setDate(day);
```

Example

```
var dateObject = new Date(); // Create new date object with today's date
dateObject.setDate(3);       // Changes the day from whatever it currently is to 3 (Wednesday)
alert(dateObject.getDate()); // Alerts 3
```

setFullYear()

The Date.setFullYear() method is used to set the year property of the Date object. The Date object will then use this value for its operations. The date and time of your system clock is not consulted with this method.

In addition, this method can be used to set the month and day properties of the Date object by providing optional month and day parameters.

The year parameter is expected to be a zero-padded four-digit year. Negative values are allowed.

The month parameter is expected to be an integer between 0 and 11. If you provide −1, the month property will set to the last month of the previous year. If you provide 12, the month property will set to the first month of the next year, and if you provide 13, the month property will set to the second month of the next year.

The day parameter is expected to be an integer between 1 and 31. If you provide 0, the day will set to the last day of the previous month. If you provide −1, the day will set to the day before the last day of the previous month. If the month has 31 days, providing 32 will result in the first day of the next month, and if the month has 30 days, providing 32 will result in the second day of the next month.

This method returns an integer representing the number of milliseconds between the new value of the Date object and midnight, January 1, 1970.

Syntax

```
exampleDate.setFullYear(year, month, day);
```

Example

```
var dateObject = new Date();       // Create new date object with today's date
dateObject.setFullYear(1999);      // Set year to 1999
alert(dateObject.getFullYear()); // Alerts 1999.
```

setHours()

The Date.setHours() method is used to set the hour of the day property of the Date object. The Date object will then use this value for its operations. The date and time of your system clock is not consulted with this method.

In addition, this method can be used to set the minutes, seconds, and milliseconds properties of the Date object by providing optional minutes, seconds, and milliseconds parameters.

The hours parameter is expected to be an integer between 0 and 23. If you provide −1, the hours property will set to the last hour of the previous day, and if you provide 24, the hours property will set to the first hour of the next day.

The minutes parameter is expected to be an integer between 0 and 59. If you provide −1, the minutes property will set to the last minute of the previous hour, and if you provide 60, the minutes property will set to the first minute of the next hour.

The seconds parameter is expected to be an integer between 0 and 59. If you provide −1, the seconds property will set to the last second of the previous minute, and if you provide 60, the seconds property will set to the first second of the next minute.

The milliseconds parameter is expected to be an integer between 0 and 999. If you provide −1, the milliseconds property will set to the last millisecond of the previous second. If you provide 1000, the milliseconds property will set to the first millisecond of the next second.

This method returns an integer representing the number of milliseconds between the new value of the Date object and midnight, January 1, 1970.

Syntax

```
exampleDate.setHours(hour, minutes, seconds, milliseconds);
```

Example

```
var dateObject = new Date();       // Create new date object with today's date
dateObject.setHours(11);           // Set the hour to 11am
alert(dateObject.getHours());      // Alerts 11.
```

setMilliseconds( )

The Date.setMilliseconds() method is used to set the milliseconds property of the Date object. The Date object will then use this value for its operations. The date and time of your system clock is not consulted with this method.

The milliseconds parameter is expected to be an integer between 0 and 999. If you provide –1, the milliseconds property will set to the last millisecond of the previous second. If you provide 1000, the milliseconds property will set to the first millisecond of the next second.

This method returns an integer representing the number of milliseconds between the new value of the Date object and midnight, January 1, 1970.

Syntax

```
exampleDate.setMilliseconds(milliseconds);
```

Example

```
var dateObject = new Date();          // Create new date object with today's date
dateObject.setMilliseconds(300);      // Sets the milliseconds value to 300
alert(dateObject.getMilliseconds());  // Alerts 300
```

setMinutes( )

The Date.setMinutes() method is used to set the minutes property of the Date object. The Date object will then use this value for its operations. The date and time of your system clock is not consulted with this method. You can also set the seconds and milliseconds of the Date object by providing optional seconds and milliseconds parameters to this method.

The minutes parameter is expected to be an integer between 0 and 59. If you provide –1, the minutes property will set to the last minute of the previous hour, and if you provide 60, the minutes property will set to the first minute of the next hour.

The seconds parameter is expected to be an integer between 0 and 59. If you provide –1, the seconds property will set to the last second of the previous minute, and if you provide 60, the seconds property will set to the first second of the next minute.

The milliseconds parameter is expected to be an integer between 0 and 999. If you provide –1, the milliseconds property will set to the last millisecond of the previous second. If you provide 1000, the milliseconds property will set to the first millisecond of the next second.

This method returns an integer representing the number of milliseconds between the new value of the Date object and midnight, January 1, 1970.

Syntax

```
exampleDate.setMinutes(minutes, seconds, milliseconds);
```

Example

```
var dateObject = new Date();          // Create new date object with today's date
dateObject.setMinutes(40);            // Sets the minutes value to 40
alert(dateObject.getMinutes());       // Alerts 40
```

setMonth()

The Date.setMonth() method is used to set the month property of the Date object. The Date object will then use this value for its operations. The date and time of your system clock is not consulted with this method. In addition, you can set the day property of the Date object by providing an optional day parameter.

The month parameter is expected to be an integer between 0 and 11. If you provide –1, the month property will set to the last month of the previous year. If you provide 12, the month property will set to the first month of the next year, and if you provide 13, the month property will set to the second month of the next year.

The day parameter is expected to be an integer between 1 and 31. If you provide 0, the day will set to the last day of the previous month. If you provide –1, the day will set to the day before the last day of the previous month. If the month has 31 days, providing 32 will result in the first day of the next month, and if the month has 32 days, providing 32 will result in the second day of the next month.

This method returns an integer representing the number of milliseconds between the new value of the Date object and midnight, January 1, 1970.

Syntax

```
exampleDate.setMonth(month, day);
```

Example

```
var dateObject = new Date();      // Create new date object with today's date
dateObject.setMonth(4);           // Sets the month value to 4
alert(dateObject.getMonth());     // Alerts 4
```

setSeconds()

The Date.setSeconds() method is used to set the seconds property of the Date object. The Date object will then use this value for its operations. The date and time of your system clock is not consulted with this method. In addition, this method can be used to set the milliseconds property of the Date object by providing an optional milliseconds parameter.

The seconds parameter is expected to be an integer between 0 and 59. If you provide –1, the seconds property will set to the last second of the previous minute, and if you provide 60, the seconds property will set to the first second of the next minute.

The milliseconds parameter is expected to be an integer between 0 and 999. If you provide –1, the milliseconds property will set to the last millisecond of the previous second. If you provide 1000, the milliseconds property will set to the first millisecond of the next second.

This method returns an integer representing the number of milliseconds between the new value of the Date object and midnight, January 1, 1970.

Syntax

```
exampleDate.setSeconds(seconds, milliseconds);
```

Example

```
var dateObject = new Date();      // Create new date object with today's date
dateObject.setSeconds(11);        // Set seconds to 11
alert(dateObject.getSeconds());   // Alerts 11.
```

setTime()

The Date.setTime() method is used to set the number of milliseconds since midnight, January 1, 1970. The date and time of your system clock is not consulted with this method.

The milliseconds parameter is expected to be a positive or negative integer value. The Date object will then calculate the day, month, year, hours, minutes, seconds, and milliseconds based on the parameter.

This method returns an integer representing the number of milliseconds between the new value of the Date object and midnight, January 1, 1970.

Syntax

```
exampleDate.setTime(milliseconds);
```

Example

```
var dateObject = new Date();        // Create new date object with today's date
dateObject.setTime(-8348438943984); // Subtract 83,848,438,943,984 milliseconds from midnight
January 1 1970
alert(dateObject.toDateString());   // Alerts "Sat Jun 13 1705"
```

setUTCDate()

The Date.setUTCDate() method is used to set the day of the month property of the Date object according to Universal Time. The Date object will then use this value for its operations. The date and time of your system clock is not consulted with this method.

UTC stands for Universal Coordinated Time and is set by the World Time Standard. It is the same as Greenwich Mean Time (GMT).

The day parameter is expected to be between 1 and 31. If you provide 0, the day of the month property will set to the last hour of the previous month. If you provide –1, the day of the month property will set to the day before the last hour of the previous month. If the month has 30 days, providing 32 will set the day of the month property to the second day of the next month. If the month has 31 days, providing 32 will set the day of the month property to the first day of the next month.

This method returns an integer representing the number of milliseconds between the new value of the Date object and midnight, January 1, 1970.

Syntax

```
exampleDate.setUTCDate(day);
```

Example

```
var dateObject = new Date();      // Create new date object with today's date
dateObject.setUTCDate(3);         // Changes the day from whatever it currently is to 3
alert(dateObject.getUTCDate());   // Alerts 3
```

setUTCFullYear()

The Date.setUTCFullYear() method is used to set the year property of the Date object according to Universal Time. The Date object will then use this value for its operations. The date and time of your system clock is not consulted with this method.

UTC stands for Universal Coordinated Time and is set by the World Time Standard. It is the same as Greenwich Mean Time (GMT).

In addition, this method can be used to set the month and day properties of the Date object by providing optional month and day parameters.

The year parameter is expected to be a zero-padded four-digit year. Negative values are allowed.

The month parameter is expected to be an integer between 0 and 11. If you provide –1, the month property will set to the last month of the previous year. If you provide 12, the month property will set to the first month of the next year, and if you provide 13, the month property will set to the second month of the next year.

The day parameter is expected to be an integer between 1 and 31. If you provide 0, the day will set to the last day of the previous month. If you provide –1, the day will set to the day before the last day of the previous month. If the month has 31 days, providing 32 will result in the first day of the next month, and if the month has 30 days, providing 32 will result in the second day of the next month.

This method returns an integer representing the number of milliseconds between the new value of the Date object and midnight, January 1, 1970.

Syntax

```
exampleDate.setUTCFullYear(year, month, day);
```

Example

```
var dateObject = new Date();        // Create new date object with today's date
dateObject.setUTCFullYear(1999);    // Set year to 1999
alert(dateObject.getUTCFullYear()); // Alerts 1999.
```

setUTCHours()

The Date.setUTCHours() method is used to set the hour of the day property of the Date object according to Universal Time. The Date object will then use this value for its operations. The date and time of your system clock is not consulted with this method.

UTC stands for Universal Coordinated Time and is set by the World Time Standard. It is the same as Greenwich Mean Time (GMT).

In addition, this method can be used to set the minutes, seconds, and milliseconds properties of the Date object by providing optional minutes, seconds, and milliseconds parameters.

The hours parameter is expected to be an integer between 0 and 23. If you provide –1, the hours property will set to the last hour of the previous day, and if you provide 24, the hours property will set to the first hour of the next day.

The minutes parameter is expected to be an integer between 0 and 59. If you provide –1, the minutes property will set to the last minute of the previous hour, and if you provide 60, the minutes property will set to the first minute of the next hour.

The seconds parameter is expected to be an integer between 0 and 59. If you provide –1, the seconds property will set to the last second of the previous minute, and if you provide 60, the seconds property will set to the first second of the next minute.

The milliseconds parameter is expected to be an integer between 0 and 999. If you provide –1, the milliseconds property will set to the last millisecond of the previous second. If you provide 1000, the milliseconds property will set to the first millisecond of the next second.

This method returns an integer representing the number of milliseconds between the new value of the Date object and midnight, January 1, 1970.

Syntax

```
exampleDate.setUTCHours(hour, miutes, seconds, milliseconds);
```

Example

```
var dateObject = new Date();          // Create new date object with today's date
dateObject.setUTCHours(11);           // Set the hour to 11am
alert(dateObject.getUTCHours());      // Alerts 11.
```

setUTCMilliseconds()

The Date.setUTCMilliseconds() method is used to set the milliseconds property of the Date object according to Universal Time. The Date object will then use this value for its operations. The date and time of your system clock is not consulted with this method.

UTC stands for Universal Coordinated Time and is set by the World Time Standard. It is the same as Greenwich Mean Time (GMT).

The milliseconds parameter is expected to be an integer between 0 and 999. If you provide –1, the milliseconds property will set to the last millisecond of the previous second. If you provide 1000, the milliseconds property will set to the first millisecond of the next second.

This method returns an integer representing the number of milliseconds between the new value of the Date object and midnight, January 1, 1970.

Syntax

```
exampleDate.setUTCMilliseconds(milliseconds);
```

Example

```
var dateObject = new Date();             // Create new date object with today's date
dateObject.setUTCMilliseconds(300);      // Sets the milliseconds value to 300
alert(dateObject.getUTCMilliseconds());  // Alerts 300
```

setUTCMinutes()

The Date.setUTCMinutes() method is used to set the minutes property of the Date object according to Universal Time. The Date object will then use this value for its operations. The date and time of your system clock is not consulted with this method. You can also set the seconds and milliseconds of the Date object by providing optional seconds and milliseconds parameters to this method.

UTC stands for Universal Coordinated Time and is set by the World Time Standard. It is the same as Greenwich Mean Time (GMT).

The minutes parameter is expected to be an integer between 0 and 59. If you provide –1, the minutes property will set to the last minute of the previous hour, and if you provide 60, the minutes property will set to the first minute of the next hour.

The seconds parameter is expected to be an integer between 0 and 59. If you provide –1, the seconds property will set to the last second of the previous minute, and if you provide 60, the seconds property will set to the first second of the next minute.

The milliseconds parameter is expected to be an integer between 0 and 999. If you provide –1, the milliseconds property will set to the last millisecond of the previous second. If you provide 1000, the milliseconds property will set to the first millisecond of the next second.

This method returns an integer representing the number of milliseconds between the new value of the Date object and midnight, January 1, 1970.

Syntax

```
exampleDate.setUTCMinutes(minutes, seconds, milliseconds);
```

Example

```
var dateObject = new Date();      // Create new date object with today's date
dateObject.setUTCMinutes(40);     // Sets the minutes value to 40
alert(dateObject.getUTCMinutes()); // Alerts 40
```

setUTCMonth()

The Date.setUTCMonth() method is used to set the month property of the Date object according to Universal Time. The Date object will then use this value for its operations. The date and time of your system clock is not consulted with this method. In addition, you can set the day property of the Date object by providing an optional day parameter.

UTC stands for Universal Coordinated Time and is set by the World Time Standard. It is the same as Greenwich Mean Time (GMT).

The month parameter is expected to be an integer between 0 and 11. If you provide −1, the month property will set to the last month of the previous year. If you provide 12, the month property will set to the first month of the next year, and if you provide 13, the month property will set to the second month of the next year.

The day parameter is expected to be an integer between 1 and 31. If you provide 0, the day will set to the last day of the previous month. If you provide −1, the day will set to the day before the last day of the previous month. If the month has 31 days, providing 32 will result in the first day of the next month, and if the month has 32 days, providing 32 will result in the second day of the next month.

This method returns an integer representing the number of milliseconds between the new value of the Date object and midnight, January 1, 1970.

Syntax

```
exampleDate.setUTCMonth(month, day);
```

Example

```
var dateObject = new Date();      // Create new date object with today's date
dateObject.setUTCMonth(4);        // Sets the month value to 4
alert(dateObject.getUTCMonth());  // Alerts 4
```

setUTCSeconds()

The Date.setUTCSeconds() method is used to set the seconds property of the Date object according to Universal Time. The Date object will then use this value for its operations. The date and time of your system clock is not consulted with this method. In addition, this method can be used to set the milliseconds property of the Date object by providing an optional milliseconds parameter.

UTC stands for Universal Coordinated Time and is set by the World Time Standard. It is the same as Greenwich Mean Time (GMT).

The seconds parameter is expected to be an integer between 0 and 59. If you provide −1, the seconds property will set to the last second of the previous minute, and if you provide 60, the seconds property will set to the first second of the next minute.

The milliseconds parameter is expected to be an integer between 0 and 999. If you provide −1, the milliseconds property will set to the last millisecond of the previous second. If you provide 1000, the milliseconds property will set to the first millisecond of the next second.

This method returns an integer representing the number of milliseconds between the new value of the Date object and midnight, January 1, 1970.

Syntax

```
exampleDate.setUTCSeconds(seconds, milliseconds);
```

Example

```
var dateObject = new Date();        // Create new date object with today's date
dateObject.setUTCSeconds(11);       // Set seconds to 11
alert(dateObject.getUTCSeconds()); // Alerts 11.
```

toDateString()

The Date.toDateString() method returns a formatted string that represents the date (not the time) of the Date object. The format is a three-letter Day abbreviation followed by MMM DD YYYY; for example, "Sun Jan 26 2013".

Syntax

```
exampleDate.toDateString();
```

Example

```
var dateObject = new Date();          // Create new date object with today's date
alert(dateObject.toDateString());    // Alerts the current date.
```

toISOString()

The Date.toISOString() method returns a string representing the value of the Date object, formatted according to ISO-8601: YYYY-MM-DDTHH:mm:ss.sssZ.

Syntax

```
exampleDate.toISOString();
```

Example

```
var dateObject = new Date();          // Create new date object with today's date
alert(dateObject.toISOString());     // Alerts today's date in ISO-8601 format.
```

toJSON()

The Date.toJSON() method will return a string representing the date formatted in JSON format. The JSON format is identical to the ISO format, so this method is identical to calling Date.toISOString().

Syntax

```
exampleDate.toJSON();
```

Example

```
var dateObject = new Date(); // Create new date object with today's date
alert(dateObject.toJSON());  // Alerts today's date in ISO-8601 format.
```

toLocaleDateString()

The Date.toLocaleDateString() method is used to return the date in a standardized format, the date for which is taken from the date specified by your operating system, and used by the Date object. The value is formatted according to locale conventions specified by the host browser, the host operating system, and possibly the user's settings. As a result, this method will behave differently in different browsers and on different operating systems

Syntax

```
exampleDate.toLocaleDateString();
```

Example

```
var dateObject = new Date(); // Create new date object with today's date
alert(dateObject.toLocaleDateString()); // Alerts today's date in a formatted
string, e.g. "Thursday, September 13, 2012"
```

toLocaleTimeString()

The Date.toLocaleTimeString() method is used to return the time portion of a Date object in a standardized format, the information for which is taken from the date specified by your operating system, and used by the Date object. The value is returned using locale conventions specified by the host browser, the host operating system, and possibly the user's settings. As a result, this method will behave differently in different browsers and on different operating systems.

Syntax

```
exampleDate.toLocaleTimeString();
```

Example

```
var dateObject = new Date();              // Create new date object with today's date
alert(dateObject.toLocaleTimeString()); // Alerts the current time, e.g. "09:17:42"
```

toLocaleString()

The Date.toLocaleString() method is used to return the value of a Date object in a standardized format, the information for which is taken from the date specified by your operating system, and used by the Date object. The value is returned using locale conventions specified by the host browser, the host operating system, and possibly the user's settings. As a result, this method will behave differently in different browsers and on different operating systems.

Syntax

```
exampleDate.toLocaleString();
```

Example

```
var dateObject = new Date(); // Create new date object with today's date
alert(dateObject.toLocaleString()); // Alerts the current time, e.g. "Thu Sep 13 2012
09:17:42 GMT-0700 (Pacific Daylight Time)"
```

toString()

The Date.toString() method is used to convert a Date object into a string.

Syntax

```
exampleDate.toString();
```

Example

```
var dateObject = new Date(); // Create new date object with today's date
alert(dateObject.toString()); // Alerts the current time, e.g. " Thu Sep 13 2012 09:17:42 GMT-0700
(Pacific Daylight Time)"
```

toTimeString()

The Date.toTimeString() method is used to convert the time portion of a Date object into a string.

Syntax

```
exampleDate.toTimeString();
```

Example

```
var dateObject = new Date();       // Create new date object with today's date
alert(dateObject.toTimeString()); // Alerts the current time, e.g. "09:17:42 GMT-0700
(Pacific Daylight Time)"
```

toUTCString()

The Date.toUTCString() method is used to convert a Date object into a string according to Universal Coordinated Time.

Syntax

```
exampleDate.toUTCString();
```

Example

```
var dateObject = new Date();       // Create new date object with today's date
alert(dateObject.toUTCString()); // Alerts the current time, e.g. " Thu Sep 13 2012 16:17:42 GMT"
```

UTC()

Unlike the other methods on the Date object, the Date.UTC() method is a static method exposed for convenience. Thus you do not have to create a new Date object in order to access it—in fact, you can't access it from a Date object. Instead, you access it directly from the global Date object.

The Date.UTC() method takes a set of parameters as follows:

- Year: The four-digit year; any year after 1900 is valid. Required.

- Month: An integer from 0 to 11 representing the desired month. Required.

- Date: An integer from 1 to 31 representing the desired day of the month.

- Hours: An integer from 0 to 23 representing the desired hour.

- Min: An integer from 0 to 59 representing the desired minutes.

- Sec: An integer from 0 to 59 representing the desired seconds.

- MS: An integer from 0 to 999 representing the desired milliseconds.

The method will return a number that represents the number of milliseconds between the date specified and midnight, January 1, 1970.

Syntax

```
Date.UTC(Year, Month, Date, Hours, Min, Sec, MS);
```

Example

```
var intMilliseconds = Date.UTC(2013,01,26); // intMilliseconds is now 1361836800000
var myNewDate = new Date(intMilliseconds);  // Create a new date object
alert(myNewDate.toUTCString()):             // Alerts "Tue, 26 Feb 2013 00:00:00 GMT".
```

valueOf()

The Date.valueOf() method returns the primitive value of a Date object, which is the number of seconds from midnight, January 1, 1970, UTC.

Syntax

```
exampleDate.valueOf();
```

Example

```
var dateObject = new Date(); // Create new date object with today's date
alert(dateObject.valueOf()); // Alerts the milliseconds from midnight January 1 1970,
e.g."1347553875570"
```

Math

The Math object provides access to various mathematical properties and functions. Unlike other objects outlined in this chapter, the Math object is not a constructor. You do not need to make a new Math object to use it; you can use its properties and methods directly.

Math Properties

The Math object has several properties that correspond to common mathematical constants:

- E: Euler's number
- LN2: The natural logarithm of 2
- LN10: The natural logarithm of 10
- LOG2E: The base-2 logarithm of E
- LOG10E: The base-10 logarithm of E
- PI: The value of pi (π)
- SQRT1_2: The square root of 1/2
- SQRT2: The square root of 2

Syntax

```
Math.E;
Math.LN2;
Math.PI;
```

Examples

```
alert(Math.E);
alert(Math.LN2);
alert(Math.PI);
```

Math Methods

The Math object has several methods, including trigonometric functions, rounding, and randomization.

abs()

The Math.abs() method is used to calculate the absolute value of the supplied parameter. Non-numeric parameters are cast as numeric for purposes of calculation.

Syntax

```
Math.abs(number);
```

Examples

```
alert(Math.abs(-1));           // will alert "1"
alert(Math.abs(0.1));          // will alert "0.1"
alert(Math.abs("Math is fun!")); // will alert "NaN"
alert(Math.abs(null));         // will alert "0"
```

acos()

The Math.acos() method returns the arccosine (in radians) of the supplied parameter. Non-numeric parameters are cast as numeric for purposes of calculation.

Syntax

```
Math.acos(number);
```

Examples

```
alert(Math.acos(1));              // will alert 0
alert(Math.acos(-1));             // will alert 3.141592653589793
alert(Math.acos(0.1));            // will alert 1.4706289056333368
alert(Math.acos("Math is fun!")); // will alert NaN
alert(Math.acos(null));           // will alert 1.5707963267948966
```

asin()

The Math.asin() method returns the arcsine (in radians) of the supplied parameter. Non-numeric parameters are cast as numeric for purposes of calculation.

Syntax

```
Math.asin(number);
```

Examples

```
alert(Math.asin(1));              // will alert 1. 5707963267948966
alert(Math.asin(-1));             // will alert -1. 5707963267948966
alert(Math.asin(0.1));            // will alert 0.1001674211615598
alert(Math.asin("Math is fun!")); // will alert NaN
alert(Math.asin(null));           // will alert 0
```

atan()

The Math.atan() method returns the arctangent (in radians) of the supplied parameter. Non-numeric parameters are cast as numeric for purposes of calculation.

Syntax

```
Math.atan(number);
```

Examples

```
alert(Math.atan(1));              // will alert 0.7853981633974483
alert(Math.atan(-1));             // will alert 0.7853981633974483
alert(Math.atan(0.1));            // will alert 0.09966865249116204
alert(Math.atan("Math is fun!")); // will alert NaN
alert(Math.atan(null));           // will alert 0
```

atan2()

The Math.atan2() method returns the arctangent of the quotient of its two parameters. The value is returned in radians between -PI/2 and PI/2. Non-numeric parameters are cast as numeric for purposes of calculation.

Syntax

```
Math.atan2(num1, num2);
```

Examples

```
alert(Math.atan2(1, 7));               // will alert 0.1418970546416394
alert(Math.atan2("Math is fun!", 8)); // will alert NaN
alert(Math.atan2(null, null));         // will alert 0
```

ceil()

The Math.ceil() method returns the parameter rounded up to the next nearest integer. Non-numeric parameters are cast as numeric for purposes of calculation. Compare to Math.floor().

Syntax

```
Math.ceil(number);
```

Examples

```
alert(Math.ceil(0.4));            // will alert 1
alert(Math.ceil(-7.9));           // will alert -7
alert(Math.ceil("Math is fun")); // will alert NaN
alert(Math.ceil("0.1"));          // will alert 1
```

cos()

The Math.cos() method returns the cosine (in radians) of the supplied parameter. Non-numeric parameters are cast as numeric for purposes of calculation.

Syntax

```
Math.cos(number);
```

Examples

```
alert(Math.cos(1));               // will alert 0.540323058681398
alert(Math.cos(0.1));             // will alert 0.9950041652780258
alert(Math.cos("Math is fun!")); // will alert NaN
alert(Math.cos(null));            // will alert 1
```

exp()

The Math.exp() method takes a numeric parameter and returns e^number as a result.

Syntax

```
Math.exp(number);
```

Example

```
alert(Math.exp(-1));          // will alert 0.36787944117144233
```

floor()

The Math.floor() method returns the parameter rounded down to the next nearest integer. Non-numeric parameters are cast as numeric for purposes of calculation. Compare to Math.ceil().

Syntax

```
Math.floor(number);
```

Examples

```
alert(Math.floor(0.4));          // will alert 0
alert(Math.floor(-7.9));         // will alert -8
alert(Math.floor("Math is fun")); // will alert NaN
alert(Math.floor("0.1"));        // will alert 0
```

log()

The Math.log() method will return the natural logarithm of the parameter. Non-numeric parameters are cast for the purposes of calculation.

Syntax

```
Math.log(number);
```

Examples

```
alert(Math.log(2));          // will alert 0.691347185599453
alert(Math.log("0"));        // will alert -Infinity
alert(Math.log(-34));        // Will alert NaN
```

max()

The Math.max() method takes a set of numeric parameters and will return the largest of them. Passing a non-numeric parameter will cause the method to return NaN. If no arguments are given, the method will return -Infinity. Compare to Math.min().

Syntax

```
Math.max(num1, num2, ..., numN);
```

Example

```
alert(Math.max(5, 0, 2, 100, 4, 68490, 4, -1, 234)); // will alert 68490
```

min()

The Math.min() method takes a set of numeric parameters and will return the smallest of them. Passing a non-numeric parameter will cause the method to return NaN. If no arguments are given, the method will return Infinity. Compare to Math.max().

Syntax

```
Math.min(num1, num2, ..., numN);
```

Example

```
alert(Math.min(5, 0, 2, 100, 4, 68490, 4, -1, 234)); // will alert -1
```

pow()

The Math.pow() method takes two parameters, numberBase and numberExponent, and returns numberBase^numberExponent. Non-numeric parameters are cast for purposes of calculation.

Syntax

```
Math.pow(numberBase, numberExponent);
```

Examples

```
alert(Math.pow(10, 10));            // will alert 10000000000
alert(Math.pow(100, 0.5));          // will alert 10
alert((Math.pow(2, 0.5) == Math.SQRT2)); // will alert true
```

random()

The Math.random() method will return a floating-point number of 16 decimal places that is greater than or equal to 0 and less than 1.

Syntax

```
Math.random();
```

Examples

```
alert(Math.random());                    // will alert a random number, such as 0.40920510
// Function to generate a random integer between 0 and intMax
function generateRandomInt(intMax) {
    return Math.floor((Math.random() * intMax) + 1);
}
alert(generateRandomInt(100));           // will alert a random integer between 0 and 100.
```

round()

The Math.round() method takes a numeric parameter and will return that number rounded to the nearest integer. Non-numeric parameters will be cast for purposes of calculation.

Syntax

```
Math.round(number);
```

Examples

```
alert(Math.round(1.49));        // will alert 1
alert(Math.round(1.5));         // will alert 2
```

sin()

The Math.sin() method returns the sine (in radians) of the supplied parameter. Non-numeric parameters are cast as numeric for purposes of calculation.

Syntax

```
Math.sin(number);
```

Examples

```
alert(Math.sin(1));             // will alert 0.8414709848078965
alert(Math.cos(0.1));           // will alert 0.09983341664682815
alert(Math.cos("Math is fun!")); // will alert NaN
alert(Math.cos(null));          // will alert 1
```

sqrt()

The Math.sqrt() method takes a numeric parameter and returns the square root of that number. Negative numbers will return NaN, and non-numeric parameters will be cast for purposes of calculation.

Syntax

```
Math.sqrt(number);
```

Example

```
alert(Math.sqrt(100));          // will alert 10
```

tan()

The Math.tan() method returns the tangent (in radians) of the supplied parameter. Non-numeric parameters are cast as numeric for purposes of calculation.

Syntax

```
Math.tan(number);
```

Examples

```
alert(Math.tan(1));              // will alert 1.5574077246549023
alert(Math.tan(0.1));            // will alert 0.10033467208545055
alert(Math.tan("Math is fun!")); // will alert NaN
alert(Math.tan(null));           // will alert 0
```

Number

The Number object is a wrapper class for numeric values. In JavaScript all numeric values are 64-bit floating point numbers.

Number Properties

The JavaScript Number object has a few properties that are useful in numeric comparisons, particularly since JavaScript is weakly typed:

- MAX_VALUE: The largest possible numeric value in JavaScript

- MIN_VALUE: The smallest possible numeric value in JavaScript

- NEGATIVE_INFINITY: Negative infinity

- NaN: The special "Not a Number" value (see Chapter 2 for details)

- POSITIVE_INFINITY: Positive infinity

Syntax

```
Number.MAX_VALUE;
Number.MIN_VALUE;
```

Example

```
alert(Number.MAX_VALUE);       // will alert 1.7976931348623157e+308
```

Number Methods
toExponential()

The Number.toExponential() method returns a string representing the number in exponential notation. The method takes an optional integer parameter between 0 and 20 that represents the number of digits after the decimal point; if it is omitted, the method will use as many digits as needed to fully represent the number.

Syntax

```
exampleNumber.toExponential(digits);
```

Examples

```
var myNumber = 4309;
alert(myNumber.toExponential());  // will alert 4.309e+3
alert(myNumber.toExponential(2)); // will alert 4.31e+3
```

toFixed()

The `Number.toFixed()` method returns a string representing the number in decimal notation and has exactly the number of digits after the decimal specified by the optional integer parameter. If the parameter is not specified, it is treated as 0 and the number will be rounded to its nearest integer.

Syntax

```
exampleNumber.toFixed(places);
```

Examples

```
var myNumber = 40.29;
alert(myNumber.toFixed());      // will alert 40
alert(myNumber.toFixed(1));     // will alert 40.3
alert(myNumber.toFixed(4));     // will alert 40.2900
```

toPrecision()

The `Number.toPrecision()` method returns a string representing the specified number rounded to the number of significant digits specified by the parameter. The result can be either fixed-point or exponential notation as needed. Typically the parameter is expected to be an integer value between 1 and 21, though this can vary depending on implementation. Parameters outside of the allowed range will throw a range error. If no numeric parameter is specified, the method simply returns a string representation of the number and is the equivalent of calling the `toString()` method.

Syntax

```
exampleNumber.toPrecision(precision);
```

Examples

```
var myNumber = 40.29;
alert(myNumber.toPrecision());    // alerts 40.29
alert(myNumber.toPrecision(1));   // alerts 4e+1 (which is 40 in exponential notation)
alert(myNumber.toPrecision(10));  // alerts 40.2900000000
```

toString()

The `Number.toString()` method returns a string that represents the value of the number. The method takes an optional parameter that is an integer between 2 and 26 and represents the radix (base) of the string. If you provide a parameter outside the accepted range, an exception will be thrown. If you do not provide a radix at all, the default is 10.

Syntax

```
exampleNumber.toString(radix);
```

Examples

```
var myNumber = 17;
alert(myNumber.toString());     // alerts 17
alert(myNumber.toString(2));    // alerts 10001
```

valueOf()

The `Number.valueOf()` method returns the primitive value of the number as a numeric data type. This method is not commonly used because direct assignment is preferred.

Syntax

```
exampleNumber.valueOf();
```

Examples

```
var myNumber = 17;
var myOtherNumber = myNumber.valueOf();
var myBetterWay = myNumber;                 // direct assignment
alert(myOtherNumber === myBetterWay);       // Will alert true, because the two are the same
```

RegExp

The JavaScript RegExp object provides the implementation for regular expressions in JavaScript. Regular expressions are a powerful tool for searching and manipulating strings of text and have their own language and methodologies. This reference covers only the JavaScript implementation of regular expressions and does not delve into how to actually build them.

In JavaScript, regular expressions are created in one of two ways: via the RegExp object constructor, or via a literal. When using the constructor, any strings present in the expression have to be escaped.

Syntax

```
var exampleRegExp = new RegExp(regularExpression);
var exampleRegExp = regularExpression;
```

Examples

```
var myConstructedRegExp = new RegExp("the", "g"); // same as myLiteralRegExp
var myLiteralRegExp = /the/g;                      // search an entire string for "the"
```

RegExp Properties

Regular expressions have several properties (global, case insensitivity, etc.) and the RegExp object has matching properties for all of them.

global

The `RegExp.global` property is a boolean that is set to true if the global flag has been set for the regular expression.

Syntax

```
exampleRegExp.global;
```

Example

```
var myRegExp = /the/g;
alert(myRegExp.global);        // will alert true
```

ignoreCase

The RegExp.ignoreCase property is a boolean indicating whether or not the ignore case flag has been set for the regular expression.

Syntax

```
exampleRegExp.ignoreCase;
```

Example

```
var myRegExp = /the/i;
alert(myRegExp.ignoreCase); // will alert true
```

lastIndex

The RegExp.lastIndex property will contain an integer representing the character position immediately after the last match found by the RegExp.match() method or RegExp.test() method. This property will only be set if the global property is set to true.

Syntax

```
exampleRegExp.lastIndex;
```

Example

```
var slogan = "Never give up, never surrender!";
var regExp = /never/gi;
while (regExp.test(slogan) === true) {
    alert("Found 'never'; index is now " + regExp.lastIndex);
}
```

multiline

The RegExp.multiline property is a boolean indicating whether or not the multiline flag has been set on the regular expression.

Syntax

```
exampleRegExp.multiline;
```

Example

```
var myRegExp = /never/m;
alert(myRegExp.multiline);  // will alert true
```

source

The RegExp.source property contains a string representing the regular expression itself.

Syntax

```
exampleRegExp.source;
```

Example

```
var myRegExp = /never/g;
alert(myRegExp.source); // will alert "/never/g" (some browsers will just alert "never" which is
equivalent)
```

RegExp Methods

The RegExp object methods are used to run the regular expression on targets.

exec()

The RegExp.exec() method takes a target string as a parameter and runs the regular expression match on it. If no match is found, the method returns null. If a match is found, the method stops and returns an array with the following properties:

- The first element in the array is the matched text.

- Subsequent elements in the array are the contents of any matching parentheses in the regular expression.

- The array will have an input property that will contain the target string.

- The array will have an index property that will contain an integer representing the index of the matched substring.

In addition, the method will update lastIndex of the RegExp object.

If the regular expression has the global flag set, subsequent calls to the match() method will continue the scanning process on the string, returning any matches found until there are no more.

Because of its iterative nature, RegExp.exec() is typically used inside a loop.

Syntax

```
exampleRegExp.exec(target)
```

Examples

```
var regExp = /never/gi;     // global case-insensitive search for "never"
var slogan = "Never give up, never surrender!";
alert(regExp.exec(slogan)); // will alert "Never"
alert(regExp.exec(slogan)); // will alert "never"
alert(regExp.exec(slogan)); // will alert null

// Demonstrate using a loop: this will alert "Never" and then "never".
var regExp = /never/gi,
    slogan = "Never give up, never surrender!",
```

```
        result;
while(result = regExp.exec(slogan)) {
    alert(result);
}
```

test()

The `RegExp.test()` method takes a target string as a parameter and runs the regular expression match on the target string. If there is a match, then the method returns true; otherwise it returns false.

Syntax

```
exampleRegExp.test(target);
```

Examples

```
var regExp = /never/g;
var slogan = "Never give up, never surrender!";
var otherSlogan = "May the force be with you!";
alert(regExp.test(slogan));      // will alert true
alert(regExp.test(otherSlogan)); // will alert false
```

String

The `String` object is a wrapper class for all strings. Whenever you access one of the properties or methods of `String` on a string literal, JavaScript will wrap that literal with a `String` object behind the scenes, giving you the functionality you requested. Your literal string will remain unchanged but will appear to have all of the properties and methods of a `String` object.

The `String` object is rarely used directly; you will almost never have call to create a `String` object using `String` as a constructor. The only advantage of creating a `String` object is that, because the result is an object, you could then give it other properties or methods.

If you should need to create a `String` object using the `String` constructor, the syntax is simple and the result is an object with all of the string properties and methods. To access the actual string you used to construct the object, use the `valueOf()` method.

Syntax

```
var exampleString = new String("desired string");
```

Examples

```
var myConstructedString = new String("Hi");
var myLiteralString = "Hi";
alert(myConstructedString === myLiteralString);          // will alert false, because literals and
objects are different types.
alert(myConstructedString == myLiteralString);           // will alert true, because JavaScript
uses the valueOf method in cast comparisons.
alert(myConstructedString.valueOf() === myLiteralString); // will alert true.
```

String Properties

The JavaScript global String object has a few properties, most of which it inherits from Object. The one property it does define for itself is length.

length

The String.length property contains an integer representing the total number of characters in the string.

Syntax

```
exampleString.length;
```

Example

```
var myString = "Hi";
alert(myString.length);          // will alert 2
```

String Methods

JavaScript provides several very useful methods for manipulating strings, including translation into arrays and regular expression scanning.

charAt()

The String.charAt() method expects as a parameter an integer representing an index within the string, and will return the character present at that index. Characters in a string are zero-indexed from left to right. If you specify an index that is outside the length of the string, the method will return an empty string.

Syntax

```
exampleString.charAt(index);
```

Example

```
var myString = "Hello World";
alert(myString.charAt(6));       // will alert "W"--spaces are characters too!
```

charCodeAt()

The String.charCodeAt() method expects as a parameter an integer representing an index within the string, and will return the numeric Unicode value of the character present at that index. Characters in a string are zero-indexed from left to right. If you specify an index that is outside the length of the string, the method will return an empty string.

Syntax

```
exampleString.charCodeAt(index);
```

Example

```
var myString = "Hello World";
alert(myString.charCodeAt(6)); // will alert "87"
```

concat()

The `String.concat()` method combines one or more strings (provided as parameters) and returns the result. The original strings are not changed.

Syntax

```
exampleString.concat(string1, string2, ..., stringN);
```

Example

```
var myString = "Hello";
var myOtherString = "World";
var mySpace = " ";
var myFullMessage = myString.concat(mySpace, myOtherString, "!");
alert(myFullMessage)                    // will alert Hello World!
```

fromCharCode()

The `String.fromCharCode()` method takes as parameters any number of Unicode character codes. It converts the codes into their associated characters and returns the resulting string.

Note that this is a static method of the `String` object, so it can be called directly; you do not need to first create a `String` object.

Syntax

```
exampleString.fromCharCode(charCode1, charCode2, ..., charCodeN);
```

Example

```
alert(String.fromCharCode(87));    // will alert W
```

indexOf()

The `String.indexOf()` method takes a substring as a parameter and searches the string from the beginning for that substring. If it is found, the method returns the index of the first character of the first occurrence; otherwise it returns −1.

The method can also take an optional integer parameter that specifies the starting index for the search. If it not specified, the default value is 0. If you specify an index outside the bounds of the string, the method returns −1.

Syntax

```
exampleString.indexOf(substring, startIndex);
```

Examples

```
var myString = "Never give up, never surrender!";
alert(myString.indexOf("up"));     // will alert 11
alert(myString.indexOf("up", 12)); // will alert -1
```

lastIndexOf()

The String.lastIndexOf() method takes a substring as a parameter and searches the string from the end for the substring. If the substring is found, the method returns the index; otherwise it returns –1.

The method can also take an optional integer parameter that specifies the index to start from. If the index is not specified, the method defaults to the length of the string.

Syntax

```
exampleString.lastIndexOf(substring, startIndex);
```

Example

```
var myString = "Never give up, never surrender!";
alert(myString.lastIndexOf("er")); // will alert 28.
```

match()

The String.match() method takes a regular expression object as a parameter, and then runs that regular expression on the string. The method returns an array of matches; if the global flag is not set, then only the first match will be returned. If there is no match, the method returns null.

Syntax

```
exampleString.match(regexp);
```

Examples

```
var regExp = /never/gi,
    slogan = "Never give up, never surrender!",
    otherSlogan = "May the force be with you!";
alert(slogan.match(regExp));      // will alert "Never, never"
alert(otherSlogan.match(regExp)); // will alert "null"
```

replace()

The JavaScript String.replace() method provides a way to search a string for a given pattern and replace it with a given substring. The search parameter can be a regular expression or a string, and the replacement can be either a string or a function. The method returns the modified string, and the original string and parameter strings are not changed.

If you provide a function as a replacement parameter, the function will be executed upon each match. The matched substring will be replaced by the output of the function. The function will be provided with the following parameters, in order:

- match: The matched substring

- paren1, paren2, ..., parenN: The substrings matched by any matching parentheses in the regular expression (if there were any)

- offset: The index in the string of the matched substring

- string: The string being searched

Functions can be supplied as either named functions or inline functions.

Syntax

```
exampleString.replace(searchParam, replaceParam);
```

Examples

```
// Simple find and replace
var slogan = "May the force be with you!";
var newSlogan = slogan.replace("force", "Force"); // newSlogan is now "May the Force be with you!"

// Using a regular expression to search and a function to replace
var slogan = "Never give up, never surrender!",
     regExp = /never/gi,
     newSlogan;
function sarrisify(matchedString) {
    if (matchedString === "Never") {
        return "Always";
    }
    if (matchedString === "never") {
        return "always";
    }
}
newSlogan = slogan.replace(regExp, sarrisify);    // newSlogan is now "Always give up, always
surrender!"
```

search()

The String.search() method takes a regular expression for a substring search as a parameter and executes that search on the string. If the substring is found, the method returns an integer representing the index of the start of the first occurrence of the substring. If the substring is not found, the method returns –1. If you provide a parameter that is not a regular expression, JavaScript will attempt to cast it as if you had created it using the RegExp constructor. (See the "RegExp" section for an explanation on creating regular expressions.)

Syntax

```
exampleString.search(regexp);
```

Example

```
var slogan = "Never give up, never surrender!",
     regexp = /up/i;
alert(slogan.search(regexp));                    // will alert 11
```

slice()

The `String.slice()` method provides a way to extract a substring from a larger string based on character indexes.
The method takes two parameters:

- `startIndex`: An integer representing the start index of the substring. Negative integers are
  permitted and represent an index counted from the end of the string.

- `endIndex`: An integer representing the end index of the substring. This parameter is optional;
  if it is omitted, the method will extract to the end of the target string. Negative integers are
  permitted, and represent indexes from the end of the string. Note that the character at this
  index is *not* contained in the returned slice.

The method returns the specified substring. The target string is not changed. Compare to `String.substr()`.

Syntax

```
exampleString.slice(startIndex, endIndex);
```

Example

```
var slogan = "Never give up, never surrender!";
var mySlice = slogan.slice(1, 5); // mySlice is now "ever"
```

split()

The `String.split()` method provides a way of converting a string to an array. The method takes as a parameter
a string that represents a delimiter. The method searches through the target string and splits it along each occurrence
of the delimiter (which is not included in the new substrings). The substrings are then placed in order into an array,
which is what the method returns. If the delimiter is not provided, the entire string is returned as the first element in
an array.
   The method also takes an optional `limit` parameter, which is an integer representing the maximum number of
elements in the returned array. If the parameter is omitted, all elements are returned.
   The target string is not altered.

Syntax

```
exampleString.split(delimiter, limit);
```

Example

```
var slogan = "Never give up, never surrender!";
var arrWords = slogan.split(" "); // split the slogan along the spaces, resulting in the array
["Never", "give", "up,", "never", "surrender!"]
```

substr()

The `String.substr()` method provides a way of extracting a substring from a larger string based on a starting
index and a length. The method takes two parameters: `startIndex`, which is an integer representing the start of the
substring, and `length`, which is an integer representing the desired length of the new substring.
   The `startIndex` parameter can be a positive or negative integer, or 0. If it is a positive integer, it represents the
index from the start of the string; if it is a negative integer, it represents the index from the end of the string.
   If the `length` parameter is omitted, the method will return the substring starting at the specified starting index all
the way to the end of the target string. If the `length` parameter would specify a substring longer than is available in the
target string, the method will return the substring through the end of the target string.

Syntax

```
exampleString.substr(startIndex, length);
```

Examples

```
var slogan = "Never give up, never surrender!";
var subString = slogan.substr(15, 5);     // subString is now "never"
var newSlogan = slogan.substr(15);        // newSlogan is now "never surrender!"
```

substring()

The `String.substring()` method provides a way to extract a substring from a larger string based on character indexes. The method takes two parameters:

- `startIndex`: An integer representing the start index of the substring. Negative integers are not permitted and will cause the method to return an empty string.

- `endIndex`: An integer representing the end index of the substring. This parameter is optional; if it is omitted, the method will extract to the end of the target string. Negative integers are permitted, and represent indexes from the end of the string. Note that the character at this index is not included in the returned substring.

The method returns the specified substring. The target string is not changed. Compare to `String.slice()`.

Syntax

```
exampleString.substring(startIndex, endIndex);
```

Example

```
var slogan = "Never give up, never surrender!";
var mySubstring = slogan.substring(1, 5); // mySubstring is now "ever"
```

toLowerCase()

The `String.toLowerCase()` method returns the target string with all characters converted to lowercase. The target string itself is not affected.

Syntax

```
exampleString.toLowerCase();
```

Example

```
var slogan = "Never give up, never surrender!";
alert(slogan.toLowerCase());              // will alert "never give up, never surrender!"
```

toUpperCase()

The `String.toUpperCase()` method returns the target string with all characters converted to uppercase. The target string itself is not affected.

Syntax

```
exampleString.toUpperCase();
```

Example

```
var slogan = "Never give up, never surrender!";
alert(slogan.toUpperCase()); // will alert "NEVER GIVE UP, NEVER SURRENDER!"
```

trim()

The String.trim() method returns the target string with all leading and trailing whitespaces removed. The original target string is not changed.

Syntax

```
exampleString.trim();
```

Example

```
var myString = "   hello world   ";
alert(myString.trim());      // will alert "hello world"
```

trimLeft()

The String.trimLeft() method returns the target string with all leading whitespaces removed. The original target string is not changed.

Syntax

```
exampleString.trimLeft ();
```

Example

```
var myString = "   hello world   ";
alert(myString.trimLeft()); // will alert "hello world   "
```

trimRight()

The String.trimRight() method returns the target string with all trailing whitespaces removed. The original target string is not changed.

Syntax

```
exampleString.trimRight();
```

Example

```
var myString = "   hello world   ";
alert(myString.trimRight()); // will alert "   hello world"
```

Miscellaneous Global Variables and Functions

This section covers the miscellaneous variables and functions that also exist within the JavaScript global scope. Many of these are not well-known but can be very useful.

Variables

JavaScript makes a few important variables available in the global scope.

Infinity

`Infinity` is a number representing infinity. There is no difference between this and `Number.POSITIVE_INFINITY`.

Syntax

```
Infinity
```

Example

```
alert(Infinity == Number.POSITIVE_INFINITY); // will alert true
```

JSON

`JSON` is a global object that collects the methods related to creating and reading JSON formatted data. We won't cover JSON in detail here; for more information about JSON, see `www.json.org`.

JSON.parse()

The `JSON.parse()` method parses a JSON string and then re-creates and returns the object it represents. The method takes a JSON string parameter. If the string does not parse as valid JSON, the method will throw a Syntax Error exception.

The method also takes an optional transformation function. The transformation function provides a way to examine JSON key/value pairs and provide a different value if desired. The function takes two parameters, key and value, and returns only the value, which is then used as the value in the `JSON` object. If the function returns `undefined` or nothing at all, the key is deleted from the JSON object.

Note that the translation function will be called on each key/value pair in the object in order. Then, once all of the key/value pairs have been processed, the translation function is called once more and given the empty string as a key and the reconstituted object itself. You can modify the object further at this point, or return it as is (if you do not handle this last step correctly, the translation will fail).

Translation functions are sometimes used to transform values from strings to objects—for example, if a value were a string that was formatted like a date, the translator could actually create a `Date` object based on that string and return that. When used in this capacity, the function is sometimes called a *reviver*.

Syntax

```
JSON.parse(jsonString, translator);
```

Examples

```
var myJsonString = '{"one" : 1, "two" : 2, "three" : 3}';
myObject = JSON.parse(myJsonString);
alert(myObject.one);                    // will alert 1

function myNumeralTranslator(key, value) {
    if (key === "one") {
        return "I";
    } else if (key === "two") {
        return "II";
    } else if (key === "three") {
        return "III"
    } else {
        return value;
    }
}
myNumeralObject = JSON.parse(myJsonString, myNumeralTranslator);
alert(myNumeralObject.two);             // Will alert "II"
```

In this example, we create a simple JSON-formatted string with three key/value pairs. First we restore it to an object as is, then we create a translation function to change the integers to Roman numerals, and then we use that to restore the same string to a different object.

```
var purchaseJsonString = '{"type" : "gift", "method" : "cash", "date" :
"2013-01-28T05:08:11.873Z"}';
function revivePurchase(key, value) {
    if (key === "date") {
        return new Date(value);
    } else {
        return value;
    }
}
var myPurchase = JSON.parse(purchaseJsonString, revivePurchase);
alert(myPurchase.method);               // will alert "cash";
alert(myPurchase.date.toUTCString()); // will alert "Mon, 28 Jan 2013 :05:08:11 GMT"
```

In this example, we create a JSON-formatted string containing some purchase information, including a value that contains a date-formatted string. We then build a simple reviver function that looks for the date and creates a new Date object with that value.

JSON.stringify()

The JSON.stringify() method takes an object as a parameter and returns the corresponding JSON string.

The method also can take an optional filter parameter, which can be use to filter the key/value pairs included in the JSON string. The parameter can be either an array or a function.

If the filter parameter is an array, then the members should represent the keys that will be included in the string. Keys that are not in the filter array will not be included in the JSON string.

If the `filter` is a function, it will be passed the key and value as parameters, and should return the desired value for that key. If the returned value is `undefined` or nothing at all, the key is not included in the JSON string.

Syntax

```
JSON.stringify(object, filter);
```

Examples

```
var myObject   = {"a" : 1, "b" : 2, "foo" : "bar"},
    arrFilter = ["a", "foo"];
function myFilter(key, value) {
    if (key === "a") {
        return undefined;
    } else {
        return value;
    }
}

var firstString = JSON.stringify(myObject ); // stringifies entire object
var secondString = JSON.stringify(myObject, arrFilter);        // Leaves out "b", only stringifies
"a" and "foo"
var thirdString = JSON.stringify(myObject, myFilter);          // leaves out "a", only stringifies
"b" and "foo"
alert(firstString + "\n" + secondString + "\n" + thirdString);  // Compare all three results.
```

NaN

The NaN property is the special "Not a Number" property in JavaScript. This property is only used internally in JavaScript and should not be used in comparisons. To determine if something is NaN, use the `isNaN()` method discussed in the upcoming "Functions" section.

undefined

The undefined property is the primitive value for undefined in JavaScript. The following things are considered undefined:

- Any variable that has been defined but not assigned a value

- Statements that attempt to evaluate such undefined variables

- Functions that do not have an explicit return value (either by not using the `return` keyword or by logic)

See Chapter 2 for an in-depth discussion of undefined and how to determine if things are undefined in JavaScript.

Note that in earlier implementations of JavaScript, this property is writable, allowing scripts to override the value. In the ECMAScript 5 standard (which corresponds to JavaScript 1.8.5), this property is read-only. Overriding such an important value is considered bad practice.

Functions

JavaScript also provides several convenience functions in the global scope.

decodeURI(), encodeURI(), decodeURIComponent(), encodeURIComponent()

These methods provide convenience routines for encoding and decoding entire URIs as well as their individual components (e.g., the query string).

The encoding methods do not encode alphanumeric characters or the characters - _ . ! ~ * ' (and). In addition, the encodeURI() method will not encode the reserved characters ; , / ? : @ & = + $ and #. All other characters will be replaced with one, two, three, or four escape sequences representing the UTF-8 encoding of that character.

Syntax

```
decodeURI(encodedURI);
encodeURI(unencodedURI);
decodeURIComponent(encodedURI);
encodeURIComponent(unencodedURI);
```

Example

```
var myURI = 'http://www.apress.com/?foo=bar&a="something new"';
alert(encodeURI(myURI)); // will alert http://www.apress.com?foo=bar&a=%22something%20new%22
```

eval()

The eval() method takes a string parameter and parses it as JavaScript. The string can contain references to objects present in the scope in which eval() was called.

For an in-depth discussion of eval and its caveats and alternatives, see Chapter 2.

Syntax

```
eval(target);
```

Example

```
var myString = "10 + 2";
var myResult = eval(myString);
alert(myResult);          // will alert 12
```

isFinite()

The isFinite() method checks the parameter and returns true if it is a finite number or false if not. This is a convenience routine for checking finite numbers instead of using equalities.

Beware: the method also returns false if the parameter is NaN.

Syntax

```
isFinite(target);
```

Examples

```
alert(isFinite(243988));                 // will alert true
alert(isFinite(Number.NEGATIVE_INFINITY)); // will alert false
```

isNaN()

The isNaN() method checks the parameter and returns true if it is NaN and false otherwise.

Under the hood, this method first coerces the parameter to a numeric value if it isn't already one. Then it checks to see if the resulting numeric value is equivalent to NaN. This behavior occasionally trips up JavaScript novices, who think the method can be used to determine if something is a numeric value or not.

Syntax

```
isNaN(target);
```

Examples

```
alert(isNaN(10));    // will alert false
alert(isNaN("10")); // will alert false even though strings are not numbers; "10" coerces to 10
which is not equal to NaN
alert(isNaN(""));    // will alert false
alert(isNaN(NaN));  // will alert true
```

parseFloat()

The parseFloat() method parses the supplied parameter and attempts to return the numeric decimal value that is contained in the beginning of the string. Basically, the method starts at the beginning of the string and builds the number. If it encounters a character that is not a number, an exponent, a decimal point, or a sign (+ or –), the method will stop and return any number it has already created. If the first character of the string cannot be converted to a number (with the exception of spaces), this method returns NaN.

Syntax

```
parseFloat(target);
```

Examples

```
var myString = "This will return NaN",
    mySecondString = "10.27 this will return 10.27",
    myThirdString = "Even though this has 10.27 in it, it will return NaN",
    myFourthString = "10.27 50.20 this will return only the first number, 10.27";
alert(parseFloat(myString) + "\n" + parseFloat(mySecondString) + "\n" +
parseFloat(myThirdString) + "\n" + parseFloat(myFourthString));
```

parseInt( )

The parseInt() method parses the parameter and returns the numeric integer value that is contained in the beginning of the string. The method starts at the beginning of the string and builds the number. If it encounters a character that is not a number, an exponent, a decimal point, or a sign (+ or –) the method will stop and return the number that has been created. If the first character of the string cannot be converted to a number (with the exception of spaces), this method will return NaN.

Syntax

```
parseInt(target);
```

Examples

```
var myString = "This will return NaN",
    mySecondString = "10.97 this will return 10",
    myThirdString = "Even though this has 10.27 in it, it will return NaN",
    myFourthString = "10.97 50.20 this will return only the first number, 10";
alert(parseInt(myString) + "\n" + parseInt(mySecondString) + "\n" + parseInt(myThirdString) + "\n" +
parseInt(myFourthString));
```

Summary

In this chapter we have covered the properties and methods of several global objects and how they are used:

- You can create arrays either by using literal notation or by using the Array object as a constructor.

- JavaScript silently wraps string and boolean literals with their associated objects when needed.

- You can create strings and booleans using their associated global objects as constructors, but there is little need to.

- The Date object provides a plethora of properties and methods for manipulating dates.

- JavaScript has a fully functional implementation of regular expressions via its RegExp global object.

- The Math object provides many static properties and methods related to mathematics.

In addition, we covered several other global functions and variables, including: the JSON object, which provides functionality for creating and manipulating JSON serializations.

In the next chapter, we'll provide a similar reference for all of the available control statements in JavaScript, and provide examples of their use.

CHAPTER 6

JavaScript Control Statements Reference

Introduction

As we discussed in Chapter 2, JavaScript has the usual control statements you would expect for a C-like language:

- do loops
- for and for/in loops
- while loops
- if-else conditionals
- switch conditionals

In addition, JavaScript provides ways to manage your loop iterations, break out of loops entirely, and even limit the scope of your loops.

In this chapter we'll provide a solid reference for all JavaScript control statements, in alphabetical order. For detailed discussions of these statements, see Chapter 2.

break

The break statement terminates the current loop or the current label or switch statement. The statement takes an optional label, which corresponds to the label of the loop to break.

Syntax

```
break label;
```

Example

```
// Set up a loop that would ordinarily alert 0 through 10, but instead breaks at 2.
var i = 0;
while (i <= 10) {
    alert(i);
    if (i === 2) {
        break;
    } else {
        i++
    }
}
```

continue

The continue statement stops the current iteration of the loop and moves on to the next. The statement takes an optional label that refers to the label of the loop to interrupt.

The continue statement can only be used inside of for loops, for/in loops, and while and do/while loops. If used within a for loop, the loop will jump back to its incrementation expression, execute it, and then check to see if it should continue.

If used within a for/in loop, the loop will proceed to the next field and continue looping from there.

If used within a while or do/while loop, the loop will immediately retest the conditional and continue or not depending on that result.

■ **Note** Use continue judiciously. It's easy to write code that uses continue that is difficult to read and maintain. It's not uncommon, in fact, to see style guides specify that continue should be avoided entirely.

Syntax

```
continue label
```

Example

```
var i;
for (i = 0; i < 11; i++) {
    if (i < 4) continue;
    alert(i);
    if (i < 7) continue;
    alert(10 * i);
}
```

In this example, we create a loop that iterates the variable i from 0 to 10 (details on for loops are provided a bit later). If i < 4, we do nothing. Once i is 5 or higher, we start to alert its value. And once i > 6, we start to alert 10 * i. So this script will alert, in order, 4, 5, 6, 7, 70, 8, 80, 9, 90, 10, and 100.

This is a somewhat contrived example, but it does illustrate one of the commonly used patterns for continue: layered tests. In this case, we are layering simple checks on the value of the iterator of our loop, but a layered test could be any test on anything that will change as your particular loop progresses.

Of course, this example could be rewritten so that it doesn't use continue at all:

```
var i;
for (i = 0; i < 11; i++) {
    if (i > 3) {
        alert(i);
    }
    if (i > 6) {
        alert(10 * i);
    }
}
```

Either way is valid.

do/while

The do/while loop creates a loop with a conditional test at the end. Because the conditional is evaluated at the end of each loop, the loop will execute at least once.

Syntax

```
do {
    // things
} while (conditional);
```

Example

```
// A way to alert only odd numbers
var i = 1;
do {
    alerti);
    i = i + 2;
} while (i <= 10);
```

for and for/in

In JavaScript, for loops can be set up as either for or for/in loops.

for

In a basic for loop, the for statement takes three parameters:

- An initializer, which is run once when the loop first starts.

- A conditional, which is tested each time the loop executes. If it evaluates as true, the loop is executed; if false, the loop terminates and control passes to the next statement after the for loop.

- An expression, which is executed at the end of every loop.

Any variables declared in the initializer have the same scope as the for statement.

Syntax

```
for (initializer, conditional, expression) {
    // do things
}
```

Example

```
// Another way to alert odd numbers
for (var i = 1; i <= 10; i = i +2) {
    alert(i);
}
```

for/in

A for/in loop iterates over an object, providing access to each property. The for statement takes two parameters, the property and the object. This provides a convenient way to enumerate objects, as discussed in Chapter 2.

Syntax

```
for (property in object) {
    // Do things
}
```

Example

```
// All-purpose enumeration loop
var testObject = {
    property1 : "this is a test object.",
    property2 : 1,
    arrIntegers : [1, 2, 3, 4],
    boolIsTrue : true
}

var strAlert = "";
for (var thing in testObject) {
    strAlert += thing + ": " + testObject[thing] + "\n";
}
alert(strAlert);
```

This example will enumerate all of the properties of our testObject in one alert:

if

The if statement provides the standard logical flow control for JavaScript. An if statement evaluates its parameter, and if that parameter is true, the statement will execute the conditional code.

An if statement can be followed by an else statement, which will execute if the parameter evaluates to false. An else statement may similarly be followed by an if statement, allowing for chaining of conditionals.

Syntax

```
if (condition) {
    // conditional code, executed if condition is true
}
```

```
if (condition) {
    // conditional code to be executed if condition is true
} else {
    // conditional code to be executed if condition is false
}

if (condition1) {
    // conditional code to be executed if condition1 is true
} else if (condition2) {
    // conditional code to be executed if condition2 is true
} else {
    // conditional code to be executed if both condition1 and condition2 are false.
}
```

Example

```
// Play with random numbers
var myNumber = Math.floor((Math.random() * 100) + 1); // Generate a random number from 1 to 100
if (myNumber <= 10) {
    alert("number is less than 10");
} else if (myNumber <=50) {
    alert("number is less than 50");
} else {
    alert("Number is frighteningly large.");
}
```

label

The label statement associates an identifier with a particular statement that can be referred to using break or continue.

Labels are considered bad practice in JavaScript because they make code difficult to read. Typically, instead of using a label, you can use a named function.

Syntax

```
label:
    statement
```

Example

```
outerloop:
for (var i =0; i < 5; i++) {
    innerloop:
    for (var j = 0; j < 5; j++) {
        if ((i == 2) && (j == 2)) {
            continue outerloop; // skip when both indices are 2
        } else {
            alert(i  + ", " + j);
        }
    }
}
```

return

The return statement is used to specify the return value of a function. The value can be any valid JavaScript data type: a string, boolean, array, function, date, regular expression, etc.

Syntax

```
return value;
```

Example

```
// Trivial function to test whether a value is less than ten or simply too large to understand.
function testValue(intValue) {
    if (intValue < = 10) {
        return "value is less than ten";
    } else {
        return "value is terrifyingly large.";
    }
}
var niceNumber = 5,
    scaryNumber = 20909239;

alert(testValue(niceNumber));  // will alert "value is less than ten"
alert(testValue(scaryNumber)); // will alert "value is terrifyingly large"
```

switch/case

switch statements provide a convenient way of providing different conditionals based on multiple values of a given expression.

A switch statement evaluates an expression, then searches for a case associated with that result. If a case is found, the associated conditional code is executed.

In addition, each conditional code block can contain an optional break statement at the end. If present, the switch statement will end immediately; if not, the switch statement will continue searching for matching case statements.

Syntax

```
switch (expression) {
    case value1:
        conditional1
        break;
    case value2:
        conditional2
        break;
    case value3:
        conditional3
        break;
    default
        default conditional
}
```

Example

```
switch(booze) {
    case "tequila":
        alert("Margarita time!");
        break;
    case "vodka":
        alert("Mr. Bond, is that you?");
        break;
    case "scotch":
        alert("Aye.");
        break;
    default:1
        alert("But why is the rum gone?");
}
```

In this example, we're switching on the ever-popular booze variable; depending on its value, we'll get an appropriate alert.

Here's a fully functional example that switches on literary subgenres:

```
var leftBehind = "religious";
var dogstar = "apocalyptic";
var kinglear = "shakespeare";

function defineSubGenre(strType) {
    var strResult = "";
    switch (strType) {
        case "religious":
            strResult += "religious ";
        case "apolcalyptic":
            strResult += "apocalyptic ";
        case "science fiction":
            strResult += "science ";
        default:
            strResult += "fiction";
    }
    return strResult;
}

alert(defineSubGenre(leftBehind)); // will alert "religious apocalyptic science fiction"
alert(defineSubGenre(dogstar));    // will alert "apocalyptic science fiction"
alert(defineSubGenre(kinglear));   // will alert "fiction"
```

In this example, we're demonstrating the use of a switch statement without break statements. This works well with cases of increasing generality that contain one another: fiction contains the subgenre science fiction; science fiction contains the subgenre apocalyptic fiction; and apocalyptic science fiction contains the subgenre religious apocalyptic science fiction.

The switch statement builds a return string, which the function returns. We try three different books: one for "religious" (which alerts "religious apocalyptic science fiction"), one for "apocalyptic" (which alerts "apocalyptic science fiction"), and one for "shakespeare" (which alerts just "fiction").

while

The while statement creates a loop that will continue to execute each time the specified expression evaluates to true. The expression is evaluated before each iteration of the loop. (Compare with do...while loops, where the conditional test is at the end.)

Syntax

```
while (expression) {
    // code to execute each time
}
```

Example

```
// alert the integers 1 through 10
var i = 0;
while (i < 11) {
    alert(i);
    i++;
}
```

with

The with statement modifies the scope chain for a given block of code. Recall that if you access a variable, JavaScript checks to see if it is defined within the immediate scope. If the variable is not found, JavaScript checks the containing scope, and so on, up to the global scope. The with statement adds the specified object to the head of the scope chain, ensuring that it gets searched for all scope lookups that happen within a given block of code.

Although it was originally included in the language as a convenience, the with statement is considered bad practice because it can make code difficult to read and maintain, and is in fact forbidden in ECMAScript 5 strict mode. If you are going to use the with statement, remember that every scope lookup that happens within the specified block of code will check the specified object first, so you should try to limit the following:

- Scope lookups in the managed block of code to the specified object

- The complexity of the object

Limiting both of these will help the efficiency of your code.

Syntax

```
with (object) {
    // statements with scope limited to object
}
```

Example

```
alert(Math.PI); // will alert the value of PI.
// Limit the scope to just Math
with(Math) {
    alert(PI);   // will alert the value of PI.
    alert(cos(PI));
}
```

Summary

In this chapter we have covered JavaScript's control statements, which are used to direct the logical flow of your programs:

- JavaScript's control statements are similar to those found in other C-like languages.

- JavaScript has two conditional flow control statements: `if` statements and `switch` statements.

- JavaScript has four different methods for looping: `do...while`, `for`, `for-in`, and `while`.

- You can modify loop execution with the `break` and `continue` statements.

- The `with` statement modifies the scope chain, but is considered bad practice.

- JavaScript has the concept of `label` statements, but they are considered bad practice as well.

In the next chapter, we'll provide a reference for JavaScript operators, including assignment operators, arithmetic operators, and comparison operators.

CHAPTER 7

JavaScript Operators Reference

In JavaScript, *operators* perform operations on expressions. The expressions that the operators operate on are called *operands*. JavaScript supports unary operators (operators that work on one expression, like the increment operator), binary operators (operators that require two expressions, like most mathematical operators), and one ternary operator (which requires three expressions).

Operators in JavaScript can be grouped into seven broad categories:

- *Assignment*: Assign values to variables
- *Comparison*: Compare values
- *Arithmetic*: Perform basic arithmetic—addition, subtraction, modulus, etc.
- *Bitwise*: Modify operands based on their binary representations
- *Logical*: Logical constructions like AND and OR
- *String*: Modifies strings (this category includes only one operator)
- *Miscellaneous*: Catch-all group for remaining operators that don't fit in the other categories

We'll cover each of these categories in order in this reference.

Assignment Operators

JavaScript assignment operators are used to assign values to their left operand based on the value of their right operand, the simplest example of which is the basic assignment operator =:

```
x = 1;
strLocation = "California";
boolSuccess = false;
```

JavaScript has several other assignment operators that are shorthand for other operations. These shorthand operators, listed in Table 7-1, provide a way to write more concise code.

Table 7-1. *Shorthand Mathematical Operators*

Shorthand Operator	Equivalent Expression
operand1 += operand2	operand1 = operand1 + operand2
operand1 -= operand2	operand1 = operand1 - operand2
operand1 *= operand2	operand1 = operand1 * operand2
operand1 /= operand2	operand1 = operand1 / operand2

Examples

```
var num1 = 5,
num2 = 9;
num1 += num2; // num1 is now 13
num1 -= num2; // num1 (which was 13) is now 5 again
num1 *= num2; // num1 is now 45
num1 /= num2; // num1 is now 5 again
```

Note that if either of the operands is a string, the shorthand operator += will perform a string concatenation rather than an arithmetical addition. If the other operand is not a string, it will be cast as one first. See "String Operator," later in the chapter, for more information.

JavaScript also supports several shorthand binary operators, listed in Table 7-2. Binary operators operate on their operands by modifying the bits that compose them. For a full discussion of binary operators, see the "Bitwise Operators" section later in the chapter.

Table 7-2. *Shorthand Bitwise Operators*

Shorthand Operator	Equivalent Expression
operand1 %= operand2	operand1 = operand1 % operand2
operand1 ^= operand2	operand1 = operand1 ^ operand2
operand1 <<= operand2	operand1 = operand1 << operand2
operand1 >>= operand2	operand1 = operand1 >> operand2
operand1 >>> operand2	operand1 = operand1 >>> operand2
operand1 |= operand2	operand1 = operand1 | operand2

Example

```
var num1 = 100,
    num2 = 50;
num1 %= num2; // num1 is now 0
```

Comparison Operators

Comparison operators are used to compare two operands. Since JavaScript is weakly typed, it has two different kinds of comparisons: strict and coerced.

In *strict* comparisons, the operator compares both the value of the operands and their type. If either doesn't match, the comparison returns false. For example, the strict comparison true === "true" evaluates to false because true is a boolean, which is a different type than "true", which is a string.

In *coerced* comparisons, the operator converts the operands to the same type before comparing their values. This conversion process, called *casting* or *coercing*, follows very specific algorithms defined in the ECMA-262 standard, so the results are perfectly predictable—as long as you're familiar with the algorithms. If you're not, the results can be counterintuitive. For example:

```
if ("true") {
    alert("true" == true);  // will alert false
    alert("true" == false); // will alert false
}
```

This example will fire both alerts, which will be `false` even though the `if` statement surrounding them must have evaluated to `true` for the alerts to even happen.

To avoid confusion, it's considered good practice when writing JavaScript to use strict comparisons whenever possible, and use coerced comparisons either when no casting will happen or when it will happen but will produce a known desirable outcome. For example, the `toString()` method on objects by definition only ever returns a string, so if you are comparing to a string literal, there is no need to do a strict comparison because casting will never happen:

```
// toString only ever returns a string, so no need for strict comparison with a string literal
if (myObject.toString() == "string literal") {
    // (do stuff)
}
// The variable testVar might change types, so a strict comparison is a good idea
if (myObject.toString() === testVar) {
    // (do stuff)
}
```

For details on the coercion algorithms that JavaScript uses, see Chapter 1.

Strict Comparisons

When using strict comparison operators, JavaScript compares both the value and the type of the operands. The two strict comparison operators are strict equality (`===`), which returns `true` if both operands are equal in value and type, and strict inequality (`!==`), which returns `true` if the operands are different in either type or value.

Syntax

```
operand1 === operand2
operand1 !== operand2
```

Examples

```
var boolOperand1 = true,
    boolOperand2 = false,
    intOperand1 = 1,
    intOperand2 = 2,
    strOperand1 = "1",
    strOperand2 = "2";

alert(boolOperand1 === boolOperand2); // will alert false
alert(boolOperand1 !== boolOperand2); // will alert true
alert(intOperand1 !== intOperand2);   // will alert true
alert(intOperand1 === strOperand1);   // will alert false
alert(strOperand1 === strOperand2);   // will alert false
```

Coerced Comparisons

When doing coerced comparisons, JavaScript first converts the operands to the same data type before comparing their values (see Table 7-3 for more information). For details on how JavaScript performs type coercion, see Chapter 1.

Table 7-3. *Coerced Comparison Operators*

Operation	Syntax	Returns
Equality	operand1 == operand2	true if the values of the operands are the same. If both operands are objects, this operator returns true if the two objects refer to the same object in memory.
Inequality	operand1 != operand2	true if the values of the operands are not the same. If both operands are objects, this operator returns true if they refer to different objects in memory.
Greater than	operand1 > operand2	true if operand1 is greater than operand2.
Less than	operand1 < operand2	true if operand1 is less than operand2.
Greater than or equal to	operand1 >= operand2	true if operand1 is greater than or equal to operand2.
Less than or equal to	operand1 <= operand2	true if operand1 is less than or equal to operand2.

Examples

```
var strOperand1 = "1",
    intOperand1 = 1,
    boolOperand1 = true;
alert(strOperand1 == intOperand1);  // will alert true
alert(intOperand1 == boolOperand1); // will alert true
alert(strOperand1 == boolOperand1); // will alert true
```

Arithmetic Operators

JavaScript has a set of basic arithmetic operators, listed in Table 7-4, that perform the specified arithmetical operation on the operands.

Table 7-4. *Arithmetic Operators*

Operation	Syntax	Returns
Addition	operand1 + operand2	The sum of operand1 and operand2.
Subtraction	operand1 - operand2	The difference of operand1 and operand2.
Multiplication	operand1 * operand2	The product of operand1 and operand2.
Division	operand1 / operand2	The quotient of operand1 divided by operand2.
Modulus	operand1 % operand2	; returns operand1 modulo operand2.

(continued)

Table 7-4. (*continued*)

Operation	Syntax	Returns
Increment by 1	operand1++ (or ++operand)	operand1++ returns the value of operand1 before incrementing, while ++operand1 returns the value of operand1 after incrementing.
Decrement by 1	operand1-- (or --operand)	operand1-- returns the value of operand1 before decrementing, while --operand1 returns the value of operand1 after decrementing.
Negative value	- operand1	The negative value of operand1. operand1 remains unchanged.
Positive value	+ operand1	The positive value of operand1. operand1 remains unchanged.

Note that all arithmetic operators in JavaScript will attempt to perform type coercion for non-numeric operands, which can have nonintuitive results. See Chapter 1 for more information about JavaScript's type coercion rules.

Examples

```
var intOperand1 = 1,
    intOperand2 = 2,
    boolOperand1 = true;
alert(intOperand1 + intOperand2);  // will alert 3
alert(intOperand1 + boolOperand1); // will alert 2
var testResult = intOperand1++;
alert(testResult);                 // will alert 1
alert(intOperand1);                // will alert 2
testResult = ++intOperand2;
alert(testResult);                 // will alert 3
alert(intOperand2);                // will alert 3
```

Bitwise Operators

JavaScript's bitwise operators take integer operands and perform operations on them based on their 32-bit representations. Non-integer operands are first coerced (see Chapter 1). And although the bitwise operators perform on a bit level, they return integers.

A Bit About Binary Numbers

JavaScript's bitwise operators, see Table 7-5, all convert their operands into signed 32-bit integers. In general, 32-bit integers can have their most significant bit on the left, with bits decreasing in significance from left to right, or they can have their most significant bit on the right, with significance decreasing from right to left. The former is referred to as *big-endian* notation, while the latter is referred to as *little-endian* notation. The origin of these terms is Jonathan Swift's novel *Gulliver's Travels*, which tells the tale of the ongoing tensions between the rival kingdoms of Lilliput (whose inhabitants crack their soft-boiled eggs on the small end) and Blefescu (whose inhabitants crack their soft-boiled eggs on the large end).

Table 7-5. *Bitwise Operators*

Operation	Syntax	Details
Bitwise AND	`operand1 & operand2`	Compares each bit position in both operands and returns a new number formed by placing a 1 in each bit position where both operands have a 1.
Bitwise OR	`operand1	operand2`	Compares each bit position in both operands and returns a new number formed by placing a 1 in each bit position where either operand has a 1.
Bitwise XOR	`operand1 ^ operand2`	Compares each bit position in both operands and returns a new number formed by placing a 1 in each position where either operand (but not both) has a 1.
Bitwise NOT	`~ operand1`	Returns a new number formed by inverting the bits of `operand1`.
Bitwise left shift	`operand1 << operand2`	Returns a new number formed by shifting `operand1`'s bits to the left by the number of positions specified by `operand2`, with zeros padded on the right.
Bitwise sign-propagating right shift	`operand1 >> operand2`	Returns a new number formed by shifting `operand1`'s bits to the right by the number of positions specified by `operand2`. Bits that are shifted off are discarded rather than wrapped (thus preserving the sign bit).
Bitwise zero-fill right shift	`operand1 >>> operand2`	Returns a new number formed by shifting `operand1`'s bits to the right by the number of positions specified by `operand2`. Bits that are shifted off are discarded. Zeros are filled in from the left.

JavaScript's 32-bit integers are big-endian, so the largest bit is always to the left, and *two's complement*, meaning negative numbers are the bitwise inversion of their positive value, plus one.

As a practical example, let's convert the number 5 into a JavaScript binary number. In binary, 5 is represented as 101. In big-endian format, the most significant bit is on the left. 101 is only 3 bits; to make it a 32-bit number, we have to pad it with zeros:

`00000000000000000000000000000101`

That's the 32-bit big-endian representation of the number 5. JavaScript converts operands into this format before performing any bitwise operations on them.

Bitwise operations are fairly uncommon in JavaScript. For some useful nontrivial examples, see Chapter 4.

Logical Operators

JavaScript has a set of logical operators, listed in Table 7-6, that are used to implement boolean logic. Typically these are used in conjunction with flow-control statements.

Table 7-6. *Logical Operators*

Operation	Syntax	Returns
Logical AND	operand1 && operand2	true if both operands are true.
Logical OR	operand1 || operand2	true if either operand is true.
Logical NOT	!operand1	false if operand is true and returns true if operand is false.

Examples

```
if (expression1 && expression2) {
    // Do something if both expression1 and expression2 are true
}
var boolFalse = !true;
alert(boolFalse); // will alert false
if (expression1 && !expression2) {
    // Do something if expression1 is true and expression2 is false
}
```

String Operator

JavaScript has a single string operator: the concatenation operator +. This operator returns both operands concatenated together. If one of the operands is not a string, it will be converted to a string by this operator.

Example

```
var strString1 = "Hello",
    strString2 = "World";
alert(strString1 + " " + strString2); // will alert Hello World
```

Miscellaneous Operators

Now that we've covered the major categories of operators, we're left with a few operators that don't quite fit but are nonetheless important. These operators include the only ternary operator in JavaScript, the conditional operator, as well as some useful operators for examining data types and manipulating objects and their properties.

Conditional Operator

The conditional operator is JavaScript's only ternary operator. It provides a shorthand for if/then/else statements.

Some JavaScript style guides recommend avoiding the conditional operator in favor of explicit if/then/else statements to make code more readable.

Syntax

```
conditional ? trueOperand : falseOperand // If conditional is true, evaluate trueOperand, otherwise
evaluate falseOperand
```

Example

```
(3 > 4) ? alert("Three is greater than four") : alert("Three is not greater than four"); // will
alert Three is not greater than four.
```

Comma Operator

The JavaScript comma operator (,) takes two operands. It evaluates both operands and returns the value of the second one. The two most common uses of the comma operator are to define multiple variables in one var statement and to supply multiple parameters in for loops.

Syntax

```
operand1, operand2
```

Examples

```
// Initialize an array of integers
var myArray = [];
for (var i = 0, j = 100; i <= 100; i++, j--) {
    myArray[i] = j;
}

// Multiple variable declarations with one var statement.
var myVar = "one",
    numericVar = 1,
    booleanVar = true;
```

delete Operator

The delete operator takes an object property as an operand and deletes it from its parent object. It returns false if it was unable to delete the property and returns true otherwise.

Syntax

```
delete myObject.myProperty;
delete myObject[myProperty];
delete myArray[index];
```

Examples

```
var myObject = {
    "prop1" : 1,
    "prop2" : "two",
    "prop3" : true
};
alert(delete myObject.prop1);      // will alert true
alert(myObject.prop1);             // will alert undefined
alert(delete myObject["prop2"]);   // will alert true
alert(myObject.prop2);             // will alert undefined
```

Note that you cannot delete properties of predefined objects like Math (so delete Math.PI will return false and not delete the property).

If you delete an overridden property on an object, the original property from the object's prototype will be restored. Also, you cannot delete a property from an object that was inherited from the object's prototype, though you can delete the property directly from the prototype. (See Chapter 1 for a detailed discussion of objects and their prototypes.)

If you delete elements from an array by index, the length of the array will not be affected. The deleted property will simply be undefined:

```
var myArray = [0, 1, 2];
alert(delete myArray[1]); // will alert true
alert(myArray[1]);        // will alert undefined
alert(myArray.length);    // will alert 3
```

function Operator

The JavaScript function operator is used to declare a new function expression. (For an in-depth discussion of functions, function expressions, and function statements, see Chapter 1.)

Syntax

```
function identifier(param1, param2, ..., paramN) {
    // body
}
```

Example

```
var newFunctionExpression = function() {
    alert('This is my new function expression.');
}
newFunctionExpression(); // Will alert "This is my new function expression."
```

get Operator

The JavaScript get operator provides an interface for accessing data within an object. You can use it to define a getter method on an object that can return a value or execute another method.

Syntax

```
// Object literal notation
var myObject = {
    prop1: value,
    get prop1: function() {
        return this.prop1;
    }
}
// object notation
function myObject() {
    // Constructor.
}
myObject.prototype = {
    prop1: value,
    get prop1 : function() {
        return this.prop1;
    }
}
```

Example

```
var myObject = {
    "privateValue" : 10,
    "units" : "degrees",
    get angle () {
        return this.privateValue + " " + this.units;
    }
}
alert(myObject.angle); // will alert "10 degrees"
```

in Operator

The in operator takes two operands: a target object and a target property. It returns true if the target property is in the target object, and returns false otherwise.

Syntax

```
targetProperty in targetObject;
```

Examples

```
var myObject = {
    "prop1" :1,
    "prop2" : "two"
}
alert("prop1" in myObject); // will alert true
alert("two" in myObject);   // will alert false; there is no property named "two"
```

instanceof Operator

The instanceof operator takes two operands: an object and a constructor. It returns true if the object has the constructor in its prototype chain, and returns false if it doesn't.

Syntax

```
targetObject instanceof targetConstructor;
```

Example

```
// Everything in JavaScript is an Object--or maybe not.
var myArray = new Array();
var myBool = true;
alert(myArray instanceof Object);  // will alert true
alert(myBool instanceof Object);   // will alert false--primitives are not objects.
myBool = new Boolean(true);
alert(myBool instanceof Object);   // will alert true, because we constructed a new boolean object,
not just a primitive.
```

In this example, we're demonstrating that primitive values are not objects in JavaScript, while arrays and boolean objects are.

new Operator

The new operator takes an object constructor function as an operand. It then creates a new empty object whose prototype inherits from the operand, sets the context of the constructor function to the empty object (so within the function the keyword this will refer to the empty object), and then invokes the function. If the constructor function does not explicitly return the resulting object, the new keyword will do it for you, allowing you to create and assign new objects as desired. This syntax resembles the syntax for instantiating classes in other languages, but don't forget: JavaScript has no classes and instead has a prototypal inheritance model. For details on JavaScript's inheritance model, see Chapter 1.

Syntax

```
var myNewObject = new objectConstructor;
```

Example

```
var myNewArray = new Array(); // Creates a new array object.
function myConstructor() {
    this.message = "hello world"
}
var myObject = new myConstructor();
alert(myObject.message);        // will alert "hello world"
```

set Operator

The set operator provides an interface for mutating values in an object. Compare it to the get operator described earlier in the chapter.

Syntax

```
// Object literal notation
var myObject = {
    prop1: value,
    get prop1: function() {
        return this.prop1;
    },
    set prop1: function(newVal) {
        this.prop1 = newVal;
    }
}
// object notation
function myObject() {
    // Constructor.
}
myObject.prototype = {
    prop1: value,
    get prop1 : function() {
        return this.prop1;
    },
    set prop1 : function(newVal) {
        this.prop1 = newVal;
    }
}
```

Example

```javascript
var myAngle = {
    "privateValue" : 10,
    "privateUnits" : "degrees",
    get angle() {
        return this.privateValue + " " + this.units;
    },
    set units(newVal) {
        // Allow the user to set the units to either degrees or radians
        if ((newVal !== "degrees") && (newVal !== "radians")) {
            alert("Allowed units are degrees and radians.");
        }
        if (newVal !== this.privateUnits) {
            this.privateUnits = newVal;
            if (newVal === "radians") {
                // Need to convert our value from degrees to radians
                this.privateValue = (this.privateValue * 0.01745);
            } else {
                // need to convert our value from radians to degrees
                this.privateValue = (this.privateValue * 57.3);
            }
        }
    }
}
alert(myAngle.angle); // will alert "10 degrees"
myAngle.units = "radians";
alert(myAngle.angle); // will alert "0.1745 radians"
```

In this example, we're building an object that will automatically convert the angle's units when the units are changed. This is a great example of using a setter in an object to do more than just set an internal value. You could do anything here, including firing a custom event or even modifying properties on other objects. For a great example of using getters and setters for advanced operations, see Chapter 4.

typeof Operator

The typeof operator returns the data type of the operand. A common misconception is that the typeof operator has to be used as a function and its operand has to be placed within parentheses. That's unnecessary. The typeof operator returns the data type of its operand. Novice JavaScript developers commonly mistake typeof as a function, and enclose the operand within parentheses. However, parentheses only serve to group expressions into a single statement, and are thus unnecessary for single operands.

Syntax

```javascript
typeof operand;
```

Examples

```javascript
var myObject = new Object();
var myBoolean = true;
alert(typeof myObject);  // will alert Object
alert(typeof myBoolean); // will alert Boolean
```

void Operator

The void operator evaluates its operand and then returns undefined.

Syntax

```
void operand;
```

Example

```
alert(void 0);           // will alert "undefined"
alert(void(alert("hi"))); // Will alert "hi" first, then will alert "undefined"
```

Summary

In this chapter we've covered JavaScript's various operators in detail:

- Most of JavaScript's operators are unary or binary; the single exception is the comparison operator, which is a ternary operator.

- JavaScript operators include bitwise operators, assignment operators, mathematical operators, string operators, comparison operators, and logic operators.

- You can use the get and set operators to modify properties on objects.

In the next chapter we'll provide a reference for the DOM, including the window and document objects.

■ ■ ■

CHAPTER 8

The DOM Reference

As described in Chapter 3, the DOM isn't JavaScript and it isn't part of the ECMA-262 standard. Instead, the DOM is specified by the W3C across multiple specifications. However, much of what you'll be doing with JavaScript will involve the DOM, so it's important to cover it.

We've already covered the important aspects of the DOM in Chapter 3, including:

- The history of the DOM and the different specifications that comprise it

- Accessing elements in the DOM

- Creating, deleting, and modifying elements in the DOM

- DOM events: handlers, custom events, etc.

This chapter provides a reference for the topics covered in Chapter 3, as well as several other common features of the DOM that we didn't cover in Chapter 3. Because the DOM specifications are quite large, this chapter won't be exhaustive. Instead, we'll focus on the features that are the most commonly used. We'll also cover features that offer highly useful functionality but perhaps aren't commonly used, either because they're new or because they're not often covered in references.

Browser Support

As mentioned in Chapter 3, the DOM has varying support across browsers, and between versions of individual browsers. This reference presumes so-called "modern" browsers: Internet Explorer 9 and later, and the latest versions of auto-updating browsers such as Safari, Firefox, and Chrome. If a particular feature has support problems in these target browsers, we'll mention it. If your project needs to target older browsers, you should make sure the features you want to use are supported in your target browsers. A good reference for ensuring this are the compatibility tables at the QuirksMode.org web site: DOM features are covered at `www.quirksmode.org/dom/w3c_core.html`, and DOM events are covered at `www.quirksmode.org/dom/events/`.

DOM Objects

The most common work you'll be doing with the DOM will involve accessing and manipulating documents and their elements. In this reference we'll focus on the DOM objects that are the most relevant to those tasks:

- `window`: The `window` object models the browser window itself, where the document is loaded. It includes properties and methods to handle scrolling the window, positioning the browser, etc.

- `document`: The `document` object models the document. It has properties and methods for accessing and modifying the contents of the document.

- element: The element object is an abstract object (meaning it is not something you access directly, like window or document, but rather serves as a template from which other objects inherit) that defines the properties and methods exposed on the elements contained within a document. As you work with DOM elements, all of element's properties and methods will be available on them.

We'll cover these objects in the preceding order (rather than alphabetically, as we did for the main JavaScript objects in the reference in Chapter 5) because it represents a progression of containers: the window object contains the document object, and the document object contains element objects.

The Window Object Reference

The window object is the top of the DOM tree and represents a document loaded into the browser. Typically you'll have only one document at a time loaded into the browser, but you can load more than one through the use of iframes. Since each document needs its own window object, by default the window object is an array-like object: the main object represents the main document, the indexed entries represent subdocuments loaded within iframes, and a length property represents the number of subdocuments. Thus, if you have only the main document with no subdocuments, the window.length property will be 0. Each iframe is its own window object, and if a given iframe has subdocuments within it, then it too will have indexed elements with the number of subdocuments represented in its length property as well.

Subdocuments can be accessed via their indices; they are in the same order as they appear in the document. Through the window.parent property, a script in a subdocument can access its parent document. As a result, any script in a document loaded into the browser can have access to any other document loaded into the browser. For security reasons, this access is limited by the Single Origin Policy.

■ **Note**   The Single Origin Policy is a security feature in browsers that is designed to prevent malicious scripts from accessing content they shouldn't. The policy basically says that scripts served from a particular site can access only documents served from that same site. More specifically, both documents must have been served using the same protocol (HTTP or HTTPS) and port (if one was specified), from the same host. If any of those are different, access between documents is not permitted.

The window object also serves as the global context for JavaScript. Each document therefore has its own global context. Because the window object is the global context, you do not need to preface any of its properties or methods with the window. identifier. For example, to access the location property, you can simply use location rather than window.location. However, some properties and methods are accessed with the window. identifier for the sake of explicitness. (For details on creating and managing your own properties and methods in the global scope, see Chapter 2.) In this section we'll explicitly use the window. reference.

Properties

In addition to serving as the global context for JavaScript, the window object has its own properties that you can access with your scripts. These properties represent the various aspects of the browser window and the document loaded within: the URL of the document, the geometry of the window, etc.

window.document

The `window.document` property is the reference to the HTML document that has been loaded into the browser window. (See "The document Object Reference" section later in the chapter.) The document object is one of the properties that traditionally is not referenced using the `window.` identifier.

Syntax

```
document.propertyName;
document.method();
```

window.frames

The `window.frames` property is just a reference to the `window` object itself, and provides a way to explicitly access the different subdocuments loaded into the main document (if any). This property is a holdover from older versions of HTML that supported loading multiple documents in a single window using a frameset, a feature that is no longer supported. Note that since `window.frames` is just a reference to `window`, `window === window.frames` and `window[3] === window.frames[3]` if subdocuments are present.

Syntax

```
window.frames[intIndex];
```

window.history

The `window.history` property is a reference to the `History` object, which is exposed by browsers to provide access to the session history. It is basically a model of the pages that have been visited, along with some useful methods for manipulating them.

Properties

The `History` object has one property, `length`.

length

The `length` property refers to the length of the history—the number of pages that have been loaded into the window. A new window (or tab) that has had a single document loaded into it would have a `window.history.length` of 1.

Syntax

```
var myLength = window.history.length;
```

Methods

The `History` object has three methods to navigate the browser history.

back()

The `back()` method moves back one entry in the browser history. If you're already at the beginning of the history, calling this method has no effect. Calling this method is the equivalent of clicking the browser's Back button.

Syntax

```
window.history.back();
```

forward()

The `forward()` method moves forward one entry in the browser history. If you're already at the end of the browser history, this method does nothing. Calling this method is the equivalent of clicking the browser's Forward button.

Syntax

```
window.history.forward();
```

go()

The `go()` method traverses the browser history by the specified number of entries. A positive number moves forward in the history (and is the equivalent of clicking the browser's Forward button), and a negative number moves back (and is the equivalent of clicking the browser's Back button).

Syntax

```
window.history.go(intDelta);
```

Examples

```
var myHist = window.history; // Get a reference to the history object--saves a bit of typing.
myHist.back();     // goes back 1 entry in the history.
myHist.go(-3);     // goes back 3 more entries in history.
myHist.forward();  // goes forward 1 entry in history.
myHist.go(3);      // returns to the most recent page.
```

window.innerHeight

The `window.innerHeight` property contains the height of the actual rendering viewport of the browser, in pixels. The value includes the horizontal scrollbar, if present. (Compare with `window.outerHeight` and `window.innerWidth`.) This property is read-only; if you wish to change the height of the window, use the `window.resizeBy()` and `window.resizeTo()` methods.

Syntax

```
var currentHeight = window.innerHeight;
```

Example

```
<!DOCTYPE html>
<html>
        <head>
        <title>JavaScript Programmer's Reference</title>
        <style>
#centerme {
    width: 100px;
    height: 100px;
    position: absolute;
```

```
        top: 0px;
        left: 0px;
        background-color: #ccc;
}
        </style>
    </head>
    <body>
        <div id="centerme"></div>
        <script>
var centerMe = document.getElementById("centerme");
// Center vertically
var newPos = (window.innerHeight - 100) / 2;
centerMe.style.top = newPos + "px";
        </script>
    </body>
</html>
```

This example creates a gray box with a width of 100 pixels and a height of 100 pixels and centers it vertically on the screen.

window.innerWidth

The window.innerWidth property contains the width of the actual rendering viewport of the browser, in pixels. This value will include the vertical scrollbar, if present. (Compare with window.outerWidth and window.innerHeight.) This property is read-only; if you wish to change the width of the window, use the window.resizeBy() and window.resizeTo() methods.

Syntax

```
var currentWidth = window.innerWidth;
```

Example

```
<!DOCTYPE html>
<html>
    <head>
        <title>JavaScript Programmer's Reference</title>
        <style>
#centerme {
    width: 100px;
    height: 100px;
    position: absolute;
    top: 0px;
    left: 0px;
    background-color: #ccc;
}
        </style>
    </head>
    <body>
        <div id="centerme"></div>
        <script>
```

```
var centerMe = document.getElementById("centerme");
// Center horizontally
var newPos = (window.innerWidth - 100) / 2;
centerMe.style.left = newPos + "px";
        </script>
    </body>
</html>
```

This example creates a gray box with a width of 100 pixels and a height of 100 pixels and centers it horizontally on the screen.

window.length

The window.length property returns the number of subdocuments loaded via iframes. If no subdocuments are present, this property will be 0.

Syntax

```
var numberOfSubdocuments = window.length;
```

Example

```
<!DOCTYPE html>
<html>
    <head>
        <title>JavaScript Programmer's Reference</title>
    </head>
    <body>
        <iframe name="frame1"></iframe>
        <iframe name="frame2"></iframe>
        <iframe name="frame3"></iframe>
        <script>
alert(window.length); // will alert 3
        </script>
    </body>
</html>
```

In this example, we create three iframes, to set window.length to 3.

window.location

The window.location property provides a Location object that represents the URL of the loaded document. A Location object has the following properties::

- hash: The part of a URL that follows the #, if present. Includes the #. For example, for the URL http://www.example.com:8080/subdirectory/index.html?prop=value#anchor, the hash is "#anchor".

- host: The host part of a URL, including the port number (if specified). For example, for the URL http://www.example.com:8080/subdirectory/index.html?prop=value#anchor, the host is "www.example.com:8080".

- hostname: The host part of the URL without the port number. For example, for the URL
  `http://www.example.com:8080/subdirectory/index.html?prop=value#anchor`, the
  hostname is `"www.example.com"`.

- href: The full URL. For example, for the URL
  `http://www.example.com:8080/subdirectory/index.html?prop=value#anchor`, the href is
  `"http://www.example.com:8080/subdirectory/index.html?prop=value#anchor"`.

- origin: The protocol, host, and port. For example, for the URL
  `http://www.example.com:8080/subdirectory/index.html?prop=value#anchor`,
  the origin is `"http://www.example.com:8080"`.

- pathname: The path relative to the host. For example, for the URL
  `http://www.example.com:8080/subdirectory/index.html?prop=value#anchor`,
  the pathname is `"/subdirectory/index.html"`.

- port: The port of the URL, if specified. If no port is specified, this property is `""`.
  For example, for the URL
  `http://www.example.com:8080/subdirectory/index.html?prop=value#anchor`,
  the port is `"8080"`.

- protocol: The transfer protocol used. For example, for the URL
  `http://www.example.com:8080/subdirectory/index.html?prop=value#anchor`,
  the protocol is `"http:"`.

- search: The part of the URL that follows the first ?, if any. Includes the question mark.
  For example, for the URL
  `http://www.example.com:8080/subdirectory/index.html?prop=value#anchor`,
  the search is `"?prop=value"`.

A `Location` object has the following methods:

- `assign(targetURL)`: Loads `targetURL` into the browser.

- `reload(boolIgnoreCache)`: Reloads the current URL. If `boolIgnoreCache` is true, the browser
  reloads the document fresh from the server; otherwise it may reload the document from its
  cache if appropriate.

- `replace(targetURL)`: Deletes the current document's entry from the browser history and
  replaces it with `targetURL`. Also loads `targetURL` into the browser. See `window.history`,
  above, for more information on handling browser history.

- `toString()`: Returns the full URL as a simple string.

Syntax

```
var currentLocation = window.location;
```

Individual properties:

```
var currHash = currentLocation.hash;
var currHost = currentLocation.host;
var currHostname = currentLocation.hostname;
etc.
```

Individual methods:

```
currentLocation.reload(true);                           // Reloads the current document, bypassing the cache.
currentLocation.assign("http://www.google.com"); // Loads the Google front page.
etc.
```

Example

```
<!DOCTYPE html>
<html>
    <head>
        <title>JavaScript Programmer's Reference</title>
    </head>
    <body>
        <h1>Hello World</h1>
        <script>
var currentLocation = window.location;
alert(currentLocation.toString()); // Will alert the URL of this page.
        </script>
    </body>
</html>
```

This example alerts the URL of the document as soon as it is loaded.

window.localStorage

The window.localStorage property provides an interface to the Local Storage feature (also referred to as "DOM Storage") in modern browsers. Specified as part of HTML5, the Local Storage feature provides an alternative to cookies for storing arbitrary data within the browser in the form of key/value pairs. (See document.cookie for details on cookies.) Local Storage persists across browser sessions, meaning the user can close their web browser and even reboot their computer and the data will persist. Access is limited by the Same Origin Policy, just like cookies; scripts from one origin will not be able to access the data stored by scripts from another origin.

The localStorage interface provides three methods for accessing Local Storage:

- localStorage.getItem(key): Returns the value previously stored with key. If no such value was stored, this method returns null.

- localStorage.removeItem(key): Removes the key/value pair specified by key from Local Storage.

- localStorage.setItem(key, value): Saves the data value under key for later retrieval.

- localStorage.clear(): Clears all key/value pairs in Local Storage.

Note that Local Storage can only store strings; it cannot store things like arrays or objects. You can, however, convert such items to JSON strings first using JSON.stringify() and then store the resulting string in Local Storage. When you retrieve the string later, you can reconstitute the item using JSON.parse(). For details on JSON.stringify() and JSON.parse(), see Chapter 5.

Also note that even if you use Local Storage in your application, there's no guarantee that your data will be there later. Most modern browsers implement some form of "private browsing," wherein each session starts with no data and at the end of the session all data, including Local Storage, is wiped. Users can also manually wipe out their Local Storage. So if you are planning on using Local Storage in your application, you should code with this in mind.

Syntax

```
var storedValue = localStorage.getItem(key);
localStorage.removeItem(key);
localStorage.setItem(key, valueToStore);
```

Example

```
<!DOCTYPE html>
<html>
    <head>
        <title>JavaScript Programmer's Reference</title>
    </head>
    <body>
        <h1>Hello World!</h1>
        <script>
// Check to see if we've visited this page before.
var myValue = localStorage.getItem("test");
if (myValue == null) {
    alert('This is your first time here!');
    localStorage.setItem("test", "true");
} else {
    alert('You have been here before!');
}
        </script>
    </body>
</html>
```

In this example, we check to see if a particular key has been used to store a value in Local Storage. If there isn't a value, we assume the user hasn't visited the site yet, and store a value using that key. If there is a value stored, we assume the user has visited the site. Test this example as follows:

1. Load it normally. It will alert "This is your first time here!"

2. Click the Reload button. It will alert "You have been here before!"

3. If your browser supports tabbed browsing, open a new tab and load the example again. It will alert "You have been here before!"

4. Close your browser and restart it. Reload the example, and it will alert "You have been here before!"

Perform these tests again in private browsing mode, if your browser supports it. You should see that the value has been deleted each time you close the browser and reopen it.

See Chapter 4 for an example using Local Storage.

window.opener

If this window was opened by a script using the window.open() method, the window.opener property will contain a reference to the window that contained that script. If this window was opened manually by the user (e.g., by starting the browser, or opening a new tab), then this property will be null.

Syntax

```
var myOpener = window.opener;
```

window.outerHeight

The `window.outerHeight` property contains the total height of the browser, including all chrome, toolbars, etc., in pixels. (Compare with `window.outerWidth` and `window.innerHeight`.) This value is read-only; if you want to change the dimensions of the browser, use the `window.resizeBy()` and `window.resizeTo()` methods.

Syntax

```
var totalHeight = window.outerHeight;
```

window.outerWidth

The `window.outerWidth` property contains the total width of the browser, including all chrome, toolbars, etc., in pixels. (Compare with `window.outerHeight` and `window.innerWidth`.) This value is read-only; if you want to change the dimensions of the browser, use the `window.resizeBy()` and `window.resizeTo()` methods.

Syntax

```
var totalWidth = window.outerWidth;
```

window.pageXOffset

The `window.pageXOffset` property contains the value of the number of pixels that the document has been scrolled horizontally. (Compare with `window.pageYOffset`.) This value is read-only; if you want to scroll the document, use the `window.scroll()`, `window.scrollBy()`, `window.scrollByLines()`, `window.scrollByPages()`, and `window.scrollTo()` methods.

■ **Note** The `window.pageXOffset` and `window.scrollX` properties both reference the same value. The `pageXOffset` property predates `scrollX`, but most browsers implement both…except Internet Explorer. Prior to version 9, Internet Explorer did not provide either property and instead provided the `document.body.scrollLeft` property.

Syntax

```
var horizScroll = window.pageXOffset;
```

window.pageYOffset

The `window.pageYOffset` property contains the value of the number of pixels that the document has been scrolled vertically. (Compare with `window.pageXOffset`.) This value is read-only; if you want to scroll the document, use the `window.scroll()`, `window.scrollBy()`, `window.scrollByLines()`, `window.scrollByPages()`, and `window.scrollTo()` methods.

■ **Note** The `window.pageYOffset` and `window.scrollY` properties both reference the same value. The `pageYOffset` property predates `scrollY`, but most browsers implement both…except Internet Explorer. Prior to version 9, Internet Explorer did not provide either property and instead provided the `document.body.scrollTop` property.

Syntax

```
var vertScroll = window.pageYOffset;
```

window.parent

If this window is an iframe, the `window.parent` property will contain a reference to the window that contains it. Otherwise, it will be `null`.

Syntax

```
var myParent = window.parent;
```

window.scrollX

The `window.scrollX` property contains the value of the number of pixels that the document has been scrolled horizontally. (Compare with `window.scrollY` and `window.pageXOffset`.) This value is read-only; if you want to scroll the document, use the `window.scroll()`, `window.scrollBy()`, `window.scrollByLines()`, `window.scrollByPages()`, and `window.scrollTo()` methods.

▓ **Note**   The `window.pageXOffset` and `window.scrollX` properties both reference the same value. The `pageXOffset` property predates `scrollX`, but most browsers implement both…except Internet Explorer. Prior to version 9, Internet Explorer did not provide either property and instead provided the `document.body.scrollLeft` property.

Syntax

```
var horizScroll = window.scrollX;
```

window.scrollY

The `window.scrollY` property contains the value of the number of pixels that the document has been scrolled vertically. (Compare with `window.scrollX`.) This value is read-only; if you want to scroll the document, use the `window.scroll()`, `window.scrollBy()`, `window.scrollByLines()`, `window.scrollByPages()`, and `window.scrollTo()` methods.

▓ **Note**   The `window.pageYOffset` and `window.scrollY` properties both reference the same value. The `pageYOffset` property predates `scrollY`, but most browsers implement both…except Internet Explorer. Prior to version 9, Internet Explorer did not provide either property and instead provided the `document.body.scrollTop` property.

Syntax

```
var vertScroll  = window.scrollY;
```

window.sessionStorage

The Session Storage feature is similar to the Local Storage feature, except that data stored using Session Storage will be lost when the session ends. Like Local Storage, access to Session Storage data is limited by the Single Origin Policy, and like Local Storage, Session Storage can only store strings. See `window.localStorage`, earlier in the chapter, for more details and an example.

Syntax

```
var storedValue = sessionStorage.getItem(key);
sessionStorage.removeItem(key);
sessionStorage.setItem(key, valueToStore);
sessionStorage.clear();
```

window.top

In the case of nested iframes, the `window.top` property provides a reference to the topmost window that is the parent to all iframes. In the topmost window, or in the case of a window with no subdocuments, this will be a reference to the window object itself.

Syntax

```
var myTopWindow = window.top;
```

Methods

The `window` object has several important methods, which can be used to set timers, communicate with the user, scroll the document, and even move the browser window.

window.addEventListener()

The `window.addEventListener()` method allows you to add event listeners to the `window` object itself. Otherwise, this method behaves the same as `element.addEventListener()`. See that entry for details and examples.

Syntax

```
window.addEventListener(strEventType, eventHandler, boolCapture);
```

window.alert()

The `window.alert()` method opens an alert pop-up dialog containing the specified text. Note that this is one method that is often accessed without the `window.` identifier.

Syntax

```
alert(strMessage);
```

Example

```
alert("We've been using alerts throughout the book.");
```

window.clearTimeout()

The window.clearTimeout() method takes a timer ID as a parameter and clears the timeout specified by the ID: that is, it removes it without executing its function. The ID is the value returned when the timer is created with the window.setTimeout() method or the window.setInterval() method. (See the entries for the window.setTimeout() and window.setInterval() methods for details.)

Syntax

```
window.clearTimeout(timeoutID);
```

Example

```
<!DOCTYPE html>
<html>
    <head>
        <title>JavaScript Programmer's Reference</title>
    </head>
    <body>
        <h1>Hello World</h1>
        <script>
// Set a timeout that will result in an alert after a 5 second delay
var myID = setTimeout(function() {
    alert('Five seconds has passed!');
}, 5000);

// Clear the timeout so it will never execute.
clearTimeout(myID);
        </script>
    </body>
</html>
```

This example sets a timer that would cause an alert after a 5-second delay, and then clears the timer so that the alert never happens. To verify, comment out the clearTimeout() call and rerun the script. After the delay, the alert will happen.

window.close()

The window.close() method closes the window. Only windows that have been opened with the window.open() method can be closed.

Syntax

```
var windowRef = window.open(strURL);
windowRef.close();
```

Example

```
<!DOCTYPE html>
<html>
    <head>
        <title>JavaScript Programmer's Reference</title>
    </head>
```

```
    <body>
        <p id="opener">Click here to open a search window.</p>
        <p id="closer">Click here to close the search window.</p>
        <script>
var opener = document.getElementById("opener"),
    closer = document.getElementById("closer"),
    windowRef = false;

opener.addEventListener("click", function() {
    // If the search window isn't open, we should open it.
    // If the search window is open, we should let the user know.
    if (windowRef === false) {
        windowRef = window.open("http://www.google.com");
    } else {
        alert("The search window is already open.");
    }
});

closer.addEventListener("click", function() {
    // If the search window is open, we should close it.
    // If the search window isn't open, we should let the user know.
    if (windowRef !== false) {
        windowRef.close();
        windowRef = false;
    } else {
        alert("The search window isn't open.")
    }
})
        </script>
    </body>
</html>
```

In this example, we first get references to the two paragraphs. For the opener reference, we add a click event handler that will open a search window if one isn't already open, and store the reference to that window in a variable. If one is already open, we alert the user. For the closer reference, we add a click event handler that will close the search window if it's open and set the reference variable back to false. If the search window isn't open, we'll alert the user.

window.confirm()

The window.confirm() method opens a confirm pop-up dialog containing the text specified as the parameter. Confirm pop-up dialogs have an OK button and a Cancel button; when the user clicks OK, the method returns true, and when the user clicks Cancel, the method returns false.

Syntax

```
var returnVal = confirm(message);
```

Example

```
<!DOCTYPE html>
<html>
    <head>
        <title>JavaScript Programmer's Reference</title>
    </head>
    <body>
        <p id="opener">Click here to open a search window.</p>
        <p id="closer">Click here to close the search window.</p>
        <script>
var opener = document.getElementById("opener"),
    closer = document.getElementById("closer"),
    windowRef = false;

opener.addEventListener("click", function() {
    // If the search window isn't open, we should open it.
    // If the search window is open, we should let the user know.
    if (windowRef === false) {
        windowRef = window.open("http://www.google.com");
    } else {
        var returnVal = confirm("The search window is already open. Would you like to close it?");
        if (returnVal === true) {
            windowRef.close();
            windowRef = false;
        }
    }
}, false);

closer.addEventListener("click", function() {
    // If the search window is open, we should close it.
    // If the search window isn't open, we should let the user know.
    if (windowRef !== false) {
        windowRef.close();
        windowRef = false;
    } else {
        var returnVal = confirm("The search window isn't open. Would you like to open it?");
        if (returnVal === true) {
            windowRef = window.open("http://www.google.com");
        }
    }
}, false);
        </script>
    </body>
</html>
```

This example extends our previous example: instead of using an alert to communicate with the user in the error conditions, we use a confirm dialog to ask the user what they would like to do.

window.getComputedStyle()

When provided an element reference (required) and an optional pseudo-element, the `window.getComputedStyle()` method returns the styles that are actually used to display the element. The return value is a read-only Style object of the same format as the element's `style` property: each CSS property that is set on the element has a corresponding property in the object.

Syntax

```
var appliedStyles = window.getComputedStyle(targetElement, pseudo);
```

Example

```
<!DOCTYPE html>
<html>
    <head>
        <title>JavaScript Programmer's Reference</title>
        <style>
.styledElement {
    background-color: #ccccff;
    border: 1px solid #000000;
    color: #0000FF;
}
#testElement {
    border-width: 50px;
    color: #00FF00;
}
p#testElement {
    border-width: 5px;
}
        </style>
    </head>
    <body>
        <p id="testElement" class="styledElement" style="border=color: #FF0000;">This is a test
paragraph.</p>
        <script>
var myTarget = document.getElementById("testElement"),
    appliedStyles = window.getComputedStyle(myTarget);

alert(appliedStyles.backgroundColor); // Will alert something like "rgb(204, 204, 255)"
alert(appliedStyles.borderWidth);     // Will alert 5
alert(appliedStyles.color);           // Will alert something like "rgb(0, 255, 0)"
alert(appliedStyles.margin);          // Will alert something like "16px 0px"
alert(appliedStyles.padding);         // Will alert something like "0px"
        </script>
    </body>
</html>
```

In this example, we apply some styles using rules in a style sheet and an inline style. Note that we can examine both the styles that we set and the default styles on the element: we didn't set either margins or padding on the element, but they are present in the `appliedStyles` object. (Exactly what margin and padding are applied will vary from browser to browser because each browser has its own default style sheet; in Chrome, the margin is 16px 0px and the padding is 0px.)

Note that what is actually alerted can vary from browser to browser. In some browsers, for example, colors are alerted as RGB values; in others, they are alerted as hexadecimal values. The values are correct, just formatted differently. In addition, some browsers attempt to provide shorthand values whenever possible. This can be problematic when trying to compare style values—if you're expecting an RGB value string for a color but instead get a hexadecimal string, then that can cause comparisons to fail.

window.open()

The `window.open()` method opens a window with the specified parameters. In browsers that implement tabbed browsing, new windows that have no features set will open as new tabs. Setting the features string usually forces the browser to open the window as a stand-alone window rather than as a new tab, though users can override that behavior as well and specify that all new windows open as tabs.

The valid parameters for the `window.open()` method are as follows:

- `url`: The URL of the desired document to display within the new window.

- `strName`: The name of the window (optional). This does not specify the title of the window—that is specified by the `<title>` tag of the document loaded into the new window. This name can be used as the target of links and forms using their `target` attribute.

- `strFeatures`: A comma-delimited list of desired window features, in the form of `feature=value` pairs. Available features and their implementation vary from browser to browser, but the most common are as follows:

  - `left`: The left position of the new window in the user's workspace, relative to the left edge of the monitor. Valid values are integers; many browsers only permit positive integers.

  - `top`: The top position of the new window in the user's workspace, relative to the top edge of the monitor. Valid values are integers; many browsers only permit positive integers.

  - `height`: The desired height of the content window in pixels; equivalent to `window.innerHeight`. Valid values are integers; minimum value is 100.

  - `width`: The desired width of the content window in pixels; equivalent to `window.innerWidth`. Valid values are integers; minimum value is 100.

  - `menubar`: When set to yes, causes the new window to render its menu bar (the menu bar contains the File, Edit, View, etc. menus of the browser). If you use a features parameter and do not set this property, it will be set to no and the menu bar will not display. Valid values are yes or no.

  - `toolbar`: When set to yes, causes the new window to render its toolbar (the toolbar contains the Back, Forward, Reload, Stop, etc. buttons). If you use a features parameter and do not set this property, it will be set to no and the tool bar will not display. Valid values are yes or no.

  - `location`: When set to yes, causes the new window to render its location bar (the location bar contains the URL entry field). If you use a features parameter and do not set this property, it will be set to no and the location bar will not display. Valid values are yes or no.

  - `status`: When set to yes, causes the new window to render its status bar (the bar at the bottom of the browser window). If you use a features parameter and do not set this property, it will be set to no and the status bar will not display. Valid values are yes or no.

  - `resizable`: If set to yes, will allow the user to resize the new window. If you use a features parameter and do not specify the resizable property, it will be set to no and the window will not be resizable. For good usability, you should always specify this value as yes. Valid values are yes or no.

- scrollbars: If set to yes, allows the new window to show horizontal and vertical scrollbars if the content is too large for the specified area. If you use a features parameter and do not specify the scrollbars property, it will be set to no and the scrollbars will not be added to the window, leaving no way for the user to scroll the content. For good usability, you should always specify this value as yes. Valid values are yes or no.

The window.open() method returns a reference to the window that was opened.

Of all the methods in the DOM, window.open() is probably one of the most abused, both by malicious spammers and by careless programmers. As a result, many browsers now allow the user to override specified settings and even disallow its use altogether through the use of pop-up blocking parameters and plug-ins. If the pop-up is prevented by a browser's internal blocking parameter, then the method will return null instead of a window reference. If the pop-up is blocked by a plug-in, often you will not be able to tell (which is why many applications that rely on pop-up windows advise users to disable pop-up blockers).

Because of these limitations, if you want to use pop-up windows in your application, you should test carefully to make sure users who are using pop-up blockers won't be denied access to important areas of your application.

Syntax

```
var strFeatures = "left=0,right=0,scrollbars=true,resizable=true";
var windowRef = window.open(URL, strName, strFeatures);
```

Example

```
<!DOCTYPE html>
<html>
    <head>
        <title>JavaScript Programmer's Reference</title>
    </head>
    <body>
        <p id="opener">Click here to open a search window.</p>
        <p id="closer">Click here to close the search window.</p>
        <script>
var opener = document.getElementById("opener"),
    closer = document.getElementById("closer"),
    windowRef = false;

opener.addEventListener("click", function() {
    // If the search window isn't open, we should open it.
    // If the search window is open, we should let the user know.
    if (windowRef === false) {
        windowRef = window.open("http://www.google.com", "searchwindow",
"left=0,top=0,resizable=true,scrollbars=true");
    } else {
        var returnVal = confirm("The search window is already open. Would you like to close it?");
        if (returnVal === true) {
            windowRef.close();
            windowRef = false;
        }
    }
}, false);
```

```
closer.addEventListener("click", function() {
    // If the search window is open, we should close it.
    // If the search window isn't open, we should let the user know.
    if (windowRef !== false) {
        windowRef.close();
        windowRef = false;
    } else {
        var returnVal = confirm("The search window isn't open. Would you like to open it?");
        if (returnVal === true) {
            windowRef = window.open("http://www.google.com");
        }
    }
}, false);
        </script>
    </body>
</html>
```

This example extends our previous example by specifying a window name and some features for the new window. If your browser implements tabbed browsing, chances are the previous version of the example opened the new window as a tab. In this version of the example, setting the features should cause your browser to open the search window as a stand-alone window. The features we specify should cause the window to open in the upper-left corner of your screen, and be both resizable and have scrollbars. Since we didn't specify the menubar, toolbar, location, or status features, those should default to no and not display, but whether or not that will be honored by the browser depends on which browser you are using and the settings for that browser. (In our version of Chrome, the new window opens as a stand-alone window, but the specified position isn't honored and the location bar displays; in our version of Firefox, the window opens at the desired position and both the location bar and the status bar display.) Try opening the example in different browsers with different settings and see how its behavior changes.

window.postMessage()

The Post Message feature is new to HTML5 and provides a secure way of sending strings from one frame to another, even if direct access between the frames in question would be forbidden by the Single Origin Policy. When you call the postMessage() method, it will dispatch a message event in the target window, with the string you specify as the data attribute of the resulting Event object. The receiving iframe will need to have a document loaded that implements an event listener for the message event, and it can then receive the Event object and read the message.

When you call the postMessage() method, you specify not only the string you wish to send, but also the desired origin of the document loaded into the iframe as a URL. If the document loaded into the iframe comes from a different origin, the event is not dispatched. This security feature enables you to ensure that only a document from the origin you desire will be able to receive your message. You can opt to send the message to all domains (as we do in the next example by using the asterisk, "*"), but doing so would leave a security hole in your application that a malicious site could exploit by listening for message events.

In the receiving window, the event handler receives an Event object that has a data attribute containing the message. It also has a source attribute that will contain the origin of the document that dispatched the message. You should always check the source to make sure the message you have received has come from the expected origin. If the origin doesn't match, you can discard the message. This way you prevent malicious sites from injecting potentially harmful data into your site.

According to the DOM standard, the message can be anything, and the latest versions of some browsers will permit sending objects. Most browsers only support sending strings. Even so, you can first serialize objects and arrays and other things with the JSON.stringify() method, and then reconstitute them on the receiving end with JSON.parse().

The Post Message feature is new to HTML5 but enjoys wide support among modern browsers. In Internet Explorer, however, Post Message only works between iframes, and not windows opened with the `window.open()` method.

Syntax

In the sending window:

```
windowRef.postMessage(strMessage, targetOrigin);
```

In the receiving window:

```
function handleMessage(event) {
    // Check event.source to make sure it comes from the desired origin
    // The message is in event.data
}
window.addEventListener("message", handleMessage, false);
```

To create an example, we'll need two pages, which we'll call the Main Page and the Target Page. The Main Page will contain an iframe that loads the Target Page.

Main Page

```
<!DOCTYPE html>
<html>
    <head>
        <title>JavaScript Programmer's Reference</title>
    </head>
    <body>
        <iframe src="target-page.html" id="targetFrame"></iframe>
        <p id="clickme">Click to send a message to the iframe.</p>
        <script>
var strMessage = "Hello, main window here, are you receiving?",
    clickme = document.getElementById("clickme"),
    targetFrame = document.getElementById("targetFrame");

clickme.addEventListener("click", function() {
    targetFrame.contentWindow.postMessage(strMessage, "*");
})

function handleMessage(event) {
    var strAlert = "Main Window:\n";
    strAlert += event.data;
    alert(strAlert);
}
window.addEventListener("message", handleMessage, false);
        </script>
    </body>
</html>
```

Target Page

```
<!DOCTYPE html>
<html>
    <head>
        <title>JavaScript Programmer's Reference</title>
    </head>
    <body>
        <h1>Target iframe</h1>
        <script>
function handleMessage(event) {
    var strAlert = "Target iframe:\n";
    strAlert += event.data;
    alert(strAlert);
    window.top.postMessage("Hello, target iframe here, I received your message.", "*");
}
window.addEventListener("message", handleMessage, false);
        </script>
    </body>
</html>
```

To run this example, save the Main Page under any name, and then save the Target Page in the same directory, under the name `target-page.html`. When you load the first page into your browser, it will load the second page in the iframe.

Both documents bind `message` event handlers to their `window` objects, and both handle any message by alerting it.

When you click the text to send the message to the iframe, the script will use `postMessage()` to send the message "Hello, main window here, are you receiving?" The iframe will receive the message and process it using its `handleMessage()` event handler, which will alert the message we just sent. Then, the Target Page will send a message back to the Main Page via the `window.top` reference (see `window.top`, above, for details). The Main Page will handle the resulting `message` event and alert the message.

Note that in this example we are not specifying the target origin in our calls to `postMessage()`, nor are we checking the source origin in our event handlers. We do this because this is a test case, and we don't know how you will be running these examples. You should always specify the target origin and check the source origin in any scripts that will be released into the wild—it is very important for security. In fact, we encourage you to modify these scripts so that they do specify the target origin and check the source origin according to your specific environment. Also, try setting them to different values to verify for yourself that the examples behave as expected.

window.print()

The `window.print()` method opens the print dialog for the browser, just as if the user had chosen File ➤ Print from the menu. For security reasons, you cannot access any of the features of the print dialog from JavaScript, including closing a print dialog once it is open.

Syntax

```
window.print();
```

Example

```
<!DOCTYPE html>
<html>
    <head>
        <title>JavaScript Programmer's Reference</title>
    </head>
    <body>
        <h1>Hello World</h1>
            <script>
window.print();
            </script>
    </body>
</html>
```

As soon as you load this example, it will open your browser's print dialog, giving you the opportunity to print the page.

window.prompt()

The window.prompt() method opens a prompt dialog, which will display a specified string and provide the user with a text entry field. The prompt dialog has two buttons, OK and Cancel. Clicking OK will close the dialog and cause the method to return whatever the user entered in the text entry field. Clicking Cancel will close the dialog and cause the method to return null.

Syntax

```
var strReturnValue = prompt(strMessage);
```

Example

```
<!DOCTYPE html>
<html>
    <head>
        <title>JavaScript Programmer's Reference</title>
    </head>
    <body>
        <h1></h1>
        <script>
var header = document.querySelector("h1"),
    userName = prompt("Hey there, what's your name?");

if ((userName !== null) && (userName !== "")) {
    header.innerText = "Pleased to meet you, " + userName + "!";
} else {
    header.innerText = "I wish I knew your name. :(";
}
        </script>
    </body>
</html>
```

In this example, we prompt the user for their name. If they click Cancel, or if they enter nothing and click OK, we tell them how sad that makes us. Otherwise, we tell them we are pleased to meet them.

window.removeEventListener()

The `window.removeEventListener()` method removes an event listener previously registered on the window. Otherwise it behaves exactly like `element.removeEventListener()`. See `element.removeEventListener()` for details and examples.

Syntax

```
window.removeEventListener(strEventType, eventHandler, boolCapture);
```

window.resizeBy()

The `window.resizeBy()` method changes the width and height of the window by the specified number of pixels. A positive number causes the dimension to increase in size, while a negative number causes the dimension to decrease. (Compare with `window.resizeTo()`.)

Most browsers allow you to resize only windows that have been opened using the `window.open()` method and that are stand-alone windows (not tabs, if the browser implements tabbed browsing). Some browsers also give the user the option of explicitly disabling this feature.

Syntax

```
window.resizeBy(changeInWidth, changeInHeight);
```

Example

```
<!DOCTYPE html>
<html>
    <head>
        <title>JavaScript Programmer's Reference</title>
    </head>
    <body>
        <h1>Hello World!</h1>
        <script>
var myWindow = window.open("http://www.google.com", "searchWindow",
"top=10,left=10,width=500,height=500");
myWindow.resizeBy(-100, -100); // Shrinks the window's width and height by 100 px each.
        </script>
    </body>
</html>
```

In this example, we open a search window that is 500 pixels wide and 500 pixels high. Then we resize it by reducing both the width and the height by 100 pixels. You may see a brief flash as the browser first opens at the 500x500 size and then shrinks to the 400x400 size. See `window.open()` for details on that method, including browser dependencies and limitations.

window.resizeTo()

The `window.resizeTo()` method resizes the window to the dimensions (in pixels) specified. (Compare with `window.resizeBy()`.) Most browsers allow you to resize only windows that have been opened using the `window.open()` method and that are stand-alone windows (not tabs, if the browser implements tabbed browsing). Some browsers also give the user the option of explicitly disabling this feature.

Syntax

```
window.resizeTo(intWidth, intHeight);
```

Example

```
<!DOCTYPE html>
<html>
    <head>
        <title>JavaScript Programmer's Reference</title>
    </head>
    <body>
        <h1>Hello World!</h1>
        <script>
var myWindow = window.open("http://www.google.com", "searchWindow",
"top=10,left=10,width=500,height=500");
myWindow.resizeTo(200, 200); // Resize the window to 200 pixels by 200 pixels.
        </script>
    </body>
</html>
```

In this example, we open a search window that is 500 pixels wide and 500 pixels high. Then we resize it to 200 by 200 pixels. You may see a brief flash as the browser first opens at the 500x500 size and then shrinks to the 200x200 size. See `window.open()` for details on that method, including browser dependencies and limitations.

window.scroll()

The `window.scroll()` method scrolls the document in the window to the specified x and y coordinates, in pixels, with the origin (0, 0) being the top left of the document. Both parameters are required.

Syntax

```
windowRef.scroll(intX, intY);
```

window.scrollBy()

The `window.scrollBy()` method scrolls the window by the specified offsets, in pixels. A positive number scrolls the window down (or to the right), while a negative number scrolls the window up (or to the left).

Syntax

```
windowRef.scrollBy(intX, intY);
```

window.scrollByLines()

The `window.scrollByLines()` method scrolls the window vertically by the specified number of lines of text. A positive number scrolls down, while a negative number scrolls up.

Syntax

```
windowRef.scrollByLines(intLines);
```

window.scrollByPages()

The `window.scrollByPages()` method scrolls the window vertically by the specified number of pages of text. A positive number scrolls down, while a negative number scrolls up.

Syntax

```
windowRef.scrollByPages(intPages);
```

window.scrollTo()

The `window.scrollTo()` method functions the same as `window.scroll()`.

Syntax

```
windowRef.scrollTo(intX, intY);
```

window.setInterval()

The `window.setInterval()` method allows you to set up a timer that will call a specified function once every specified number of milliseconds. The method returns the ID of the timer, which when provided as a parameter to the `window.clearTimeout()` method will cancel the timer. If not canceled, the timer will continue to run, calling the specified function every interval, until the window is closed (by closing the tab or the browser itself) or a new document is loaded into the window.

Note that a timer will run its function every specified number of milliseconds regardless of how long it takes for the function to execute. If the function takes longer than the interval to execute, you can end up with your function executing simultaneously. For example, if the function takes 700 milliseconds to run, and you schedule it to be run every 500 milliseconds, you'll end up with simultaneous executions of the function.

Syntax

```
var timerID = setInterval(functionToExecute, intMilliseconds);
```

Example

```
<!DOCTYPE html>
<html>
    <head>
        <title>JavaScript Programmer's Reference</title>
    </head>
```

```
    <body>
        <h1>JavaScript Clock</h1>
        <h2>hh : mm : ss</h2>
        <p><button>Start</button></p>
        <script>
var clockID = null,
    buttonRef = document.querySelector("button");

// Create a function that can be called every second to update the clock.
function updateClock() {
    var ptrClock = document.querySelector("h2"),
        myTime = new Date(),
        strTime;

    // Build a string with the current time
    strTime = myTime.getHours() + " : ";
    strTime += myTime.getMinutes() + " : ";
    strTime += myTime.getSeconds();

    // Update the clock
    ptrClock.innerText = strTime;
}

// Handle clicks on the button to either start or stop the clock.
function handleButtonClick() {
    // If the clockID is null, then we need to start the clock.
    // Otherwise, we need to stop the clock.
    if (clockID == null) {
        updateClock();                          // Set the clock to the correct time
        clockID = setInterval(updateClock, 1000); // start the timer
    } else {
        clearTimeout(clockID);                  // Stop the timer
        // Clear the ID so that the next time we click on the
        // button we'll know there is no timer running
        clockID = null;
    }
}

// Bind the event handler to the button.
buttonRef.addEventListener("click", handleButtonClick, false);
        </script>
    </body>
</html>
```

In this example, we create a simple clock that you can start and stop by clicking the button. First, we create a function that can be called every second by the timer, called updateClock(). This function gets the current time using the Date object and builds a string representing the time using Date methods (see Chapter 5 for details on the Date object and its methods). Then, it updates the text of the clock.

When the user clicks the button, we want to start the clock if it is stopped, or stop the clock if it is started, so we create an event handler that checks to see if the clockID is set. If the clock isn't stopped, the event handler updates the clock and then starts the timer. If the clock is stopped, the event handler stops the timer and clears the clockID.

window.setTimeout()

The window.setTimeout() method works similarly to the setInterval() method in that it allows you to specify a function to run after a specified number of milliseconds. However, unlike setInterval(), setTimeout() only executes the function once. Like setInterval(), setTimeout() returns an ID that represents the new timer, which can be cleared using the clearInterval() method.

Syntax

```
var timerID  = setTimeout(functionRef, intMilliseconds);
```

Example

```
<!DOCTYPE html>
<html>
    <head>
        <title>JavaScript Programmer's Reference</title>
    </head>
    <body>
        <h1>Hello World</h1>
                <script>
// This will alert "Hello World" after 5 seconds.
var timerID  = setTimeout(function() {
    alert('Hello World!');
}, 5000);
        </script>
    </body>
</html>
```

In this example, we create a simple timeout to alert "Hello World" five seconds after the page is loaded.

window.sizeToContent()

The window.sizeToContent() method sizes a window to its content. It is useful for sizing a pop-up window to be the size needed to fit its content. Note that the DOM has to be loaded and ready before this method is called. If you call it before the DOM is loaded, it may resize the window to the incorrect size.

Syntax

```
windowRef.sizeToContent();
```

The document Object Reference

The document object represents the document that has been loaded into the window. The document object is a property of the window object, so you can access it as window.document. Since the window object also serves as the global context for JavaScript, you can omit specifying the window. identifier and simply use document (which is a very common convention).

Properties

The properties on the document object provide information about the document itself, such as the URL and cookies.

document.activeElement

The document.activeElement property provides a read-only reference to the element in the document that currently has keyboard focus. If there is nothing with focus, this property returns a reference to the body element.

Syntax

```
var myElementReference = document.activeElement;
```

document.body

The document.body property provides a reference to the body element of the document.

Syntax

```
var bodyRef = document.body;
```

Example

```
var myDiv = document.createElement("div"); // Creates a new element.
document.body.appendChild(myDiv); //Appends the new DIV to the document at the end.
```

document.compatMode

The document.compatMode property returns the compatibility mode used to render the document. Browsers can render documents according to different levels of compatibility, and with the document.compatMode property, you can tell which was used to render the current document. The values are:

- CSS1Compat: The browser rendered the document in strict mode, meaning it rendered the document's markup according to the relevant standards to produce predictable results.

- BackCompat: The document was rendered using quirks mode. Quirks mode is a rendering mode designed to maintain backward compatibility with older, nonstandard markup. Because quirks mode is a departure from the standard, results can be unpredictable.

Note that all modern browsers (and even most older browsers) automatically render HTML5 documents in strict mode.

Syntax

```
var strCompat = document.compatMode;
```

Example

```
<!DOCTYPE html>
<html>
    <head>
        <title>JavaScript Programmer's Reference</title>
    </head>
```

```
    <body>
        <h1>Hello World</h1>
        <script>
var strCompat = document.compatMode;
alert(strCompat); // will alert "CSS1Compat" because this is an HTML 5 document.
        </script>
    </body>
</html>
```

This example alerts the rendering mode of the document. Because it's an HTML5 document (as specified by the doctype tag on the first line), the browser is rendering in standards-compliant mode.

document.cookie

The document.cookie property provides access to the cookies associated with this document. Cookies provide a way of storing small amounts of information on the user's system for later retrieval. This information can persist across browser sessions, enabling you to retrieve the stored data even after the user has closed their browser or rebooted their computer. Access to cookies is limited by the Single Origin Policy, so scripts from one origin cannot access cookies set by scripts from another origin. It is possible, however, for a script from one origin to set a cookie with a different origin than its own, resulting in a cookie with a different origin (and which the original script would be unable to read, but which scripts from the specified origin could access). Such cookies are referred to as third-party cookies. Third-party cookies are commonly employed to track users across web sites: each domain employs a script to write a cookie for a third domain, and also loads a script for that domain that can read that cookie. In that way, a third domain can monitor users and their activities as they move from domain to domain. Third-party cookies carry with them some serious privacy concerns, and can be used as a security hole by malicious scripts.

The stored cookie is a string consisting of a single key/value pair, followed by the following optional attributes:

- domain: The domain of the document that can read the resulting cookie. You can specify an exact domain (e.g., "www.apress.com", which would allow the cookie to be read only from scripts served from the www.apress.com domain) or subdomains (e.g., .apress.com, which allows the cookie to be read from any subdomain of apress.com: www.apress.com, my.apress.com, examples.my.apress.com, etc.).

- expires: A date in GMT format that specifies when the data expires. If you are managing the dates in your application using Date objects, the Date.toUTCString method will produce a string of the correct format. If neither the expires value nor the max-age value is set, the cookie will expire at the end of the session.

- max-age: The maximum age of the cookie, in seconds. If neither the expires value nor the max-age value is set, the cookie will expire at the end of the session.

- path: Specifies the path of the document that can read the resulting cookie. If not set, this defaults to the path of the current document.

- secure: If this key is included (it does not need a value, just inclusion in the string), then the cookie can only be read over a secure (HTTPS) connection.

Cookies can contain only text, not objects, and cannot contain semicolons, commas, or spaces. You can set more than one cookie for a given domain.

Syntax

```
var myCookie = document.cookie; // reads the cookie string that has been set
document.cookie = myCookie;     // sets the cookie string for the document
```

For an example, consider a common use case for cookies: storing user preferences. On your hypothetical site, users are allowed to customize their user interface by specifying a theme and a language. You can store this information as cookies so that when the users return to your site, their settings will persist. You also want to specify that the cookies should last 5 days (or 432000 seconds) and be read on any subdomain.

Example

```
// Set the cookies
document.cookie = "username=uberuser;max-age=432000;domain=.yourdomain.com";
// Sets a cookie for username.
document.cookie = "theme=greenapple;max-age=432000;domain=.yourdomain.com";
// Sets a cookie for theme.
```

Reading a cookie is a slightly more complex matter because you get all cookies sent back at once in a semicolon-delimited string. So for the preceding example, accessing document.cookie would return the string username=uberuser; theme=greenapple. To handle multiple cookies, you need a way to search that string for a given key/value pair. The solution is the fact that the format of the string follows a very specific schema: given a particular key, you need to search for the value associated with it, which means you need to look for the text between the first occurrence of the string "key=" and the next semicolon. There are many ways of doing that, but the most succinct is to use a regular expression. A regular expression can search for a substring delimited by a beginning and an end delimiter: (?:^|;)\\s?key=(.*?)(?:;|$) This regular expression specifies that from the beginning of the string, we'll search for the substring "key=" and, once it is found, return the substring between that and the next semicolon. Here's a function that uses that regular expression:

```
// Returns the value associated with strKey within the document's cookie, or null if not found.
function readCookie(strKey) {
    var myCookie = document.cookie,
        cookieReg = new RegExp('(?:^|;)\\s?' + strKey + '=(.*?)(?:;|$)'),
        myVal = myCookie.match(cookieReg);
    if(myVal == null) {
        return myVal;
    } else {
        return myVal[1];
    }
}
```

Here's an example that puts everything together:

Example

```
<!DOCTYPE html>
<html>
    <head>
        <title>JavaScript Programmer's Reference</title>
        <script>
// Returns the value associated with strKey within the document's cookie, or null if not found.
function readCookie(strKey) {
    var myCookie = document.cookie,
        cookieReg = new RegExp('(?:^|;)\\s?' + strKey + '=(.*?)(?:;|$)'),
        myVal = myCookie.match(cookieReg);
```

```
        if(myVal == null) {
            return myVal;
        } else {
            return myVal[1];
        }
}

var myCookie = document.cookie;
if (readCookie("username") != null) {
    // We have been here before!  Use the readCookie function to get our preferences
    var myUsername = readCookie("username"),
        myTheme = readCookie("theme");
    alert("Hello " + myUsername + ", your theme is " + myTheme);
} else {
    // We have not been here before.  Set new cookies.
    document.cookie = "username=uberuser"; // Sets a cookie for username.
    document.cookie = "theme=greenapple";  // Sets a cookie for theme.
    alert('Cookie set.  Reload the browser to see the results.')
}
        </script>
    </head>
    <body>
        <h1>Testing Cookies</h1>
    </body>
</html>
```

In this example, we set cookies for username and theme. We don't set either max-age or expires values on them, though, so they are session cookies and will be erased as soon as you close the browser. Try setting a max-age on one of the cookies of a few minutes to verify that the cookie persists as expected and then is not available after it expires. (Most browsers will not access cookies for pages loaded from the filesystem, so if you wish to run this example you will probably need to serve it using a personal web server.)

Cookie strings are limited in size to 4kb total, so you are limited in the amount of data you can store. In addition, many browsers provide users with fine control over their cookies, including overriding their expiration or content or even disallowing them altogether.

For a modern alternative to cookies, see the discussion of window.sessionStorage and window.localStorage, earlier in the chapter.

document.head

The document.head property returns a reference to the head element of the document. This property can be used as a shortcut for accessing elements within the head, such as scripts, style sheets, etc.

Syntax

```
var myHead = document.head;
```

Example

```
var docTitle = document.head.title;
```

document.location

The document.location property behaves the same as window.location, returning a Location object. See window.location for full details.

document.referrer

In the case where the user came to the current page by clicking a link on another page, the document.referrer property returns the URL of the referring page. Otherwise, it returns an empty string ("").

Syntax

```
var myReferrer = document.referrer;
```

document.title

The document.title property returns a string containing the contents of the document's title tag.

Syntax

```
var myTitle = document.title;
```

document.URL

The document.URL property returns a string containing the URL of the document.

Syntax

```
var myUrl = document.URL;
```

Methods

The document object has several methods that are useful for manipulating document content, accessing elements, and managing events.

document.addEventListener()

The document.addEventListener() method adds an event listener to the document. Otherwise it behaves exactly the same as element.addEventListener(); see that entry for details and examples.

Syntax

```
document.addEventListener(strEventType, eventHandler, boolCapture);
```

document.createComment()

The document.createComment() method creates a new comment element with the specified text. This element can then be inserted into the DOM using any of the DOM manipulation methods.

Syntax

```
var myCommentEl = document.createComment("This is my comment.");
```

Example

```
var myCommentEl = document.createComment("END OF DOCUMENT");
document.body.appendChild(myCommentEl); // appends the new comment to the end of the document.
```

document.createDocumentFragment()

The document.createDocumentFragment() method creates a new document fragment. Document fragments are generic containers that can serve as a staging area for new elements that you are creating. After you configure the document fragment to your liking, you can append it to the main document at the desired location.

Syntax

```
var myFrag = document.createDocumentFragment();
```

Example

```
var myFrag = document.createDocumentFragment(),
    myPar = document.createElement("p"),
    myText = document.createTextNode("Hello world!");
myPar.appendChild(myText);          // append the text to the paragraph.
myFrag.appendChild(myPar);          // Append the paragraph to the document fragment.
document.body.appendChild(myFrag); // Append the total fragment to the end of the document body.
```

document.createElement()

The document.createElement() method creates a new DOM element of the specified type. The type is a string enclosed in quotes, and if you supply an invalid type, the method throws an error.

Syntax

```
var myEl = document.createElement(tagName);
```

document.createEvent()

The document.createEvent() method creates a DOM Event object of the specified type that can then be configured and dispatched on a target using target.dispatchEvent(). For details and examples, see Chapter 3.

Syntax

```
var myEvent = document.createEvent(eventType);
```

document.createTextNode()

The document.createTextNode() method creates a text node with the desired text. This node can then be appended to another node.

Syntax

```
var myTextNode = document.createTextNode(strText);
```

Example

```
var myParagraph = document.createElement("p"),
    myTextNode = document.createTextNode("This is a dynamically added paragraph.");

myParagraph.appendChild(myTextNode);
document.body.appendChild(myParagraph); // Appends the paragraph to the very end of the document.
```

document.getElementById()

The document.getElementById() method returns a reference to the element with the specified ID. IDs are presumed to be unique within a document; if there are duplicate IDs within a document, this method returns the reference to the first element it encounters with the specified ID.

Syntax

```
var targetEl = document.getElementById(strID);
```

document.getElementsByClassName()

The document.getElementsByClassName() method searches through the document for all elements that have the specified class and returns an array-like object containing their references. Each match will be present as an indexed element in the object, and the length property will represent the total number of elements. If no elements match, this method returns an array-like object with no members and a length property set to 0.

Syntax

```
var myTags = document.getElementsByClassName(strClass);
```

Example

```
<!DOCTYPE html>
<html>
    <head>
        <title>JavaScript Programmer's Reference</title>
    </head>
    <body>
        <h1>Hello World</h1>
        <ul>
            <li>This should stay visible.</li>
            <li class="hideme">This should be hidden.</li>
            <li>This should stay visible.</li>
            <li>This should stay visible.</li>
            <li class="hideme">This should be hidden.</li>
            <li>This should stay visible.</li>
            <li class="hideme">This should be hidden.</li>
            <li class="hideme">This should be hidden.</li>
            <li>This should stay visible.</li>
        </ul>
```

```
        <p>This should stay visible.</p>
        <p class="hideme">This should be hidden.</p>
        <div class="hideme">
            <p>This div and everything within it should be hidden.</p>
        </div>
        <div>
            <p>This div and everything within it should be visible.</p>
        </div>
        <script>
var myEls = document.getElementsByClassName("hideme"),
    i;
for (i = 0; i < myEls.length; i++) {
    myEls[i].style.display = "none";
}
        </script>
    </body>
</html>
```

In this example, we get a reference to all of the items that have the class "hideme" and then we loop through the collection and set the display property of each one to be hidden.

document.getElementsByTagName()

The document.getElementsByTagName() method returns an array-like object containing references to all elements of the specified tag name. Each match will be present as an indexed element in the object, and the length property will represent the total number of elements. If no elements match, this method returns an array-like object with no members and a length property set to 0.

Syntax

```
var myEls = document.getElementsByTagName(strTagName);
```

document.querySelector()

The document.querySelector() method returns a reference to the first element that matches the specified CSS selector. If there is no match, the method returns null. (Compare to document.querySelectorAll().) For details on querySelector(), see the Chapter 3 section "Accessing Elements in the DOM."

Syntax

```
var myEl = document.querySelector(strSelector);
```

document.querySelectorAll()

The document.querySelectorAll() method returns an array-like object whose members are elements that match the specified CSS selector. Each match will be present as an indexed element in the object, and the length property will represent the total number of elements. If no elements match, this method returns an array-like object with no members and a length property set to 0. (Compare to document.querySelector().) For details on querySelectorAll(), see the Chapter 3 section "Accessing Elements in the DOM."

Syntax

```
var myEls = document.querySelectorAll(strSelector);
```

Example

```
<!DOCTYPE html>
<html>
    <head>
        <title>JavaScript Programmer's Reference</title>
    </head>
    <body>
        <h1>Hello World</h1>
        <table>
            <tr>
                <td>1</td>
                <td>1</td>
                <td>1</td>
                <td>1</td>
                <td>1</td>
            </tr>
            <tr>
                <td>1</td>
                <td>1</td>
                <td>1</td>
                <td>1</td>
                <td>1</td>
            </tr>
            <tr>
                <td>1</td>
                <td>1</td>
                <td>1</td>
                <td>1</td>
                <td>1</td>
            </tr>
            <tr>
                <td>1</td>
                <td>1</td>
                <td>1</td>
                <td>1</td>
                <td>1</td>
            </tr>
            <tr>
                <td>1</td>
                <td>1</td>
                <td>1</td>
                <td>1</td>
                <td>1</td>
            </tr>
            <tr>
                <td>1</td>
                <td>1</td>
```

```
                <td>1</td>
                <td>1</td>
                <td>1</td>
            </tr>
        </table>
        <script>
var myEls = document.querySelectorAll("tr:nth-child(odd)"),
    i;
for (i = 0; i < myEls.length; i++) {
    myEls[i].style.backgroundColor = "#ccc";
}
        </script>
    </body>
</html>
```

In this example, we use `querySelectorAll()` to access all the odd-numbered rows of the table and then give them a different background color.

The `element` Object Reference

Unlike the `window` and `document` objects, the `element` object is an abstract object: you don't access it directly. Instead, it serves as a template object from which other objects can inherit. Any HTML element in the DOM inherits from the `element` object, so any element in the DOM will have all of `element`'s properties and methods.

Properties

Many of the properties on an HTML element (`class`, `ID`, `href`, `target`, etc.) are exposed as properties on its associated DOM `element` object. In addition, DOM `element` objects have properties that provide access to the element's children, siblings, and parents, as well as its position in the page.

element.childNodes

The `element.childNodes` property provides an array-like object, the members of which are the immediate child nodes of the element. This includes child elements as well as other children such as comments, cdata sections, and even text nodes representing whitespace in the HTML markup. Each node will be present as an indexed element in the object, and the `length` property will represent the total number of child nodes. If the element has no child nodes, this property returns an array-like object with no members and a `length` property set to 0. (Compare with `element.children`.)

Syntax

```
var targetElement = document.getElementById("myId");
var myChildNodes = targetElement.childNodes;
```

element.children

The `element.children` property provides an array-like object, the members of which are the immediate child elements of the target element. Each element will be present as an indexed element in the object, and the `length` property will represent the total number of child elements. If the element has no child nodes, this property returns an array-like object with no members and a `length` property set to 0. (Compare with `element.childNodes`.)

Syntax

```
var myChildren = targetElement.children;
```

element.classList

The element.classList property provides an interface to the CSS classes that have been applied to an object. When accessed by itself, this property provides an array-like collection, the members of which are the individual classes on the element. Each class will be present as an indexed element in the object, and the length property will represent the total number of classes. If the element has no classes, this property provides an array-like object with no members and a length property set to 0.

In addition, the classList interface has several useful methods:

- add(className): Adds the specified class to the element.

- remove(className): Removes the specified class from the element.

- toggle(className): Removes the class from the element if present; adds the class if not present.

- contains(className): Returns true if the specified class is on the element; returns false if not.

The element.classList feature is relatively new. Internet Explorer 9 and lower does not support it, nor does Safari 5.0 and lower. In older browsers, you can access an element's class through the className property.

Syntax

```
var myClasses = targetElement.classList;
targetElement.classList.add(strClass);
targetElement.classList.remove(strClass);
targetElement.classList.toggle(strClass);
var boolHasClass = targetElement.classList.contains(strClass);
```

element.className

The element.className property provides access to the classes that have been applied to the element. When accessed, it provides a string that is a space-delimited list of all the classes, or an empty string if none. When used in an assignment, it changes the classes on the element to the specified list of space-delimited classes.

Syntax

```
var myClasses = targetElement.className;
targetElement.className = myClasses;
```

Example

```
var targetElement = document.getElementById("myId");
targetElement.className = "class1 class2"); // Add 2 classes to the element
```

element.contentEditable

The element.contentEditable property sets the contentEditable property on an element. Setting this value to true enables editing, while setting it to false disables editing. Setting the value to inherit causes the element to inherit its parent element's contentEditable value. To determine if the element is editable or not, use the element.isContentEditable property.

According to the HTML5 specs, almost any element can be editable. (Actually, this is an old feature, but it wasn't a part of the standards until HTML5.) All you have to do is set the contentEditable property on the element, and the user can modify the text content it contains.

Syntax

```
targetElement.contentEditable = true;
targetElement.contentEditable = false;
targetElement.contentEditable = "inherit";
```

Example

```
<!DOCTYPE html>
<html>
    <head>
        <title>JavaScript Programmer's Reference</title>
    </head>
    <body>
        <h1>Hello World</h1>
        <script>
var headline = document.querySelector("h1");
headline.contentEditable = true;
        </script>
    </body>
</html>
```

In this example, the headline is editable. The user can click it and then change its content.

element.id

The element.id property provides access to the ID that has been applied to the element. Changing this property changes the ID on the element.

Syntax

```
var elID = targetElement.id;
targetElement.id = differentID;
```

element.innerHTML

The element.innerHTML property provides access to the HTML contained within the target element. When used as an accessor, it returns a string containing the serialized HTML within the element. When used in an assignment, it takes the HTML string provided, removes the element's descendents, deserializes the provided HTML, and inserts the resulting elements into the DOM as descendents of the target element.

Setting this property to `null` or an empty string removes all the target element's child elements. In older browsers this can result in memory leaks; see the Chapter 3 section "Deleting Elements" for details.

Note that any valid HTML can be inserted into the element this way, including scripts. When working with user-provided content or content that you're not sure is safe, you should be careful to sanitize the HTML before inserting it, to avoid compromising the security of your application.

Syntax

```
var strHtml = targetElement.innerHTML;
targetElement.innerHTML = strDifferentHtml;
```

Example

```
document.body.innerHTML = ""; // completely erase a document
var strHtml = '<h1>Hello World</h1><p>This is dynamically created.</p>';
document.body.innerHTML = strHtml; // Add our content.
```

element.isContentEditable

The `element.isContentEditable` property is a read-only property that is set to `true` if the element's `contentEditable` property is set to `true`, or if it is set to "`inherit`" and the element's parent element's `contentEditable` is set to `true`.

Syntax

```
var boolEditable = targetElement.isContentEditable;
```

element.lastChild

The `element.lastChild` property provides a read-only pointer to the last child node of the target element. If the element has no child nodes, this is set to `null`. Nodes include elements, tags, cdata sections, or even text nodes representing whitespace in the markup. (Compare with `element.lastElementChild`.)

Syntax

```
var childNode = targetElement.lastChild;
```

element.lastElementChild

The `element.lastElementChild` property provides a read-only pointer to the last HTML element child of the target element. If the element has no child elements, this is set to `null`. (Compare with `element.lastChild`.)

Syntax

```
var childNode = targetElement.lastElementChild;
```

element.name

The `element.name` property provides access to the element's name property.

Syntax

```
var myName = targetElement.name;
targetElement.name = myName;
```

element.nextSibling

The element.nextSibling property provides a read-only pointer to the node that is the immediate next sibling of the target element. If the element has no siblings, this is set to null. Nodes include elements, tags, cdata sections, or even text nodes representing whitespace in the markup. (Compare with element.nextElementSibling.)

Syntax

```
var mySeebl = targetElement.nextSibling;
```

element.nextElementSibling

The element.nextElementSibling property provides a read-only pointer to the HTML element that is the immediate next sibling of the target element. If the element has no sibling elements, this is set to null. (Compare with element.nextSibling.)

Syntax

```
var mySeebl = targetElement.nextElementSibling;
```

element.offsetHeight

The element.offsetHeight property provides read-only access to the height of the target element, calculated by adding the height of the content plus the top and bottom padding plus the top and bottom border width. It does not include the top or bottom margins.

Syntax

```
var elHeight = targetElement.offsetHeight;
```

element.offsetLeft

The element.offsetLeft property provides read-only access to the number of pixels the target element's top-left border is offset from the top-left border of its offset parent. An element's offset parent is the first parent element that has its CSS position property set to either relative or absolute.

Syntax

```
var elLeft = targetElement.offsetLeft;
```

element.offsetParent

The element.offsetParent property provides a read-only pointer to the target element's offset parent, which is the first parent element that has its CSS position property set to either relative or absolute.

Syntax

```
var ptrOffsetParent = targetElement.offsetParent;
```

element.offsetTop

The `element.offsetTop` property provides read-only access to the number of pixels the target element's top-left border is offset from the top-left border of its offset parent. An element's offset parent is the first parent element that has its CSS position property set to either `relative` or `absolute`.

Syntax

```
var elTop = targetElementoffsetTop;
```

element.offsetWidth

The `element.offsetWidth` property provides read-only access to the target element's offset width, which is calculated by adding the element's content width plus the left and right padding plus the left and right border width. It does not include the left or right margins.

Syntax

```
var elWidth = targetElement.offsetWidth;
```

element.outerHTML

The `element.outerHTML` property provides access to the HTML of the target element and all of its descendents. When used as an accessor, it returns a string containing the serialized HTML of the element and its descendents. When used in an assignment, it takes the HTML string provided, removes the element and its descendents, deserializes the provided HTML, and inserts the resulting elements into the DOM.

Setting this property to `null` or an empty string removes the target element and all of its descendents. In older browsers this can result in memory leaks; see the Chapter 3 section "Deleting Elements" for details.

Note that any valid HTML can be inserted into the element this way, including scripts. When working with user-provided content or content that you're not sure is safe, you should be careful to sanitize the HTML before inserting it, to avoid compromising the security of your application.

Syntax

```
var strHtml = targetElement.outerHTML;
targetElement.outerHTML = strHtml;
```

Example

```
<!DOCTYPE html>
<html>
    <head>
        <title>JavaScript Programmer's Reference</title>
    </head>
```

```
    <body>
        <h1>Hello World</h1>
        <ul>
            <li>Apples</li>
            <li>Oranges</li>
            <li>Bananas</li>
        </ul>
        <script>
var myList = document.querySelector("ul"),
    strToDo = '<ol><li>Laundry</li><li>Grocery Store</li><li>Dry cleaning</li></ol>';

myList.outerHTML = strToDo;  // Replace the list and all of its children with our to-do list.
        </script>
    </body>
</html>
```

In this example, we want to replace the list of fruits with our to-do list. We begin by getting a reference to the list, and then we create a string containing the HTML we wish to insert into the document. Then we use outerHTML to replace the target element with our new markup.

element.parentNode

The element.parentNode property provides a read-only pointer to the element's parent node. If the element is within a DOM fragment or has not been added to the DOM, it will be set to null.

Syntax

```
var myParent = targetElement.parentNode;
```

element.previousSibling

The element.previousSibling property provides a read-only pointer to the node that is the immediate previous sibling to the target element. If there is no previous sibling, this will be null. Nodes can be elements or they can be cdata sections, comments, or even text nodes representing the whitespace in the markup. (Compare with element.previousElementSibling.)

Syntax

```
var mySeebl = targetElement.previousSibling;
```

element.previousElementSibling

The element.previousElementSibling property provides a read-only pointer to the element that is the immediate previous sibling to the target element. If there is no previous sibling, this will be null. (Compare with element.previousSibling.)

Syntax

```
var mySeebl = targetNode.previousElementSibling;
```

element.scrollHeight

The `element.scrollHeight` property provides read-only access to the element's height plus the top and bottom margins. This is equivalent to the minimum height a containing element would have to be to display all of the element's content without scrolling.

Syntax

```
var myHeight = targetElement.scrollHeight;
```

element.scrollLeft

The `element.scrollLeft` property provides access to the left scroll offset of the target element. When used as an accessor, this returns the number of pixels that the target element's content has scrolled horizontally. When assigned a value, it causes the target element's contents to scroll to the specified position.

Syntax

```
var scrollPos = targetElement.scrollLeft;
targetElement.scrollLeft = scrollPos;
```

element.scrollTop

The `element.scrollTop` property provides access to the vertical scroll offset of the target element. When used as an accessor, this returns the number of pixels that the target element's content has scrolled vertically. When assigned a value, it causes the target element's contents to scroll to the specified position.

Syntax

```
var scrollPos = targetElement.scrollTop;
targetElement.scrollTop = scrollPos;
```

element.scrollWidth

The `element.scrollWidth` property provides read-only access to the width of the content of the element plus the left and right padding. It does not include the left or right margins. This is equivalent to the minimum width a containing element would have to be to display all of the element's content without horizontal scrolling.

Syntax

```
var myWidth = targetElement.scrollWidth;
```

element.style

The `element.style` property provides access to the element's `style` attribute via a `Style` object. The `Style` object has attributes representing all of the CSS properties set in an element's `style` attribute. New ones can be added as desired. These attributes can be used to read the current values or to set them to new values.

Syntax

```
var myValue = targetElement.style.desiredCssAttribute;
targetElement.style.desiredCssAttribute = myValue;
```

Example

```
<!DOCTYPE html>
<html>
    <head>
        <title>JavaScript Programmer's Reference</title>
    </head>
    <body>
        <h1 style="border: 1px solid red;color: #00F;background-color: #ccc">Hello World</h1>
        <script>
var headline = document.querySelector("h1");

alert(headline.style.backgroundColor); // will alert something like "rgb(204, 204, 204)"
headline.style.fontStyle = "italic";   // will make the text within the headline italic.
        </script>
    </body>
</html>
```

In this example, we set some inline styles on the headline element and then use the element's style attribute to both examine the background color and to italicize the text.

element.tabIndex

The element.tabIndex property provides access to the element's tabindex attribute. The browser maintains a default tabbing order for form elements in the document—by default it is the order in which they are marked up in the HTML. You can override this order by using this property. In addition, you can force the browser to include non-form elements in the tabbing order by setting this property. The value is an integer that starts at 0. Setting the value to –1 means the element cannot be accessed with the Tab key.

Syntax

```
var myTabIndex = targetElement.tabIndex;
targetElement.tabIndex = newTabIndex;
```

element.tagName

The element.tagName property is a read-only property that returns a string that is the tag of the element.

Syntax

```
var strTag = targetElement.tagName;
```

Example

```
<!DOCTYPE html>
<html>
    <head>
        <title>JavaScript Programmer's Reference</title>
    </head>
```

```
    <body>
        <h1>Hello World</h1>
        <script>
var headline = document.querySelector("h1");

alert(headline.tagName); // will alert "H1"
        </script>
    </body>
</html>
```

element.title

The element.title property provides access to the element's title property. This is the text that appears in a tool tip when the user mouses over the element.

Syntax

```
var myTitle = targetElement.title;
targetElement.title = myTitle;
```

Methods

The element object's methods provide useful functionality for managing elements and the events that happen on them.

element.addEventListener()

The element.addEventListener() method registers an event handler for a specified event type on the target element. Every time an event of the specified type is dispatched to the element (whether by the browser, or manually by a script), the event handler will execute. The method takes the following parameters:

- strEventType: The event type for which you are registering the handler.

- eventHandler: An object that will receive the event notification. This object can be a function (which will be executed when the event occurs) or it can be an object that implements an event listener interface (see Event Handler Objects, below, for details on the event listener interface). The event handler can be a named function or an anonymous inline function expression.

- useCapture: A boolean that, if set to true, indicates that the event handler should execute during the capture phase. If set to false (or if omitted), the event handler will execute during the bubble phase. This parameter is marked as optional in the standard, but many browsers required it until quite recently, so specifying it is a good idea.

Event Handler Objects

Typically you'll see functions as event handlers, but the DOM standard specifies that the handler could be an object as well, as long as the object implements what the DOM standard calls a listener interface. A listener interface is a method named handleEvent() and which receives an Event object as a parameter. When the method is called to handle the event, the execution context (referred to by the this keyword) is set to the object that is the parent of the listener interface.

For details on DOM events, see Chapter 3.

Syntax

```
targetElement.addEventListener(strEventType, eventHandler, useCapture);
```

Example

```
<!DOCTYPE html>
<html>
    <head>
        <title>JavaScript Programmer's Reference</title>
    </head>
    <body>
        <h1>Hello World</h1>
        <p id="functionHandler">Click me to test an event handler function!</p>
        <p id="objectHandler">Click me to test using an object that implements a listener
interface!</p>
        <script>
var functionHandler = document.getElementById("functionHandler"),
    objectHandler = document.getElementById("objectHandler"),
    objHandleClick;

// Implement the listener interface on objHandleClick
objHandleClick = {
    handleEvent: function(event) {
        alert('This is the event listener interface!');
        alert(this == objHandleClick);  // Will alert true
    }
}

// Create an event handler function
function fctHandleClick(event) {
    alert('This is the function event handler!');
    alert(this == functionHandler);      // Will alert true
}

functionHandler.addEventListener("click", fctHandleClick, false);
objectHandler.addEventListener("click", objHandleClick, false);
        </script>
    </body>
</html>
```

In this example, we create two different event handlers: one is a function, and the other is an object that implements a listener interface. We bind each handler to its own target.

See the example under element.dispatchEvent() for another example of using an object to handle events.

element.appendChild()

The element.appendChild() method appends the specified DOM fragment or element as the last child of the target element.

Syntax

```
targetElement.appendChild(fragment);
```

Example

```
<!DOCTYPE html>
<html>
    <head>
        <title>JavaScript Programmer's Reference</title>
    </head>
    <body>
        <h1>Hello World</h1>
        <div id="myTarget">
            <p>This paragraph was already here.</p>
        </div>
        <script>
var myTarget = document.getElementById("myTarget"),
    textNode = document.createTextNode("This one is new."),
    myPar = document.createElement("p");

myPar.appendChild(textNode); // Append the text node to the paragraph
myTarget.appendChild(myPar); // Append the paragraph to the div as the last child
        </script>
    </body>
```

In this example, we create a new text node and a new paragraph, and then we append the text node to the paragraph. Then we append the paragraph to the DOM as the last child of the target <div>, so that it appears after the original paragraph.

element.blur()

The element.blur() method removes keyboard focus from the element. (Compare with element.focus().)

Syntax

```
targetElement.blur();
```

element.click()

The element.click() method simulates a click event on the element. This is a convenient shorthand method for firing click events without using the standard way of manually dispatching events.

Syntax

```
targetElement.click();
```

element.cloneNode()

The element.cloneNode() method returns a clone of the target element. If the optional parameter is set to true, a "deep" clone is performed and all the target element's descendant nodes are cloned as well. The result is a DOM fragment that can be further manipulated if desired or appended to the document.

This method does not clone any event handlers that have been registered on the target element or its descendants, but it does clone attributes, including IDs (so be careful not to introduce duplicate IDs in your document).

Syntax

```
var newClone = targetElement.cloneNode(boolDeep);
```

Example

```
<!DOCTYPE html>
<html>
    <head>
        <title>JavaScript Programmer's Reference</title>
    </head>
    <body>
        <h1>Hello World</h1>
        <div id="myTarget">
            <p>This paragraph was already here.</p>
        </div>
        <script>
var myTarget = document.getElementById("myTarget"),
    myClone = myTarget.cloneNode(true);

myClone.id="myNewTarget"; // update the ID so it is not a duplicate
myClone.querySelector("p").innerText = "This is a new clone."
// Update the text in the paragraph.
document.body.appendChild(myClone);
// Appends the clone to the document as the last child.
        </script>
    </body>
</html>
```

In this example, we perform a deep clone of the target div. Then we change the clone's ID (to prevent introducing duplicate IDs in the document) and change the text in the paragraph. Then we append the clone to the document as the last child.

element.dispatchEvent()

The element.dispatchEvent() method manually dispatches the specified event to the target element. It can be used to simulate user interactions or to dispatch custom events. See Chapter 3 for details on manually dispatching events.

Syntax

```
targetElement.dispatchEvent(eventObject);
```

Example

```
<!DOCTYPE html>
<html>
    <head>
        <title>JavaScript Programmer's Reference</title>
    </head>
    <body>
        <h1>Hello World</h1>
        <p id="targetMouseup">On mouseup here there will be an alert.</p>
        <p id="targetClick">Clicking here will manually dispatch a mouseup event to the
paragraph above.</p>
```

```
        <script>
var targetMouseup = document.getElementById("targetMouseup"),
    targetClick = document.getElementById("targetClick"),
    eventObject;

// Implement an event listener interface on our object
eventObject = {
    handleEvent : function(event) {
        // Route the event to the correct handler
        if (event.type === "click") {
            this.handleClick(event);
        } else if (event.type === "mouseup") {
            this.handleMouseup(event);
        }
    },
    handleClick: function(event) {
        var myCustomEvent = document.createEvent("Event"); // use the generic event module
        myCustomEvent.initEvent("mouseup", true, true);    // Initialize the event as a mouseup event
        targetMouseup.dispatchEvent(myCustomEvent);        // Dispatch the event.
    },
    handleMouseup: function(event) {
        alert('A mouseup event was dispatched to this element!');
    }
}

targetMouseup.addEventListener("mouseup", eventObject, false);
targetClick.addEventListener("click", eventObject, false);

        </script>
    </body>
</html>
```

In this example, we're using a single eventObject to handle all our event-handling needs. The event listener interface (the handleEvent() method) detects the type of event and routes the event to the correct method. Then we implement methods for handling click and mouseup events.

Within the click event handler, we manually create an Event object using the generic event module. (We could have used the MouseEvent module, but generic events are simpler.) Then we initialize the new Event object to be a mouseup event, and then dispatch the event to the target element.

element.focus()

The element.focus() method sends keyboard focus to the target element. (Compare to element.blur().)

Syntax

```
targetElement.focus();
```

element.getAttribute()

The element.getAttribute() method returns the value of the specified attribute. If the attribute does not exist on the element, it returns null. (Compare with element.setAttribute().)

Note that in most browsers, accessing an attribute by its named property on the element (if there is one) is faster than using the getAttribute() method.

Syntax

```
var myAttrValue = targetElement.getAttribute(strAttributeName);
```

Example

```
<!DOCTYPE html>
<html>
    <head>
        <title>JavaScript Programmer's Reference</title>
    </head>
    <body>
        <h1 id="headline" class="myclass" name="greeting">Hello World</h1>
        <script>
var headline = document.getElementById("headline");
alert(headline.getAttribute("id"));     // Will alert "headline"
alert(headline.getAttribute("name"));   // will alert "greeting"
alert(headline.getAttribute("class"));  // will alert "myclass"
alert(headline.getAttribute("href"));   // will alert null
        </script>
    </body>
</html>
```

In this example, we use getAttribute to query the ID, class, and name of an element. We also used getAttribute to query the href property on the element, but found that it was null (not set).

element.getElementsByClassName()

The element.getElementsByClassName() method behaves the same as document.getElementsByClassName() but the search is limited to the descendants of the target element. See document.getElementsByClassName() for an example.

Syntax

```
var myEls = targetElement.getElementsByClassName(strClass);
```

element.getElementsByTagName()

The element.getElementsByTagName() method behaves the same as document.getElementsByTagName() but the search is limited to the descendants of the target element. See document.getElementsByTagName() for an example.

Syntax

```
var myEls = targetElement.getElementsByTagName(strTagName);
```

element.hasAttribute()

The element.hasAttribute() method returns true if the target element has the specified attribute, or false if it does not.

Syntax

```
var boolHasAttribute = targetElement.hasAttribute(strAttribute);
```

Example

```
<!DOCTYPE html>
<html>
    <head>
        <title>JavaScript Programmer's Reference</title>
    </head>
    <body>
        <h1 id="headline" class="myclass" name="greeting">Hello World</h1>
        <script>
var headline = document.getElementById("headline");
alert(headline.hasAttribute("id"));    // Will alert true
alert(headline.hasAttribute("href")); // will alert false
        </script>
    </body>
</html>
```

In this example, we are querying the target element to see if it has an ID (which it does, so hasAttribute("id") returns true) or an href (which it does not, so hasAttribute("href") returns false).

element.hasAttributes()

The element.hasAttributes() method returns true if the target element has any attributes at all, and returns false if it does not.

Syntax

```
var boolHasAttributes = targetElement.hasAttributes();
```

Example

```
<!DOCTYPE html>
<html>
    <head>
        <title>JavaScript Programmer's Reference</title>
    </head>
    <body>
        <h1 id="headline" class="myclass" name="greeting">Hello World</h1>
        <h2>JavaScript is awesome</h2>
        <script>
var headline = document.getElementById("headline"),
    subHead = document.querySelector("h2");
alert(headline.hasAttributes()); // Will alert true
alert(subHead.hasAttributes());  // will alert false
        </script>
    </body>
</html>
```

In this example, we check to see if the headline has attributes (it does, so hasAttributes() returns true) and if the subheadline has attributes (it does not, so hasAttributes() returns false).

element.hasChildNodes()

The element.hasChildNodes() method returns true if the target element has any child nodes, and returns false if it does not. Child nodes can be HTML elements as well as comments, cdata sections, or even text nodes representing whitespace in the markup.

Syntax

```
var boolHasChildNodes = targetElement.hasChildNodes();
```

Example

```
<!DOCTYPE html>
<html>
    <head>
        <title>JavaScript Programmer's Reference</title>
    </head>
    <body>
        <h1 id="headline" class="myclass" name="greeting">Hello World</h1>
        <div id="div1">

        </div>
        <div id="div2">
            <p>JavaScript is awesome.</p>
        </div>
        <div id="div3"></div>
        <script>
var headline = document.getElementById("headline"),
    div1 = document.querySelector("#div1"),
    div2 = document.querySelector("#div2"),
    div3 = document.querySelector("#div3");
alert(headline.hasChildNodes()); // Will alert true; the headline has a text node as a child
alert(div1.hasChildNodes());     // will alert true; div1 has a text node representing empty space
                                 // in the markup
alert(div2.hasChildNodes());     // will alert true; div2 has a paragraph as a child node
alert(div3.hasChildNodes());     // will alert false.
        </script>
    </body>
</html>
```

In this example, we have several different elements, and we check them all to see if they have child nodes. The H1 tag has a text node as a child node; div1 has a text node representing the empty space in the markup as a child node; div2 has a paragraph as a child node; and div3 has no child nodes.

element.insertBefore()

The element.insertBefore() method inserts a new element as a child of the target element before the reference element. If no reference element is provided, the new element is appended to the end of the child elements of the target element.

Syntax

```
targetElement.insertBefore(newElement, referenceElement);
```

Example

```
<!DOCTYPE html>
<html>
    <head>
        <title>JavaScript Programmer's Reference</title>
    </head>
    <body>
        <h1>Hello World</h1>
        <ul>
            <li>1</li>
            <li>2</li>
            <li>4</li>
            <li>5</li>
        </ul>

        <script>
var targetList = document.querySelector("ul"),
    referenceElement = document.querySelectorAll("li")[2],
    myTextNode = document.createTextNode("3"),
    myLi = document.createElement("li");

myLi.appendChild(myTextNode);
targetList.insertBefore(myLi, referenceElement);
        </script>
    </body>
</html>
```

In this example, we have a list of consecutive numbers missing the number 3, so we need to create a new list item for the number 3 and insert it as a child of the unordered list before list item 4.

First we get a reference to the unordered list, and then we get a reference to list item 4 by querying all list items and using the one at index 3. Then we create a text node and a new list item, append the next node to the list item, and then use insertBefore() to insert the list item as a child of the unordered list before our chosen reference item.

element.querySelector()

The element.querySelector() method behaves the same as document.querySelector(), except the search is limited to descendent nodes of the target element. See document.querySelector() for details and examples.

Syntax

```
var myEl = targetElement.querySelector(strSelector);
```

element.querySelectorAll()

The element.querySelectorAll() method behaves the same as document.querySelectorAll() except the search is limited to the descendent nodes of the target element. See document.querySelectorAll() for details and examples.

Syntax

```
var myEls = targetElement.querySelectorAll(strSelector);
```

element.removeAttribute()

The element.removeAttribute() method removes the specified attribute from the target element.

Syntax

```
targetElement.removeAttribute(strAttribute);
```

Example

```
<!DOCTYPE html>
<html>
    <head>
        <title>JavaScript Programmer's Reference</title>
    </head>
    <body>
        <h1 name="headline">Hello World</h1>
        <script>
var targetEl = document.querySelector("h1");
alert(targetEl.hasAttributes());  // will alert true
targetEl.removeAttribute("name"); // removes the name.  Now the H1 should have no attributes.
alert(targetEl.hasAttributes());  // Will alert false
        </script>
    </body>
</html>
```

In this example, we are removing the name attribute from the headline. The hasAttributes() method returns true the first time because the name attribute is present, and returns false the second time because the name attribute has been removed.

element.removeChild()

The element.removeChild() method removes the specified child element from the target element. If the specified element is not a child of the target element, this method throws an exception.

Syntax

```
targetElement.removeChild(childElement);
```

Example

```
<!DOCTYPE html>
<html>
    <head>
        <title>JavaScript Programmer's Reference</title>
    </head>
    <body>
        <h1>Hello World</h1>
        <ul>
            <li>1</li>
            <li>2</li>
            <li>3</li>
            <li>4</li>
            <li>5</li>
        </ul>

        <script>
var targetList = document.querySelector("ul"),
    targetElement = document.querySelectorAll("li")[2];

targetList.removeChild(targetElement);
        </script>
    </body>
</html>
```

In this example, we are removing the third item from the list using removeChild(). First we get a reference to the list, and to the element we want to remove, and then we use removeChild() to remove the element.

element.removeEventListener()

The element.removeEventListener() method "undoes" the element.addEventListener() method. As such, it takes the same parameters, and will remove the event handler that was added with those parameters. If no event handler matches the parameters provided, the method does nothing.

Syntax

```
targetElement.removeEventListener(strEventType, eventHandler, useCapture);
```

Example

```
<!DOCTYPE html>
<html>
    <head>
        <title>JavaScript Programmer's Reference</title>
    </head>
    <body>
        <h1>Hello World</h1>
        <p>Click me!</p>
        <script>
var myPar = document.querySelector("p"),
    myEventObject;
```

```
// Implement a listener interface on myEventObject
myEventObject = {
    handleEvent : function(event) {
        alert('You clicked on the paragraph!');
        event.target.removeEventListener("click", this, false); // Unregister the event handler
    }
}

myPar.addEventListener("click", myEventObject, false);
        </script>
    </body>
</html>
```

In this example, we create an event handler that executes only once, because it removes itself when it executes. We begin by creating an object that implements a DOM listener interface (see element.addEventListener() for details). Within the listener interface, we have an alert to indicate that the handler fired, and then we remove the event handler from the target element. Note that within a listener interface, the value of this is set to the object that contains the interface; that's why in the removeEventListener() call we refer to the event handler as this, and in the addEventListener() call we refer to the event handler as myEventObject—they refer to the same thing.

element.replaceChild()

The element.replaceChild() method replaces the specified child of the target element with the specified new element.

Syntax

```
targetElement.replaceChild(newElement, oldElement);
```

Example

```
<!DOCTYPE html>
<html>
    <head>
        <title>JavaScript Programmer's Reference</title>
    </head>
    <body>
        <h1>Hello World</h1>
        <ul>
            <li>1</li>
            <li>2</li>
            <li>3</li>
            <li>4</li>
            <li>5</li>
        </ul>

        <script>
var targetList = document.querySelector("ul"),
    targetElement = document.querySelectorAll("li")[2],
    newTextNode = document.createTextNode("three"),
    newLi = document.createElement("li");
```

```
newLi.appendChild(newTextNode);

targetList.replaceChild(newLi, targetElement);
        </script>
    </body>
</html>
```

In this example, we replace the third list item with a generated one. First we get a reference to the unordered list (the parent element), and then a reference to the element we want to replace. Then we build our new list item, and use replaceChild() to replace the target element.

element.scrollIntoView()

If the target element is outside of the viewport as a result of scrolling, the element.scrollIntoView() method causes the element to scroll into view and align with the top of the viewable area. If the optional boolean parameter is provided, true causes the element to scroll to the top of the viewable area (default behavior), while false causes the element to align with the bottom of the viewable area.

Syntax

```
targetElement.scrollIntoView(boolAlignWithTop);
```

Example

```
<!DOCTYPE html>
<html>
    <head>
        <title>JavaScript Programmer's Reference</title>
        <style>
.container {
    width: 300px;
    height: 500px;
    overflow: auto;
    border: 1px solid #000;
}
        </style>
    </head>
    <body>
        <div class="container">

        </div>
        <script>
// Create many elements to induce scroll.
var myDocFrag = document.createDocumentFragment();
for (var i = 0 ; i < 200; i++) {
    var newParagraph = document.createElement("p"),
        newTextNode = document.createTextNode("This is paragraph #" + i);
    newParagraph.id = "id" + i;
    newParagraph.appendChild(newTextNode);
    myDocFrag.appendChild(newParagraph);
}
```

```
// Get a reference to our container and append the fragment.
var targetDiv = document.querySelector(".container");
targetDiv.appendChild(myDocFrag);

// Get a reference to the element we want to scroll into view.
var targetParagraph = document.getElementById("id150");
targetParagraph.scrollIntoView();
        </script>
    </body>
</html>
```

In this example, we first have a document that has a single div, which we have styled to be a specific width and height. Then we create many paragraphs and append them as children to the div. Then we get a reference to one of those paragraphs and scroll it into view using its scrollIntoView() method.

element.setAttribute()

The element.setAttribute() method sets the specified attribute to the specified value. If the attribute does not exist on the target element, it will be added. Note that changing attributes through their named properties on the element is faster than setting their values using setAttribute().

Syntax

```
targetElement.setAttribute(strAttribute, strValue);
```

Example

```
<!DOCTYPE html>
<html>
    <head>
        <title>JavaScript Programmer's Reference</title>
    </head>
    <body>
        <h1>Hello World</h1>
        <script>
var headline = document.querySelector("h1");

alert(headline.hasAttribute("name"));        // Will alert false, the headline has no name attribute.
headline.setAttribute("name", "headline"); // Sets the name.
alert(headline.hasAttribute("name"));        // Will alert true
        </script>
    </body>
</html>
```

In this example, we are adding the name attribute to the headline. At first, the headline has no name attribute, so hasAttribute("name") returns false. Then we set the attribute and check again, and hasAttribute("name") returns true.

Summary

In this chapter, we have provided a basic reference for three of the most commonly used objects specified by the DOM:

- `window`, which models the window where the document is loaded and displayed, and also includes references to other windows. It also serves as the global scope for JavaScript.

- `document`, which models the document that has been loaded into the window. The `document` object has properties and methods for accessing elements in the document and modifying them.

`element`, which provides the abstract template for elements. DOM elements have properties and methods for accessing and modifying an element's contents, as well as for managing events. For detailed discussions of many of the topics covered here, along with more examples, see Chapter 4.

This concludes the reference section of the book. We hope that you find both this reference section and the discussion section (consisting of Chapters 1 through 4) to be helpful in your JavaScript programming. Good luck!

Index

■ Y, Z

CPSIA information can be obtained at www.ICGtesting.com
Printed in the USA
LVOW110202070613

337430LV00004B/75/P